Law and Internet Cultures

Law and Internet Cultures raises the profile of socio-political questions about the global technology and information market. It is a close study of communication flows, networks, nodes, biopolitics and the fragmentations of power. It brings to life the role played by personalities, corporate interactions, industry compromises and the regulatory incompetencies affecting the technological world we all live in.

US technology powers the internet and disseminates American culture on an unprecedented scale. Assessing this power requires an analysis of the diffuse ways that US practice, policy and law dominate, and a consideration of how influence is negotiated and resisted locally. This involves a discussion about how ideas about trade and innovation circulate; of the social power of engineers who establish conventions and protocols; of the reach of leviathan corporations; and questions about global marketing and consumer tastes.

This book is for readers interested in intellectual property law, information technology, cultural studies, globalisation and mass communications.

Kathy Bowrey is a senior lecturer in the Faculty of Law at the University of New South Wales.

Law and Internet Cultures

KATHY BOWREY

CAMBRIDGE
UNIVERSITY PRESS

CAMBRIDGE UNIVERSITY PRESS
Cambridge, New York, Melbourne, Madrid, Cape Town, Singapore, São Paulo

Cambridge University Press
477 Williamstown Road, Port Melbourne, VIC 3207, Australia

Published in the United States of America by Cambridge University Press, New York

www.cambridge.org
Information on this title: www.cambridge.org/9780521600484

First published 2005

Printed in Australia by BPA Print Group

A catalogue record for this book is available from the British Library

National Library of Australia Cataloguing in Publication data

Bowrey, Kathy.
Law and internet cultures.
Bibliography.
Includes index.
ISBN 0 521 60048 0.
ISBN-13 978-0-521-60048-4 paperback
ISBN-10 0-521-60048-0 paperback
1. Internet – Law and legislation – United States.   2. Internet – Law and legislation.
3. Internet – Political aspects.   4. Globalization.   I. Title.
343.7309944

ISBN-13 978-0-521-60048-4 paperback
ISBN-10 0-521-60048-0 paperback

Contents

Illustrations and tables

Illustrations

Tables

Acknowledgements

This book would not have been possible without the warm hearts, sparkling wits, thoughts, and long patience of Lloyd Sharp, Val Kerruish, Jill McKeough, Jane Anderson, Natalie Fowell, Martin Hardie, Matt Rimmer, Nicole Graham, Maurice Bailey, Tamsin Clarke and Lleu Sharp.

Thanks also to Eben Mogler, Volker Kitz, Marc Freedman, and Roger Bourke and, at Cambridge University Press, Jill Henry and Susan Keogh.

1
Defining internet law

A friend of mine set up an email server. He was really relieved at how easy it had been. It only took a few online searches, downloading some free software and following the steps. Now all he wanted to do was check to see if it was RFC compliant.

RFCs are usually described as technical standards for computer networking. RFCs establish protocols, procedures and conventions used in or by the internet. RFC 2026 says they are designed to help facilitate best practice in terms of:

- technical excellence;
- prior implementation and testing;
- clear, concise and easily understood documentation;
- openness and fairness; and
- timeliness.[1]

RFCs date back to the development of ARPANET in 1969 and the decision to document the process of designing networking applications. It is partly due to the success of these networking applications, and the take up of these early documentation practices, that now over thirty years later, it is relatively easy to set up your own email server from your home computer, if you want to. But that the internet is easy to access and easy for users to develop their own nodes or networks is only partly due to the successful distribution of good technical standards.

RFC actually means 'request for comments'. This terminology signals something of the ethos of those involved in the original developments.

Stephen Crocker, who wrote RFC 1, says in RFC 1000:

> The precise usage of the ARPANET was not spelled out in advance, and the research community could be counted on to take some initiative . . . Most of us were graduate students and we expected that a professional crew would show up eventually to take over the problems we were dealing with . . . we found ourselves talking to people whose first concern was how to get bits to

flow quickly and reliably but hadn't – of course – spent any time considering the thirty or forty layers of protocol above the link level.

... it became clear to us that we had better start writing down our discussions ... I remember having great fear that we would offend whomever the official protocol designers were, and I spent a sleepless night composing humble words for our notes. The basic ground rules were that anyone could say anything and that nothing was official. And to emphasise the point, I labelled the notes 'Request for Comments'. I never dreamed these notes would be distributed through the very medium we were discussing in these notes. Talk about Sorcerer's Apprentice![2]

The 'just get on with it' approach to innovation and an unassuming attitude toward authority characterises much of the early development of internet standards.

This attitude morphed into a broader cyberlibertarian ethos that characterised the discussion of the internet of the 1990s. Richard Barbrook and Andy Cameron described it as a 'Californian Ideology':

By integrating different technologies around common protocols, something is being created which is more than the sum of its parts. When the ability to produce and receive unlimited amounts of information in any form is combined with the reach of the global telephone networks, existing forms of work and leisure can be fundamentally transformed. New industries will be born and current stock market favourites will be swept away. At such moments of profound social change, anyone who can offer a simple explanation of what is happening will be listened to with great interest. At this crucial juncture, a loose alliance of writers, hackers, capitalists and artists from the West Coast of the USA have succeeded in defining a heterogeneous orthodoxy for the coming information age: the Californian Ideology.[3]

The success of early network applications was not simply because they worked. What carried them forward and contributed to their successful adoption was the promotion of a culture associated with the use of the technology.

Discussion of the internet has been strongly influenced by this early history. The conventional wisdom is that we have since moved on from those humble, innocent days. Increasingly internet architecture has become less 'open' and surveillance and control have assumed a definitive role. The professional crew that Crocker feared would turn up and take things over did eventually arrive. But they didn't turn out to be a bevy of like-minded computer scientists interested in efficient applications. They were an army of intellectual property and contracts lawyers, practising a far more arcane science and with no interest in how quickly or reliably the information flowed. And then the lawyers got together with some of the computer scientists, which could mean the death of the internet as a commons, so the story goes.

There is something in these now familiar popularist histories of the internet and the politics of its changing cultures that is missing.

To understand what that is, we need to return to the discussion of RFCs and the peoples who develop and use them. Why do little nodes, such as my friend's small email server which is attached to a car club site, need to be RFC compliant? As the origin of the name infers, RFCs begin as humble suggestions about good design. They say no more than 'hey, adopting these standards might be a good idea'. There is no law of the internet that says your site or network must be compliant. If you are happy with how your little piece of the network works, why bother?

There is more to standards than functionality

The usual explanation for seeking compliance with RFC standards is to achieve the level of functionality that comes with adopting a tried and tested 'best practice'. But there are lots of organisations, some voluntary, others that are commercial operations, testing for RFC compliance. These organisations compile listings of non-compliant addresses and relays, and if you are not compliant, you are open to being blacklisted. These lists are very frequently updated and emailed to service providers and other intermediaries, who then deny service to blacklisted parties or locations. The point of blacklisting is to make the work of spammers, virus and worm distributors and other anti-social members of the internet community – people whose activities capitalise on sloppy network design – as difficult as possible.

The design issues RFCs address are real ones. And viruses, worms and spam are a pain that makes the technology difficult to use and a major expense for individuals and organisations to combat. As everyone who uses computers knows well, they pose a threat that can compromise the entire communications medium.

When you have a system that allows for points of entry into the network for people with relatively low levels of technical skill, you can't always be sure they realise the risks they are creating with the technical things they do, that can affect everyone else who uses the medium. That's why there is a need for RFCs and for bodies that test RFC compliance. These people don't tidy up after poor designers, but by setting standards and by creating blacklists, they try to minimise the risks of damage. And that there is no official overseer, and that there are many that are running different compliance checks, is in keeping with the original engineering philosophy.

But this openness to authority structures can itself create problems.

Recently a blacklist operated by 'RFC-ignorant.org' listed the whole of the '.com.au' domain space. RFC-ignorant is:

> the clearinghouse for sites who think the rules of the internet don't apply to *them*. We maintain a number of lists . . . which contain domains or IP networks whose administrators choose not to obey the RFCs, the building block 'rules' of the net. It is important to note that NOTHING requires ANYONE to comply with an RFC (pedantically a 'Request for Comments'), however, the 'cooperative interoperability' the net has enjoyed is based upon everyone having the same 'rule book' and following it . . . RFC-ignorant.org does not block anyone. We document who has chosen not to implement certain protocols described in the RFCs, and provide a means for allowing people to determine for themselves if they wish to communicate with non-compliant systems.[4]

A consequence of the listing by RFC-ignorant was that email to and from some '.com.au' addresses started to bounce. This caused serious concern amongst affected Australian businesses. They felt that their access to customers had been severely compromised, because of a decision made by unknown persons, from somewhere else, about a technical matter that they had little understanding of. And in any case, they had no ability to remedy a problem that affected an entire top level domain. There was nothing that they could do themselves about getting a blacklisting of '.com.au' lifted.

Australia was not the only country affected. RFC-ignorant also blacklisted '.cl' and '.pl' domains, affecting email addresses in Chile and Poland.

The most practical solution offered to Australian businesses was to try to buy a US '.com' domain name, and get the word out to their customers of the change of address. Of course it is most unlikely that were the same compliance problem to affect the '.com' top level domain that RFC-ignorant would presume to deal with it in the same way. And even if they did, it is hard to believe administrators would avail themselves of this clearing house's services any longer. Can you imagine the consequences of administrators of email servers choosing to exclude the entire '.com' domain space?

The reason given for the blacklisting of the '.com' domain was non-compliance with RFC 954 NICNAME/WHOIS, October 1985. This is a protocol about the listing of necessary contact and ownership details of registered domains.

From the beginning of the development of ARPANET it was recognised that there would be a need to be able to learn about the origin of the resources distributed over the network. To service this information need, a directory service run by the Network Information Center (NIC) was established at Stanford Research Institute. Each domain registration record usually has basic details about the registrant and the administrative and technical contact. The registrant 'owns' the domain. The other contacts may provide day-to-day maintenance of the domain details, such as where the domain is hosted on a server. Whilst a website often also has a contact email address listed on it, there is always some uncertainty about who this party actually is, and what kind and level of responsibility they have for the site.

To locate the appropriate persons responsible for the domain it is common to conduct an online search in a 'who-is' database. There are numerous who-is databases on the internet dealing with a wide range of top level and sub-domains. The information a who-is search may provide about a domain registration could simply be an email address and a NIC-name. The term NICNAME has come to refer to an alphanumeric code created at the time of registration, that provides a short cut to a fuller record of contact details of the domain registration. The full records may include a postal address, phone number, fax, and email addresses.

Some Australian domain name registrars, in accordance with the policy of the licensing and accrediting body, the Australian Domain authority (auDA), had removed public access to much of the contact information for registered domains, citing privacy concerns. There have been cases where, for example, personal contact details of a celebrity author were obtained from a 'who-is' database search conducted by an earnest fan. The author's website had been set up with an administrator as the email contact, precisely to try to keep unsolicited contact with her fan base at a distance.

Whereas 'open architecture' could be described as the internet culture of the 1980s and 1990s, with the pervasive spread of quite intrusive communications technologies privacy has emerged as a major concern. Privacy and open architecture are not necessarily at odds. There are also many RFCs dealing with aspects of privacy. However unfortunately RFC 954 NICNAME/WHOIS does not address privacy. This and related problems with the protocol has led to requests to replace it, including some by administrators of country code top level domains who have implemented privacy policies and then found their domains listed as non-compliant.

The role of drafting and publishing RFCs is now undertaken by the Internet Engineering Task Force (IETF).[5] The organisation describes itself as 'a large open international community of network designers, operators, vendors, and researchers concerned with the evolution of the Internet architecture and the smooth operation of the Internet. It is open to any interested individual.' An IETF Working Group is looking at the drafting of a replacement protocol, recognising the lack of a privacy policy as one of the weaknesses of RFC 954.[6]

That the issue is being addressed attests to the open consultative processes of the IETF, and their well-developed sense of responsibility toward best facilitating the operation of the network as a whole, and attention to interoperability within it. However IETF only sets standards, and has no interest in hearing disputes about ways these are interpreted and used downstream. That is not their game. But given the way the network has evolved to date, nor is it anyone else's.

RFC-ignorant also values the 'co-operative interoperability' of internet architecture. However they see this dynamism articulated as rules established by a respected community of technical peers. Their services draw attention to those they believe are compromising the spirit of the enterprise in not conforming to the expert's rule book. They only point the finger, of course. But to creators, owners and administrators of domains, at whatever networking level, this subtle detail is hardly a relevant point.

There are many kinds of lists, but finding out who subscribes to what services, and why to those, is very difficult to determine. It is not something systems administrators are keen to openly discuss, fearing the discussion would in itself create some vulnerability. Administrators take advantage of various kinds of listings hoping to keep the spaces they bear responsibility for operating as their clients expect – with minimal intrusions and maximum network efficiency. Systems are continually tested for myriads of weaknesses, and no system can ever be presumed as secure, reliable or invulnerable. Blocking is not a simple exercise, and spammers and the like can be constantly moving targets. It is well recognised that one of the consequences of using lists may well be the blocking of legitimate users from time to time and place to place.

Responsibility for 'collateral damage' produced by the network is always deferred. 'Co-operative interoperatibility' is partly a messy war of attrition, and those fraternising with poor practice are cast as co-conspirators in a flagrant theft of resources. Network resources are assumed to really only be the natural inheritance of those that can be tested and proven as technically worthy.

As the provider of one aggressive Mail Abuse Prevention System says:

> The Mail Abuse Prevention System's Realtime Blackhole List (MAPS RBL) can be used by any interested party in the configuration of their own network or mail relay, toward the goal of limiting theft of resources by spammers. This step must not be taken lightly – the MAPS RBL creates intentional loss of connectivity for anyone who chooses to use it. While we try to limit that connectivity loss to only networks which are friendly or neutral toward spam, sometimes a spammer hides in and amongst nonspammers so as to share a more positive fate with those nonspammers. What actually happens is that the nonspammers share an unpleasant and negative fate with spammers in that case. In other words, if you are not willing to occasionally throw out a baby with the bathwater (figuratively speaking, of course), then the MAPS RBL is not for you.[7]

The hope is that eventually the nonspammers, finding themselves thrown out, will force their service providers to take the action required to rectify whatever is deemed to be the cause of the potential spamming problem. And if the provider doesn't act, their disconnected clients are exhorted to go elsewhere.

Despite the salient advice that may be offered, not only administrators that share a hardline approach will necessarily subscribe to these kinds of lists. There is a strong pragmatic interest in using whatever tools are available to help with the job – so long as it shows results. The desired situation is to draw neither spammers nor anti-spam vigilantes to your system. A successful system is one that in technical terms goes unnoticed. To help with this objective, increasingly email software comes with settings already determined to gather various kinds of default listings that facilitate the spread of preferred technical 'solutions'.

Whilst businesses struggling with bouncing email will be fuming, these people are also likely to share an interest in opening their email and finding the inbox filled with messages actually relevant to the business or their other lives. The real source of anger is frustration at finding oneself unceremoniously dumped from a network you have come to depend upon. Some of the disconnected may well have a gut-expectation that modern notions of administrative fairness and accountability in decision-making would apply before draconian steps were taken. But these particular legal ideals are alien to this diffuse, global network.

The interface between law and technology is difficult because despite little in the way of formal authority structures, there are clearly forces that operate very much like laws. However the culture that has grown up around the internet uses references to the voluntariness of the 'protocols', the virtues of 'decentralisation' and 'openness', and 'choice' about compliance, about subscribing to lists and taking action. This language, used especially by those technicians and managers whose actions power the system, deflects any address toward the reality of decision-making structures existing. It also destroys any practical expectation of formal responsibility being taken for those hit with the friendly fire produced by the maintenance of smooth operations.

The other kinds of laws

We are accustomed to thinking of laws in terms of formal mechanisms of governance, of centralised rules, run by hierarchically organised bureau-cracies, with courts and other legal personnel that serve the public. And the problem is that this level also permeates the network at various points. For example, to act constructively against RFC-ignorant it would be use-ful to know who is using their lists, and thereby be able to contact these parties directly with news of the fallout from the recent initiative, and tell them about the privacy problems associated with complying with RFC 954. However the client list of RFC-ignorant is commercially valuable informa-tion. Quite ironically, in these circumstances this means that the privacy of RFC-ignorant and their clientele could be protected under trade secret or confidential information laws. If a third party were to find a means of accessing these details, the courts could be asked to prevent the disclosure and use of that information, because disclosure could harm the commercial interests of the clearing house and its clients.

The information contained in who-is databases might also be regulated by more specific privacy legislation. This area of jurisprudence is relatively new and strongly influenced by the European Union (EU) directive on the protection of personal data adopted in July 1995. This directive regulates transfer of data to non-EU countries, who are required to provide an ade-quate level of protection for personal information as a condition of the free flow of information from all EU states. Out of a concern for the privacy issues raised by new technologies, and for the trade implications of not hav-ing acceptable privacy laws, many EU trading partners have found it essential to develop them. Australia, for example, has national and state legislation that creates obligations concerning the collection and use of personal information obtained by government departments, agencies and many private sector organisations. There are principles governing how personal data is to be stored, made secure, the conditions under which it may be disclosed, and the rights of the individual to access the information. auDA's *WHOIS Policy No: 2002–06* says: '4.2 In order to comply with Australian privacy legislation, the street address, telephone and facsimile numbers of registrants will not be disclosed.' It is the application of this policy, which is in accordance with national law, that created the non-compliance issue noticed by RFC-ignorant.

Whilst the openness of the network emphasises global interoperability and global technical norms that operate like 'rules', there is also a need to attend to the layers of domestic laws that could apply. Clearly these laws can affect the operations of all parties resident within the state or country, and parties are not free to ignore them without risking legal consequences.

It was commonly thought that online operations need only concern themselves with complying with domestic laws where their business has a significant presence, such as an office and assets. However this has proven not necessarily to be the case, as Dow Jones, the US-based publisher of the financial publication *Barron's Magazine*, found out. In 2001 Dow Jones was sued under an Australian state defamation law over comments made concerning the dealings of an Australian businessman, Joseph Gutnick. The article was made available to subscribers of the Barron's news service on Dow Jones' website. A small number of subscribers downloaded the publication in Victoria where Mr Gutnick is a resident and where he sought to defend his reputation.

The Australian High Court considered the question of local jurisdiction and legal responsibility in a global communications medium in 2002.[8] In addressing these issues Justices Gleeson CJ, McHugh, Gummow and Hayne noted:

> Dow Jones submitted that it was preferable that the publisher of material on the World Wide Web be able to govern its conduct according only to the law of the place where it maintained its web servers, unless that place was merely adventitious or opportunistic . . . The alternative, so the argument went, was that a publisher would be bound to take account of the law of every country on earth, for there were no boundaries which a publisher could effectively draw to prevent anyone, anywhere, downloading the information it put on its web server.

However as their Honours saw it:

certainty does not necessarily mean singularity. What is important is that publishers can act with confidence, not that they be able to act according to a single legal system, even if that system might, in some sense, be described as their 'home' legal system. Activities that have effects beyond the jurisdiction in which they are done may properly be the concern of the legal systems in each place.

Justice Kirby said:

The genius of the common law derives from its capacity to adapt the principles of past decisions, by analogical reasoning, to the resolution of entirely new and unforeseen problems. When the new problem is as novel, complex and global as that presented by the Internet in this appeal, a greater sense of legal imagination may be required than is ordinarily called for.

. . . If the place of uploading were adopted as the place of publication which also governs the choice of applicable law, the consequence would often be, effectively, that the law would assign the place of the wrong for the tort of defamation to the United States. Because of the vastly disproportionate location of webservers in the United States when compared to virtually all other countries (including Australia) this would necessarily have the result, in many cases, of extending the application of a law of the United States (and possibly the jurisdiction and forum of its courts) to defamation proceedings brought by Australian and other foreign citizens in respect of local damage to their reputations by publication on the Internet. Because the purpose of the tort of defamation (as much in the United States as in Australia) is to provide vindication to redress the injury done to a person's reputation, it would be small comfort to the person wronged to subject him or her to the law (and possibly the jurisdiction of the courts) of a place of uploading, when any decision so made would depend upon a law reflecting different values and applied in courts unable to afford vindication in the place where it matters most. At least in the case of the publication of materials potentially damaging to the reputation and honour of an individual, it does not seem unreasonable, in principle, to oblige a publisher to consider the law of the jurisdiction of that person's habitual residence.

Justice Callinan remarked:

what the appellant seeks to do, is to impose upon Australian residents for the purposes of this and many other cases, an American legal hegemony in relation to Internet publications. The consequence . . . would be to confer upon one country, and one notably more benevolent to the commercial and other media than this one, an effective domain over the law of defamation, to the financial advantage of publishers in the United States, and the serious disadvantage of those unfortunate enough to be reputationally damaged outside of the United States. A further consequence might be to place commercial publishers in this country at a disadvantage to commercial publishers in the United States.

In finding that Joseph Gutnick could sue for damage to his reputation in Victoria, the High Court asserted the ongoing relevance of the Australian common law as a body capable of mediating local precedent, values and circumstance, with global technical and business realities. They clearly affirmed a strong sense of Australian sovereignty as a feature of the global internet context.

The Gutnick decision was widely condemned in the press, who unsurprisingly pointed to the implications for publishers, the US press especially, and the 'erosion' of US First Amendment rights. The assertion of Australian legal principles was alleged to be a 'totalitarian' step, largely because this posed a challenge to the supremacy of American free speech principles. The particularity of those American values, and the potential for conflict with other established political values, was largely ignored. So for example, Justice Kirby's reference to Mr Gutnick's right of reputation, as expressed under the International Covenant on Civil and Political Rights, was dismissed as outrageous by one US corporate news group, SriMedia, in an article titled '*Dow Jones v Gutnick:* Australian Court on a very slippery slope to totalitarianism?' The report said, 'The final disappointment . . . was the separate opinion of His Honor Mr. Justice Kirby, normally a pro civil rights advocate, who, of all things, justified the Court's decision by reference to the . . . United Nations document, as the basis for *gagging* free speech.'[9] SriMedia had filed an amicus brief along with CNN, *The New York Times*, The Associated Press, Amazon and Yahoo in support of the Dow Jones case. Articles in *The New York Times* published the reaction of the lawyer acting for these interveners, David Schultz. He said:

In a nutshell, what the court said was that there is nothing wrong with an Australian court hauling Dow Jones into Australia to go to court . . . If that becomes the law of the Internet, the problem isn't that individuals will be suing all over the world – though that is a problem. The problem is that rogue governments like Zimbabwe will pass laws that effectively shut down the internet.[10]

This hysteria seems to ignore the difficulties inherent in 'rogue' jurisdictions enforcing their judgments – an issue that was itself recognised by the High Court as quite problematic.

Australians subject to black-listings may not have recourse to Australian courts for action taken by a clearing house or their clients abroad. However this does not mean that in all situations involving the internet, there is no applicable domestic law and jurisdiction. Whether there is or isn't an applicable national law will depend upon the nature of the wrong perceived – whether it is something for which there is an established legal category, even one that might need to be stretched to deal with the 'challenge' of the internet. If there isn't, there may be legislative interest in creating a new law to cover the situation. Once the hurdle of finding an actionable wrong is overcome, whether there is legal recourse will still depend upon the attitude of the courts to the cultural and jurisdictional dilemmas posed by the facts of the case.

Technical practices intersecting with national and international laws

Increasingly, and especially concerning the global information economy, new laws are required. Increasingly these laws are also informed by policies negotiated in global institutions and administered in view of global bureaucratic logics.

auDA (au Domain Administration Limited), for example, is a form of co-regulation. It was set up with the participation of the Australian government as a not-for-profit organisation incorporated under Australian company law. There is an elected Board of Directors, and auDA is expected to operate by generating its own funds from stakeholders. The preamble to its constitution describes the Internet Domain Name System as a 'public asset' that auDA will administer for the benefit of the Australian community.

auDA was modelled on the global domain name body, Internet Corporation for Assigned Names and Numbers (ICANN).[11] With the backing of the Australian government, auDA entered into a 'ccTLD Sponsorship Agreement' with ICANN. In accordance with this agreement auDA agrees to abide by ICANN policies. This includes policies concerning 'the interoperability of the Delegated ccTLD with other parts of the DNS and Internet; operational capabilities and performance of the ccTLD operator; and the obtaining and maintenance of, and public access to, accurate and up-to-date contact information for domain name registrants.' Whilst the Australian courts are busily asserting authority over aspects of internet governance, in this instance it looks like the Australian government is backing away, preferring to rely upon the relevant global expertise to inform the Australian branch office who, it is presumed, will then act in the best interests of the public.

It looks like that. But it is not that simple, because as we have already seen, auDA is also cognisant of local laws, local sensitivities and some practical possibilities that need to be taken into account. Not everyone will like how they do it, but it is not the case that auDA merely implements agendas wholly determined elsewhere.

Further, the history of ICANN has shown a high degree of sensitivity toward the specific values that might be inscribed in its policies and rulings about domain name disputes.[12] Early discussions of representation on ICANN and analysis of dispute mediations often focused on how accountable the body was. It was scrutinised for 'American' influence, 'European' influence, democratic process, and to see whether commercial imperatives were the only ones that counted, with claims that if other interests were squeezed out it would be the death of the net as a useful or interesting medium. Out of political necessity, though not unanimously welcomed, this has encouraged a reasonably conservative approach toward policy formation by ICANN.

For example, with regard to privacy policy, a May 2003 'Staff Manager's Issues Report on Privacy Issues Related to Whois'[13] noted the complexity of the issue, and 'the stark divergence of views held by different segments of the community about many, if not all, of the issues.' It also noted that 'In many cases, the divergence of views appears to be based on the lack of a common understanding of various facts and circumstances relevant to the issues.' Further 'There also appears to be an imperfect general understanding regarding the requirements concerning Whois currently established in (a) ICANN agreements and policies and (b) legal requirements established by laws and other governmental requirements.' The recommendation was that the ICANN policy development process should not proceed until a Whois/Privacy Steering Group had first clarified 'the uses and misuses of Whois, their effects on privacy concerns, and the issues and their inter-relationships.' There was recognition of a range of groups outside of ICANN already working on Whois/privacy issues including the OECD, the European Commission, the US Federal Trade Commission, and the International Working Group on Data Protection in Telecommunications. It was suggested that these agencies might assist discussions within ICANN.[14] The suggestion seems to be that with sufficient 'facts' cultural differences and the reality of competing priorities will disappear.

Where it is likely that strong national or group positions will be asserted leading to a diversity of views within ICANN, the management strategy is to move those difficult issues to the periphery, in an attempt to prevent challenges to the authority of the global organisation. This allows the normative content of difficult areas to remain inscribed in different ways, at the local levels. This strategy makes political sense in terms of ICANN's own governance problems. It does not however provide a method for actually resolving disputes, such as the current one over RFC 954.

Connecting technologies, laws, communities and cultures

The designer of a small mail server to facilitate communications between members of an online community need not bother with protocols about technical standards. But if they choose not to, this might be noticed and acted upon. It seems safer to comply. After all, you can just access a free service that will test the nominated site and report back any obvious problems. This system works pretty well, and the majority of protocols are not all that controversial.

But when the protocol is controversial and there is doubt that it does establish an appropriate internet 'rule', the conflict demonstrates the cultural and legal complexities of the global communications medium. There are different kinds of communities and associated cultures that intersect with the layers of self-regulation, voluntary schemes, co-regulation, legislation, and international agreements. Cultural attitudes and different expectations about the best possible future for the medium seem to be the cause of much of the conflict. However the intersections of technology, law, community and culture are dimensions of internet governance attracting little study to date.

Internet cultures

Richard Barbrook and Andy Cameron observed quite a while ago, and then with some irritation, that simple explanations about the internet and its communities have been listened to with great interest. And as Geert Lovink, in his somewhat bleakly titled book, *My First Recession*,[15] describes it, the earlier period's "'economy of the cool" is fading away, its cultural residues are being absorbed into the everyday, and "all-too-human" characteristics are hitting the interface surface . . . There is a rising awareness of backlash. A part of this new consciousness could be translated as Internet culture's need to write its own history. It has to leave its heroic, mythological stage behind.'[16] Lovink says: 'The current state of the internet is one of conflict.' His work calls for a different kind of cultural criticism, capable of analysing different positions and expectations that are the hallmarks of those conflicts.

I am sympathetic to that call, but want to take the quest in a slightly different direction. I am not willing to give up the matter of stories. Stories are always important, and it is only the style of their telling that has changed. Whilst in the early 90s they were written in a self-consciously loose and knowingly unconventional style,[17] they now masquerade as a more staid diet of sober net 'news'. This is just a new pantheon of myths, heroes and villains.

Whether utopian or bleak, fanciful or serious, the messages that stories contain are productive. They are essential to the creation of a community member's sense of identity and purpose. With the internet as the medium of transmission they circulate and recirculate, like unending games of whispers. They are made available for free and by subscription. They are archived and sold as pay per view. They reappear in newspapers, magazines, books and on TV. Stories are part of what the internet was, is, and the force that drives what it can be. In understanding why the current state is one of conflict, we should not dismiss studying the place of storytelling – then *and* now.

There are many internet cultures, made up by many different kinds of storytellers, all trying to maintain their own voice and identity. In the current more subdued mood, internet communities are fighting to keep their cultures alive amongst fears they are bound to be swamped – by bad code, bad businesses, bad practices, bad people, bad organisations, bad laws, bad courts and bad governments. Evil doers and dangerous idiots can be found at all levels and in all places and directions, depending upon whom you ask.

As I see it, the problem of writing about the internet in the past was not the attraction to storytelling, even when these stories were self-promoting and very incomplete. Rather the problem was, and still remains, that we have many quite different kinds of internet communities. These communities – corporate, public, open, closed, educational, legal, scientific, artistic, social, peer-to-peer, hacktivist and activist – are all fed by their own sense of history, experience and attitude. This knowledge circulates in the form of stories, and the stories influence how technological and institutional powers are exercised.

This book explores the way internet communities involved in contemporary conflicts, represent themselves and others – what they see as problems and what it is that they want to be done. The point is to look at how stories are a form of power and knowledge – to explore the interplay between stories and mechanisms of power. It is true that not all groups have the same kind of access to the same kinds of technological and institutional powers. However given the many layers of difference in interest, expertise and interactions, it is also never a zero-sum game.

Law and internet cultures

The approach taken here draws upon critical legal studies approaches that in the 1980s started to reflect upon Foucault's discourses about power.[18] In *Discipline and Punish*, Foucault argued:

> We must cease once and for all to describe the effects of power in negative terms: it 'excludes', it 'represses', it 'censors', it 'abstracts', it 'masks', it 'conceals'. In fact power produces; it produces reality; it produces domains of objects and rituals of truth.[19]

Foucault was a useful writer for some scholarly lawyers.[20] He emphasised the significance of governance by disciplinary mechanisms and the biopolitical. He argued that in modern nation states, individuals and communities police themselves without the need for formal exercises of power by others over them. To him there were far more intrusive and significant powers to be considered than the formal juridical apparatus of the modern nation state.

These insights resonated with concerns about law that legal scholars were already having. The traditional focus on law as a formal system of self-contained rules had somehow missed the point, because legal power did not necessarily rest in an unproblematic application of established rules. Significant power was vested in the more fluid and political act of their interpretation. Further, legal meaning was not necessarily communicated in a one-directional way. Social forces affected the application of the law. Another problem was that law was not just created and administered by legislature and courts. Increasingly 'legal' powers and functions were exercised within modern bureaucracies, and even by corporations. These personnel had quite different relationships with the public to 'legal officers', and there were significantly different processes of accountability. There was also the problem of dealing with the reality that citizens make choices about how they relate to the law. Some are ignorant about legal matters, and some good people are just plain disinterested in law. Others are 'too interested' in it and wanting to test legal limits or test competitors' stamina, they use various legal avenues to try to gain strategic advantage. Further, some citizens act in apparent defiance of perceived legal commands. These people do not necessarily face formal legal consequences or create a crisis, or contribute to a general feeling of anarchy.

Clearly what is represented in legislation and litigation is only a snapshot of the broader legal landscape. Predominantly focusing on legislation and litigation is really studying the levels of law most removed from everyday experience. Perhaps then, some legal scholars asked, the formal mechanisms of power weren't all that important. Maybe what the law formally was, and what the legislature and higher courts did, didn't matter as much as had conventionally been thought.

The point was not to abandon the older sense of law altogether, and Foucault's weak discussion of formal law was broadly criticised.[21] However a far broader interdisciplinary or multidisciplinary approach to the subject called law did seem like a good idea. As Foucault's work cried out for a stronger consideration of more dispersed forms of power, legal academics began to look at broader ways of thinking about what law was and about how law was being constituted.

There are various 'cultural' approaches to law:

> As Carol Weisbrod has recently noted, 'One relates to the point that law creates the conditions of culture to some degree. Another notes that law, as a cultural product, may have something in common with other cultural products. Still another focuses on the point that while law is to some degree a mandarin text, it is itself a subject of popular culture.' As these suggestions indicate, a cultural analysis/cultural studies of law not only helps in challenging traditional ideas of culture, it also may help advance new conceptions of law.[22]

The Australian High Court seeking to hold Dow Jones to account for defamation is an example of law creating the conditions of culture. The court sought to regulate what could be said and control where certain views could be circulated. More commonly the example of law creating the conditions of culture referred to is intellectual property – copyright, trade marks, celebrity rights, advertising rights, even patents. In creating private ownership rights these laws affect the way culture can be expressed, related to and how ideas circulate in the marketplace.[23]

In the second version, where law itself is seen as a cultural product, the focus is often on the role of the imaginary or the unconscious in law:

> Treating law as a cultural reality means looking at the material structure of the law to see it in play and at play, as signs and symbols, fantasies and phantasms.[24]

More simply, this may mean looking at the way law invents problems to solve, such as by adopting a metaphor of piracy, to flesh out discussions of the legal implications of file sharing. The cultural specificity and heritage of representations the law uses sets certain lines of inquiry in train, and this forecloses other concerns. But that will not necessarily be obvious to the party who advocates a particular line, and even to others who engage them. As Maureen Cain notes:

> Gramsci argued that organic intellectuals maintain institutionalized or regular relationships with a particular social class, such that they are integral members of it and have regular experiential knowledge of that class and its problems. These are also their own experiences and their own problems demanding a solution . . . they are creative. They develop new forms of relationship, new practices and, of course, new names for them and ways of thinking about them. They literally think the advance of the class they are related to.[25]

Here lawyers, like other knowledge workers, are considered as a 'productive' cultural force.

The third mode suggested draws attention to the proliferation of law stories in popular culture. Here the familiar diet is the cop shows, the 'law and order' franchises, the court dramas, the law-firm soaps, crime fiction more generally, and films about the suburban guy and gal battling against the odds for moral victories, and through the courts. There is also the way law-related stories, especially those involving exciting or controversial uses of new technologies, regularly achieve greater prominence in the mainstream media, crossing over from the specialist to the mainstream news. Even people who don't spend much time online or reading the business or technology pages know about the problems of predatory online behaviour, online pornography, Napster and related peer-to-peer packages, virus panics, online banking scams and the spam scourge. They also know that there is talk about whether new laws can meet the challenge. The point of studying these cultural sources is because mass communications have become a primary source of legal information for the public. News can also set and sell law reform agendas.

What these approaches share is a consideration of the role of culture as a form of governing. Sarat and Simon argue, 'the practices of governance help set the agenda for legal scholarship.'[26]

Because the focus is mainly on the interplay between the two, this approach can leave both culture and law as rather vague explanatory constructs. Whilst 'culture' may be 'everywhere invoked and virtually nowhere explained',[27] it could equally be said that amongst these scholars 'law' shares a similar fate. In addition, Rosemary Coombe argues that the 'relationship between law and culture should not be defined . . . An ongoing or mutual rupturing – the undoing of one term by the other – may be a more productive figuration than the image of relationship or rejoinder.'[28] Coombe argues that, 'an exploration of the nexus between law and culture will not be fruitful unless it can transcend and transform its initial categories.'[29]

For legal scholars the analytical problem has been one of trying to escape the artificial construction of autonomous categories and principles of law. However cultural analysis of law that strives to combat 'common sense' understandings of law as formal and rule-bound, and instead seek to justify a 'cultural' approach, shows the difficulty lawyers have had in 'moving beyond legal realism'.[30] Writers who engage with this terrain are reacting to a phantom created by legal discourse and perversely bringing it back to life. The approach forgets the experience and understanding of the 'everyday' people they presume to write about. Through the circulation of law stories in the form of news and entertainment, there is a very widespread awareness of the emptiness of much of the modern liberal rhetoric about legal institutions. There is much popular scepticism and cynicism about what legal institutions can reliably deliver for the regular person, as opposed to the wealthy. There is familiarity with the diverse and diffuse mechanisms of power that regulate all spheres of daily life. And especially for those of us outside of the US, there is knowledge of the weaknesses of national governments in engaging legal and political agendas in a global context, and even lower expectations of modern juridical institutions as a consequence.

In any case, in new technology areas, and especially in regard to the internet, there are few 'initial categories' to form the backdrop for a critical deconstruction of the law. Of those that do exist, like defamation and copyright, there are sufficient questions about their global application to deflect any common-sense presumption of pre-digested concepts of law being served up. It is important to keep in mind Lawrence Lessig's observation that:

In real space we recognize how laws regulate – through constitutions, statutes, and other legal codes. In cyberspace we must understand how code regulates – how the software and hardware that make cyberspace what it is regulate cyberspace as it is. As William Mitchell puts it, this code is cyberspace's 'law'. Code is law.[31]

His book, *Code and other Laws of Cyberspace*, was very influential precisely because it moderated widely held fears and elation about the presumed irrelevance of law in cyberspace. He focused on the significant ways computer architecture or code, embedded or successfully marketed to us, regulates us. Code determines what we, as users, can and cannot do with our machines. He also pointed to the way this seemingly informal mode of regulation by code was increasingly sanctioned and supported by legislative reform, for example through the provision of copyright laws that protect the technologies associated with digital rights management systems.[32]

'Internet law' is diffuse and rarely autonomous. It moves with the technological flows, and is thereby quite globally pervasive. It is intersected by the more familiar laws and courts of nation states, but these do not stand alone. Formal laws take technological controls and global realities into account, albeit in different and diverse ways. What this means is, that in relation to the internet, the idea of law changes, depending upon the context and the nature and concerns of the relevant decision-making community. In this regard it is the definition of the relevant internet community and their cultures that helps to focus and refine the relevant meaning for law.[33]

The concern in 'reading internet law' is to raise the profile of socio-political questions about the global technology and information market. In line with the insights of critical legal scholarship, the aim is to bring to life an understanding of the role played by personalities, corporate interactions, industry compromises and regulatory incompetencies affecting the technological world we live in. This involves looking at the stories communities tell about themselves and about others. As Rosemary Coombe has said, instead of focusing on the relationship between law and culture, as if they were separable objects that interact, my ambition is to write against culture(s): 'To write against culture is to focus upon practices and problems of interpretation, exploring contradiction, misunderstanding, and misrecognition, aware of interests, inclinations, motivations, and agendas.'[34]

The desire is also to reflect upon the significant influence of US technology, jurisprudence, practice and culture upon the development of information technology law more generally. To this end, this book draws upon a very broad range of literature – interviews with people involved at various levels of technology policy-making, economic analyses of the technology market, journalistic accounts of leading players and battles in the industry, the economy of technological innovation, communications theory, cultural studies, and critiques of globalisation. It is argued that this broader context is essential to understanding the mechanics of the law/technology interface.

Lloyd Sharp, *Nano-entities: actual, virtual, possible – the fluid construction of identity*

2
Defining internet cultures

It is difficult to pin down the concept of internet cultures. Whose internet? Which communities? What cultures? There are problems of definition and issues of selectivity and representativeness – matters of time, site and perspective.

One way to proceed is to reflect upon the theoretical tools developed in relation to explorations and critiques of the global information society in the eighties and nineties. This literature has been influential in constructing ideas about the internet and its cultures. Writers such as Lyotard, Deleuze and Guattari, Hardt and Negri, and Appadurai are also very sensitive to problems of definition, history and change.

However the early period of global communications and associated cyber studies also needs to be re-evaluated in view of more recent explanations of the dot com booms and deaths of the early 21st century. Dot com failures have led to significant reappraisals of assumptions made about the value of technology and the internet – to society, the economy and global trade. Further, features that previously were considered as central to internet culture, like the pace and ease of information and capital flows, are now more likely to be considered as problematic, contributing to dangerously flawed, social and economic actors and worthless ideas about productivity. In revisionist discussions however, earlier theoretical concerns about perspective and position are usually passed by with barely more than a glance.

Both theoretical concerns and more pragmatic insights need to be combined to reflect upon the challenge of defining internet cultures. To do this some assistance can be drawn from the previous chapter's discussion about technology and law. There is always going to be a problem with securing a universal definition of an internet culture, but in combination with a concern for questions of law and power, it is possible to more confidently frame the objects of inquiry. *Law and Internet Cultures* explores the way that various actors mediate the understanding and experience of the internet for others. Influential people: engineers, programmers, logicians, multinationals, consumers, cyberactivists, libertarians, the military, and lawyers create the internet realities, possibilities and impossibilities for others.

What kinds of communities do these influential people make? Communities here are defined in relation to their own decision-making processes and preoccupations; in terms of their roles as knowledge producers; and in view of interactions and antagonisms with each other. With the notable exception of the military, the selection of players is directed toward communities that consciously discuss their 'law' making and the interests that they value. These are all players with a strong sense of their own identity, and often strong negative views about others. Yet they all share an ability to affect the internet experience for the many of us beyond their immediate, chosen horizons.

Mapping global communities

Description of global communications invariably refers to networks, flows, lines, layers, strata, vectors, scapes, deterritorialisation, multilinearity, transfers, pipes, bandwidth, bits, bytes, and data. The only term that suggests some biological materiality in the medium is Deleuze and Guattari's reference to plateaus and rhizomes, but this is also meant as a reference to a machinic assemblage.[1] The mathematical, architectural, mechanical and geographical terms all emphasise the complex nature of the structures that intersect global relations.[2] The language used infers at most only a loose connection with earlier kinds of mappings of the globe.

> The world we take for granted – the real world – ... It is presented to us on the platter of the map, presented, that is, made present, so that whatever invisible, unattainable, erasable past or future can become part of our living ... now ... here ... And every map is like this, every map facilitates some living by virtue of its ability to grapple with what is known instead of what is merely seen, what is understood rather than what is no more than sensed.[3]

Lines, colours and dates once plotted and separated the course of nation states. This helped identify their subjects and outline distinct imperial and colonial linkages. These maps enabled particular presumptions about the reality of communities. The boundaries drawn upon the globe provided an easy tool for simple differentiations of economies, cultures, political interests, legal frameworks and historical groupings.

Such solid two-dimensional lines make far less sense once the boundaries are cut through by reliable, high-speed electronic transmissions. The technology itself suggests connections between, rather than the separation of, citizens.

But the whole language of citizenry is also problematic in this kind of global world. Citizens of what form of governance? The term carries too much baggage from centuries-old liberal-democratic theories of governance.[4] The preferred denotation for the human subject is invariably just a reference to the 'self'.

> A self does not amount to much, but no self is an island; each exists in a fabric of relations that is now more complex and mobile than ever before. Young or old, man or woman, rich or poor, a person is always located at 'nodal points' of specific communication circuits, however tiny these may be. Or better: one is always located at a post through which various kinds of messages pass.[5]

Lyotard wrote of this postmodern reality well before the phenomenal growth of the internet in the 1990s. He was exploring why metanarratives, that had provided unitary explanations of politics, social forces and society, had lost credibility. Attempts to describe society in terms of national identity, or conceive of it as an organic whole, as a functional system, or as a product of class antagonism, were no longer sufficient. Metanarratives were a totalising kind of thought. They secured their explanatory power by negation of the realities that failed to fit the chosen schema.

From a postmodern perspective, the order suggested by a metanarrative as 'real' is inextricably related to the production of particular 'disorders'. The realities that don't fit the chosen narrative are ignored, suppressed and denied. Deconstruction is important because it brings the disorders created by the metanarrative into view. Deconstruction proceeds by destabilising the homogenising metanarratives. It gives voice to more provisional, temporary and relative 'mini-narratives', that are able to account for some of the realities of the Other. At the same instance it reveals the metanarrative as itself no more or less than a provisional fabrication, fashioned from a particular world view.

Notions of 'Other' draw upon feminist[6] and anthropological[7] debates about interpretation of the subject. This literature is sensitive to the specificity and contingency of meaning, and questions of class, gender, race, age and (dis)ability. Paul Patton reflects upon the politics of difference, drawing upon Deleuze and Guattari's discussion of multiplicities, in these terms:

Suppose there are only two groups and suppose that there is a standard or ideal type of member of the larger collectivity: the majority is defined as the group which most clearly approximates the standard, while the minority is defined by the gap which separates its members from that standard.[8]

Postmodern and related approaches necessarily raise the profile of the subject and subjectivity. They provide a space to consider the situation of the minority. However as attention is directed to dismantling the concepts that secured boundaries, postmodernism tends to eviscerate notions of community. At best it could be said that a community of Others is formed, through the accounts of the violence being perpetrated upon them by the totalising structures of the majority. But even then, who can presume the authority to speak for that community? A postmodern self-consciousness about the status of the speaking voice leads to contingent and partial representations of community.[9]

For Lyotard technology was tied up with changes in society, but the organisational power of communications technology was not fully realised:

the historical impetus for (postmodernism) was the destruction of dysfunctional social institutions and ideologies, and the once-absolute credibility those institutions has wielded during the Modern period had been sufficiently eroded by the end of the century to permit large-scale reconstruction around more productive cultural values . . . the first epoch of the 3rd Millennium, the Network Age, was already asserting itself in increasingly powerful ways by the early 1990s, if not sooner, through the literal reorganisation of the social, political and economic infrastructure around electronic networks and the metaphorical re-structuration of human activity around social practices that mimicked the distributed character of the network.[10]

Writers on globalisation consistently refer to the internet, or at least the world wide web,[11] as a material aspect that assists the flows of trade and capital across the globe, related to the 'shrinking' of distance.[12] The materiality of global wires is invariably related to discussions about the notion of 'imagined communities'[13] and the production of fluid, sometimes unstable, multiple, and hybrid constructions of self.

Appadurai identifies five dimensions of global flows: (a) ethnoscapes; (b) mediascapes; (c) technoscapes; (d) finanscapes; and (e) ideoscapes. He says:

the individual actor is the last locus of this perspectival set of landscapes, for these landscapes are eventually navigated by agents who both experience and constitute larger formations, in part by their own sense of what these landscapes offer. These landscapes, thus, are building blocks of what, extend- ing Benedict Anderson, I would call 'imagined worlds', that is, the multiple worlds which are constituted by the historically situated imaginations of per- son and groups spread around the world.[14]

The priority of deconstruction of ideal, stable representations of identity is less relevant to this medium. Global configurations are ever fluid, with paths mapped by individual actors.

In cyberculture literature of the 1990s we are cyborg. We play with vir- tual identities, identity tourism, doppelgangers, anonymity. This makes us vulnerable to identity theft, frauds, scams and related deceptions. These navigators are not unitary centred subjects, and identities are as complex as the possible interactions with these multiple global flows allow.

This literature still discusses the 'self' in relation to the notion of online communities. But these communities are mainly defined in relation to the agency of many dynamic selves.[15] The online community is formed by the deposit of expressions by individuals. These expressions can be collated according to the possibilities permitted by the site construction and the sophistication of the database supporting it. The body of information that is open and accessible can then be used to inform the insights of cultural commentators who, in interpreting these expressions of identity, create a sense of the collective for us. But this is a knowledge of community that is confined to the records of a precise moment in time. The online community is really only produced, in the first instance, as a receptacle for collecting and relating individual contributions, and secondarily, if it is spectacular enough to attract scholarly reflection, as an interesting cultural artefact.

The deterritorialisation of space makes it difficult to construct the reality of this technologically enabled community of travellers.

Mapping Mandeville's *Travels*

According to the ancient Greek geographer Pliny, the Blemmyae, men with faces on their chests, lived in the deserts of Libya.[16] Blemmyae were also reputed to have attacked Christian settlements in North Africa between the middle of the third century and the fifth. There is speculation that the Blemmyae may have been tribes who wore ornamental shields or chest armour, leading to misperceptions of the absence of a neck and face.[17]

Spectacular images of the Blemmyae, amongst other monstrous and fab- ulous creatures, accompanied copies of the fourteenth-century manuscript

Blemmyae, Mandeville's *Travels*

The Travels of Sir John Mandeville. This text claims to be the work of an English knight who travelled from 1322 to 1356, though there is debate about whether he actually travelled at all. Mandeville claimed to have met Blemmyae:

> There are many different kinds of people in these isles. In one, there is a race of great stature, like giants, foul and horrible to look at; they have one eye only, in the middle of their foreheads. They eat raw flesh and raw fish. In another part, there are ugly folk without heads, who have eyes in each shoulder; their mouths are round, like a horseshoe, in the middle of their chest. In yet another part there are headless men whose eyes and mouths are on their backs.[18]

Mandeville's *Travels* started to circulate across Europe between 1356 and 1366. In summing up the purpose of the text, C. D. R. W. Moseley writes, 'The medieval ideal of lust and lore – pleasure and instruction – seems to be the goal.'[19]

Originally written in French, by 1400 there were versions available in every major European language. There were also picture book editions for devotional use. The work was so popular that at least 300 versions have survived. Various versions of the text are still in print today, though unfortunately few of these are illustrated.[20]

Mandeville's *Travels* illustrates the possibilities and controversies tied up with the mapping, interpreting and making real, of unfamiliar, unknowable 'realities'.

In terms of history, Mandeville's knowledge was trusted by both navigators and armchair travellers. It is suggested that Columbus took the work with him on his first voyage. Further, as Moseley and Greenblatt[21] explain, to the people of the Middle Ages literature was polysemous and knowledge of the physical world was to be reconciled with Faith and Reason. The *Travels* are a kind of anti-geography, that is:

> . . . a system of imaginary geography, a geography beyond geography, as it were – a system of fantasy with roots in classical antiquity that had a long development in early modern Europe and that continues to be observed even today, albeit in a highly modified form. In anti-geographical fantasy the imagination takes as its objects phenomenon that occupy what today we might call 'the beyond'. Sometimes serious and quasi-scientific, sometimes merely playful or comic, and often a combination of the two, a specimen of jocoserious discourse, anti-geography fills up the spaces of the beyond as if they were similar to or continuous with the world at hand, and as if contiguity guaranteed some form of continuity.[22]

The *Travels* have also been described in terms of transgression.

> 'Transgression' denotes the moment of crossing the limit between that which is known or familiar to us, the Same, and that which is unknown or does not want to be known, the Other . . .
>
> Travelling is transgression. A travel narrative, even if it portrays a purely imaginary voyage, is the verbalization and textualization of transgression, of the crossing of borders and limits. In *The Travels of Sir John Mandeville* the Mandeville narrator travels along the frontiers of the world known to medieval Christendom and traverses the terra incognita outside his culture's experience where imagination, myth, and fear blend into each other . . .[23]

The *Travels* affirms medieval world views but it also plays with these, and with the authority of Mandeville as trusted observer.[24] The text professes concern for the tales not being believed. Some of the knight's more extravagant claims include obtaining a thorn from the Crown of Thorns, serving as a soldier for the Sultan, being offered a princess in marriage by the Sultan, and drinking from the Well of Youth. His work deflects doubts about its own authority by the persona adopting a sceptical tone in parts. He also addresses the question of trust more explicitly, with reference to another story. Mandeville tells of carrying his book of *Travels* to Rome where it received Papal ratification 'in all points'. The stories are true because Mandeville, the author, tells us that he was there when the Pope and his wise counsel authenticated them by reference to another Latin text that 'contained all that and mickle more.'[25]

The popularity of the book survived serious concerns about its accuracy and relevance that date from the late sixteenth century.[26] Mandeville's disrepute amongst navigators was not just a consequence of his factual errors and irritation at his colourful exaggerations. Mandeville was also inclined to comment on the importance of abstinence, rather than of taking possession of worldly things. His reflections were always tied back to Christianity and to the Holy City of Jerusalem as the centre of the world. Greenblatt notes that unlike the accounts of Marco Polo or Columbus, his travel was distinctly unrelated to the identification of new trade opportunities.

By 1820 the critic Hugh Murray described the text as 'a pure and entire fabrication' which had been copied and pillaged from other books. 'What he added of his own', Murray concluded, 'consists quite exclusively of monstrous lies.'[27] Moseley notes in passing that 'The response to and use of the *Travels* can be used as an intellectual litmus to test the assumptions, values and perceptions of a given period.'[28]

With this in mind it is interesting to reflect upon the significance of the flurry of more recent scholarly interest in the work. The *Travels* are used to reconstruct both serious and playful accounts of medieval experience, often contrasting that time with the discoveries of Columbus, the enlightenment, colonisation, imperialism, the roots of western racism[29] and the need for sensitivity to different notions of time, space and narrative.

The pull to reinterpret the *Travels* also feeds on our transgressive desires to imagine a fantastic and novel journey. As Italo Calvino describes at the start of *If on a Winter's Night a Traveller*:

> You derive a special pleasure from a just-published book, and it isn't only a book you are taking with you but its novelty as well, which could also be merely that of an object fresh from the factory, the youthful bloom of new books, which lasts until the dust jacket begins to yellow, until a veil of smog settles on the top edge, until the binding becomes dog eared, in the rapid autumn of libraries. No, you hope always to encounter true newness, which, having been new once, will continue to be so. Having read the freshly published book, you will take possession of this newness at the first moment, without having to pursue it, to chase it. Will it happen this time? You never can tell. Let's see how it begins.[30]

Perhaps the Mandevellian attraction is of fleeing to a space away from our own narrow preoccupations – from our particular economics, expansionist intentions, the pace of change and associated shrinkings of distance. As Calvino puts it in relation to an earlier shrinkage of the world brought about by reliable air travel:

> To fly is the opposite of travelling: you cross a gap in space, you vanish into the void, you accept not being in any place for a duration that is itself a kind of void in time; then you reappear, in a place and in a moment with no relation to the where and the when in which you vanished.[31]

The dot com bubble: the ugly face of internet space and time?

There is an uneasy connection between the boastfulness of Mandeville's exploits and the unreality of the dot com bubble, which was accompanied by our own times' equivalent to Mandeville's exciting tales of discovery. Extraordinary claims about expansive new horizons were taken seriously by e-commerce explorers, their backers and the broader public, only to be later followed by revisionist denunciations of the collective stupidity associated with believing in such tales, and attempts to allocate blame for the unwarranted circulation of such ridiculous fictions.[32]

Economic data, whether compiled as individual share prices, as sector analyses or as global flows, could be considered the contemporary equivalent of Mandeville's imaginary creatures. Financial data is spectacular, foreboding or beastly, depending upon one's point of exposure.

Consider, for example, these illustrations of the global cultural trade landscape, compiled to demonstrate the down-under-side of the information technology and communications wave.

Information and communications technology (ICT) was valued at $US2.414 billion in 2001. This constituted an 86% increase on 1992 levels. ICT spending accounted for 7.6% of GDP, up from 5.6% in 1992. However the USA and Japan account for 50% of world expenditure. Australian expenditure on ICT is less than 2% of the world total, but based on population, expenditure per person is five times the world average.[33]

Increases in ICT spending can contribute to the overall trade deficit. Nonetheless this spending is often read as necessary and an indication of future efficiencies, productivity gains and increased global competitiveness in the sectors buying the technology. But are we making the most of the technological flows associated with globalisation? Are we spending enough?

Table 1 *Information and communications services: value of Australian trade 2002–2003*

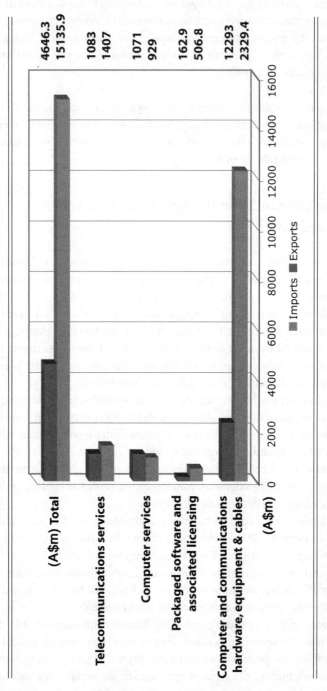

	Imports	Exports
(A$m) Total	4646.3	15135.9
Telecommunications services	1083	1407
Computer services	1071	929
Packaged software and associated licensing	162.9	506.8
Computer and communications hardware, equipment & cables	12293	2329.4

Reference: Australian Bureau of Statistics, *Trade in ICT goods and services by broad commodity group*, ABS Information Technology, Australia, 2002–03 (cat. no. 8126.0)

Table 2 *Digital media: value of Australian trade*

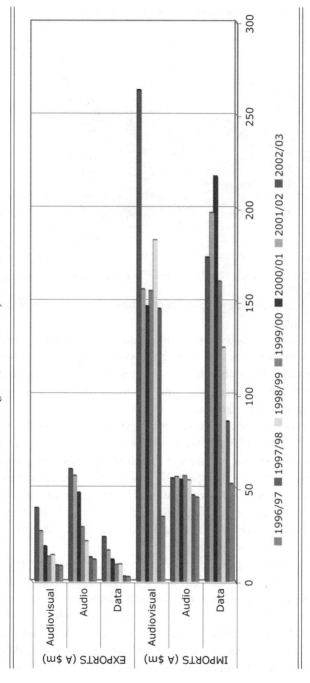

1996/97 ■ 1997/98 ■ 1998/99 ■ 1999/00 ■ 2000/01 ■ 2001/02 ■ 2002/03

Reference: Australian Film Commission, Australian Bureau of Statistics, International Trade, FASTRACCS Service, cited on <http://www.afc.gov.au/gtp/wnmiitrade.html>, viewed February 2005

Table 3 *Household and individual access to ICT*

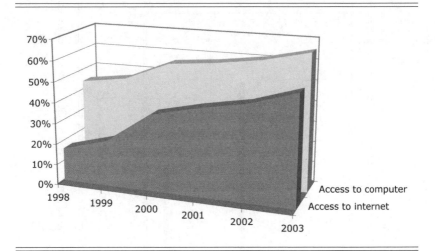

Reference: ABS, *Household Use of Information Technology,* Australia (cat. no. 8146.0)

And when does technology expenditure actually show in terms of improved financial results?

There are various 'globalisation indices' to assist with comparative readings and related analyses that suggest the significance of developments in various sectors.[34] Invariably data can read in terms of 'opportunity' and in terms of 'danger', related to speculation about what is now required for success in the global marketplace.

Analyses are not just concerned with plotting the progress of globalised markets, and viewing global flows as positive forces. The growth of the internet and related economic activity, in a climate of trade liberalisation, was not necessarily welcomed by all, especially outside of the US. The development was accompanied by prophecies of cultural imperialism, with global media conglomerates further extending their reach.[35] Internet technology simply provided another level for vertical integration, market concentration and cultural homogenisation, it was argued.[36]

Statistics and tables were compiled from material produced by the Australian Film Commission, a government agency that supports the local independent production of film, television and interactive digital media (see Table 5). They point to the realities of the economic and cultural flows already existing, and hope to inform Australian trade negotiations that could lead to changes in existing government cultural policies that currently support the local film industry, and are complained of by the US as 'protectionism'.

Table 4 *Example of vertical integration in media interests*

Time Warner 2003 Revenues = US $39.6 billion

TV/Movies

The WB network includes:

Cable Channels: HBO, CNN, Turner, TBS, Cartoon Network, Turner Classic
   Movies, Court TV (in part)

Time Warner Cable: Including cable service and RoadRunner broadband access

Production/Distribution: Warner Bros Studios, Hanna-Barbera Cartoons,
   Castle Rock Entertainment, Warner Home Video, WB Pay- TV, New Line
   Cinema

Movie Theatres: owns/operates multiplex theatres in over 12 countries.

Music

Warner Music Group includes:

Atlantic Recordings, Rhino Records, Elektra Entertainment Group, Elektra/Sire,
   Warner Brothers Records, Reprise, Warner Music International

Other Recording Interests: Warner/Chappell Music (publishing company),
   WEA Inc. (sales, distribution and manufacturing), Ivy Hill Corporation
   (printing and packaging).

Publishing

Time-Life Books: Time-Life Audiobooks, Book-of-the-Month Club, Little,
   Brown and Company, Bulfinch Press, Back Bay Books, Little, Brown and
   Company (U.K.)

Magazines: Time, Fortune, Business 2.0, Life, Sports Illustrated, Who Weekly,
   Entertainment Weekly, Asiaweek (Japan), Wallpaper (UK), Popular Science,
   Mad Magazine

Comic Books: DC Comics.

Internet

America Online, Netscape Communications, Winamp, CompuServe
   Interactive, iAmaze, Amazon.com (partial).

Other

Services: Road Runner, Warner Publisher Services, Time Distribution Services,
   Pathfinder

Retail: Warner Bros. Stores & Products

Theme Parks: Warner Brothers Recreation Enterprises

Sports: Atlanta Braves, Hawks, Thrashers, Goodwill Games, Turner Sports,
   Philips Arena

Misc.: Turner Learning, CNN Newsroom (for classrooms), Turner Adventure
   Learning (electronic field trips), Turner Home Satellite, Turner Network
   Sales.

Reference: 'Free Press: Who owns the Media?' *Columbia Journalism Review*

Table 5 *Royalties and trade deficit arising from imports and exports of cinema films, TV programs and videos in Australia*

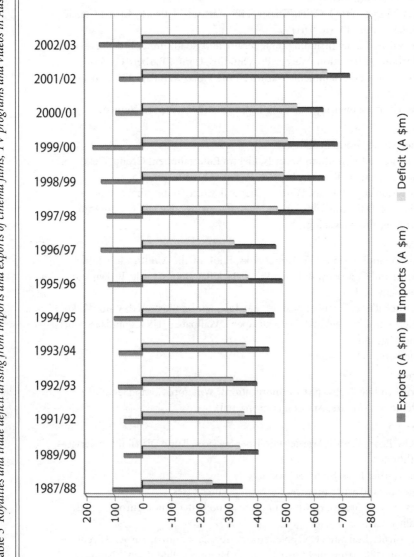

■ Exports (A $m)   ■ Imports (A $m)   ▨ Deficit (A $m)

Reference: Australian Film Commission, Australian Bureau of Statistics, *Balance of Payments and International Investment Position*

Note 2000/01 excludes earnings by the Sydney Organising Committee of the Olympic Games (SOCOG)

Internet access is anticipated to simply exacerbate the existing problems of cultural trade imbalances and monopoly power, and further reduce the visibility of and space for consumption of local efforts, once viable models for commercial online distribution of digital product are put in place.

Whilst few would argue that the might of multinational media conglomerates is clearly to be reckoned with, the retort is to point to new opportunities for two-way exchanges in cultural trade, the potential for cultural hybridisation, as well as the significance of local negotiations and resistance.[37]

E-commerce, it is often argued, offers a potential levelling power, since both multinational and small business operate in the same online space. Further the 1990s showed how hobbies could become businesses running from a garage, and once they had attracted venture capital, small businesses could quickly turn the innovators, backers and mum and dad shareholders into millionaires. Further, with the ability to access share information and trade online, there was no longer any need for other intermediaries and associated delays in calculating and reinvesting returns. This contributed to even more accelerated growth – for a time.

Many have since been blamed for encouraging delusional beliefs about the value of e-commerce to global trade throughout the 1990s. Those targeted include the IT media fronted by people like Louis Rossetto, the founder of *Wired* magazine. This class are held responsible for engendering a climate that was receptive to false beliefs about the value of technology and innovation to the future.[38] Blame is also heaped upon Wall Street analysts such as Henry Blodget. Analysts are at fault for encouraging speculation in stock they more realistically believed to be of very questionable value. The financial media that uncritically reported the overblown accounts of these opinion makers are also criticised.[39] To this, attacks on Alan Greenspan and the Federal Reserve must be added. They are held responsible for overstating the importance of information technology in the economy, encouraging unrealistic assessments about the role of technology in reducing production costs outside of the IT sector[40] and refusing to intervene in an overheated market by adjusting interest rates or warning about the dangers of excessive speculation.[41]

Many accounts blur the line between criticism of the values of neoliberal economics and of internet culture more generally. Both are considered as infected with an essentially selfish rationality, encouraging the community to gamble upon the ability to make ever quicker calculations of personal gain and disregard the consequences. For example, John Cassidy writes:

Table 6 *US technology, media and telecommunications: equity prices versus profits, March 1995–March 2000*

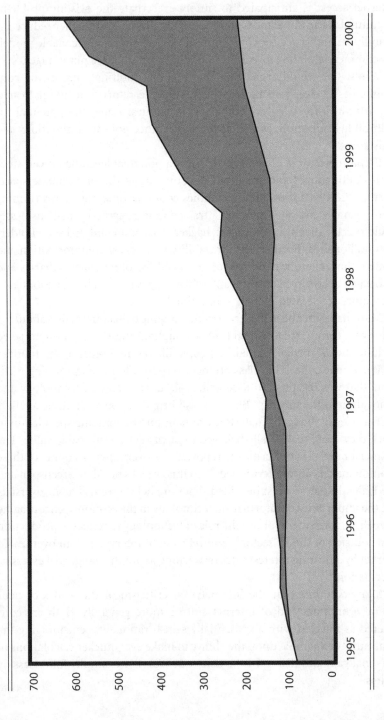

Reference: Robert Brenner, *The Boom and the Bubble: The US in the World Economy* (Verso, 2003), p. 187
Note: The upper line represents equity prices

Table 7 *Gross proceeds of initial public offerings, US economy 1975–2000*

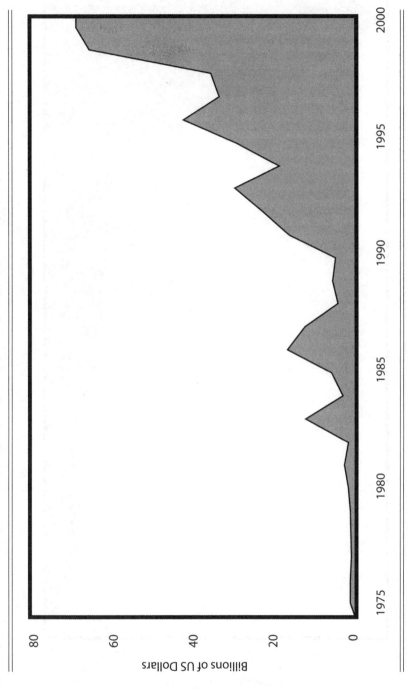

Reference: Robert Brenner, *The Boom and the Bubble: The US in the World Economy* (Verso, 2003), p. 197

Table 8 *Venture capital investment, US economy 1995–2000*

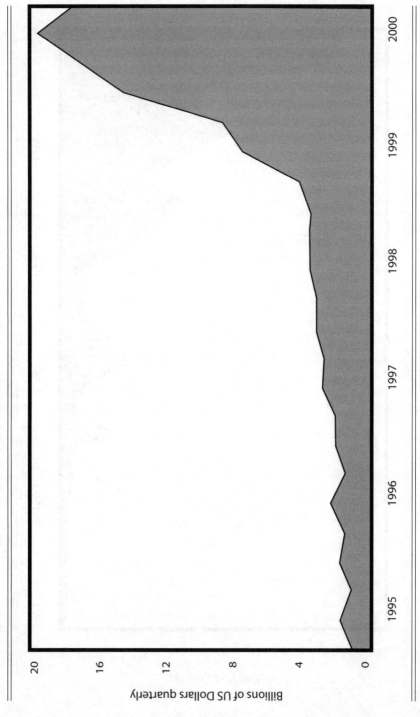

Billions of US Dollars quarterly

Reference: Robert Brenner, *The Boom and the Bubble: The US in the World Economy* (Verso, 2003), p. 227

At the height of the boom, the United States was consumed by the idea of getting rich on the Internet . . . the Internet boom and bust was like an epic miniseries that grabbed the imagination of the country and held it rapt until the final episode had ended. By quitting their jobs and joining an internet start-up, or by simply buying a few hundred shares in Yahoo!, (the public) could become actors in the ongoing drama. The desire not to feel left out fuels all mass movements. Coupled with greed it is virtually irresistible.[42]

'Pets.com because pets don't drive'

Pets.com is the paradigmatic tale, no doubt partly because its notoriety was enhanced by the success of its television advertising campaigns. Old media helped secure a solid level of recognition of the name of the virtual pet store, but the venture still failed.[43]

Pets.com was founded in 1989 by an entrepreneur who had registered hundreds of internet addresses, then in 1999 sought the backing of a Silicon Valley venture firm. Amazon.com also backed the venture. Amazon's involvement was considered important since there were other online pet stores associated with established companies that already dominated pet food retailing. At the time all these ventures were also only beginning to have an online presence. The pet food and accessory market was estimated as worth over $US 20 billion a year.

Pets.com had raised more than $US 100 million, but with costly advertising campaigns in order to establish brand presence, and with selling stock below cost and free shipping (even though pet food items can be very bulky) in order to attract customers from rivals, pets.com lost $61.8 million, with revenue of only $5.8 million in 1999. Yet projections were positive. At the pets.com stockmarket debut in February 2000, Merrill Lynch had priced 7.5 million shares at $11 each. In explaining the hype, former pets.com employee Carlotta Mast says:

> I wanted in on the dot.com dream . . . After only a year at Pets, even people with meagre option packages like mine would finally have the dough to go to graduate school.
>
> Sure the online pet market was crowded, despite the pet supply industry's slim margins. And yes, we were selling and shipping our dog food for less than we paid for it in order to make our revenue goals. But those were Old Economy considerations, and this was the Brave New Economy of the internet. Pets.com was just doing what the investment community demanded: Grabbing market share and getting big fast.[44]

The initial public offering (IPO) raised a further $US 82.5 million. The share price peaked at $14 and closed on the first day back at its opening price of $11. The price then slid over the next ten months, along with the share price of many other dot com retailers. Pets.com closed for business in mid-November 2000 with the company valued at about $6.4 million.

At the end of 2000 brand recognition and getting big fast were no longer considered enough:

> Most Internet start-ups failed because they were based on the premise that the Internet represented a revolutionary new business model, which it didn't . . . The Internet companies that had survived were those providing services that wouldn't otherwise have existed . . . The Internet's greatest strength is its capacity to process information. Any good that can be standardized and converted into ones and zeros has the potential to support online commerce.[45]

Does this mean the Brave New Economy is just an assortment of 'special cases' – of flows of spam, financial services, pornography, MP3 and maybe film?

The problem with popular dot com analyses is that, because they are focused on explaining troubling events of the past, they offer little insight into the significance of the changes that have occurred that reach into the future. They allocate blame for a pre-defined problem, rather than explore its parameters. Such analyses may further affect the confidence of investors in the technology sector,[46] but a story of unrealistic financial expectations and over-exuberance about getting rich quick isn't a full picture of the significance of the changes brought about by the internet either.

As most broader analyses discuss:

> Studies of the impact of ICT (Information and communications technology) also make it clear that ICT is not a panacea. Technology does not, on its own drive transformation – that comes from the policy environment, strategic decisions and change strategies embraced by individuals, firms and governments. The way in which ICT investments are managed, and ICTR products and services used, has a major impact on the benefits achieved.[47]

It is difficult to meaningfully quarantine the impact of ICT. It is not one industry sector because ICT goods and services permeate all the 'Old Economy' sectors. The mediascapes, technoscapes, finanscapes, ideoscapes blur the definition of the lines of the Old Economy. And the ICT policies, decisions and strategies of individuals, firms and governments affect all sectors, albeit differentially.

It's possible that I am (or you are) in the Matrix right now[48]

A more enduring concern about internet futures and productivities is the question of who controls the landscapes and the flows. The metaphors of the Matrix, the intelligent machine, with all-pervasive macro and micro presences, ever adaptive, creative, able to anticipate resistances and micro-manage desired changes, is an image with strong resonances in the 1980s and 1990s analysis of global communications. Whereas Mandeville's medieval realities framed his visions, here it is the already familiar vision of the technological landscape, and polarised good and evil, that carries the story.

In films like *The Matrix* technology is presented as a potent force, dangerous in its capacity to control – always moving actively at the edges beyond us and potentially in opposition to us. Through mechanisms of power that synchronise total control with illusions of freedom, it poses a serious threat to humanity, with humanity represented as grand-scale 'civilising' emotions and bonds that mysteriously inform militaristic-style models of command and resistance.

Technology has come to be commonly represented in opposition to community – with technological cultures blamed for further heightening alienation and loss of 'real' connections between peoples.[49] Remnants of humanity exist largely amongst the primate and feral, the recyclers of older sciences, with far more limited technological means at their disposal. New technology is presumed to be autonomous, abstract, active, clean, efficient, impersonal, potentially endless in reach and scope, and highly individualised. As a consequence, the communities that create and use new technology are represented as highly fragmented and largely impotent. In the new landscapes there are only reactive capabilities for action and interventions, not by the ordinary technology maker and user, but only by the truly exceptional and unique personalities, miraculously less affected than the rest of us, by the mainstream.

Whilst the more critical globalisation literature seeks to address the complexity of new technological modes of power, this work is nonetheless also inflected by a similar sense of hyper-reality – of technology as spectacle. This comes into writings in the conventional way discussions of technology relate, or more to the point do not relate, to community. The prevailing scepticism is that:

> the agora, the general community, has gone . . . There is no place left where people can discuss the realities which concern them, because they can never lastingly free themselves from the crushing presence of media discourse and of the various forces organized to relay it.[50]

We need to reassess this position and the machine metaphors that support it. It may not be possible to construct the idea of an internet culture that is not in some sense also an idealised and imaginary one. But there is a need to relocate analysis away from phantasms of technology, bleatings for lost community or presumptions that communities simply vanish under the weight of the wires.

Technological control is constructed through hardware and software design, and arrangement of the wires that enable connections, with power enhanced by the privileges conferred by laws such as those conferred by copyright and patent ownership. There are many sites, locations, organisations, formally and informally constituted, where the nature and consequences of these technological controls are discussed and debated.

As makers and purveyors of internet cultures, the output of technological communities can reach into far broader domains – economic, political, social and domestic. As knowledge producers whose major output translates into new products and services, and ways of managing, processing, and distributing information, these people are significant negotiators and mediators of global power and control. As discussed in the previous chapter, these are complex distributions of influence that exceed any simple, universal manifestation of control over the landscape.

Unlike their cinematic representations, communities making new technologies are not generally all that closed, most of the time. For reasons of practical dependencies on others' outputs, and conditions related to state-sponsored grants of rights and privilege, the presumption tends the other way. As with other spaces for discourse, it is true that certain kinds of competencies and literacies are assumed. But even when decision-making and deliberations are quite secret, there is still opportunity to reflect upon the 'realities' being constructed, to the extent that there are still usually various kinds of documentations and information flows that allow this. One of the advantages of the internet is that information flows tend toward excess, rather than shortage.

This is not to say that there are no controls; nor that individual agendas do not exist; or that discourse is not manipulated, is unaffected by greed, corruption, various manifestations of self-interest and related seductions. It is also the case that through an extraordinary level of participation in making, and perhaps more influentially, through talking about the meaning of technology, what outsiders intuitively recognise as 'US cultural influence' tends to predominate. However in every forum even this culture presents in different aspects.

There are always different possibilities, influences, priorities, ideologies and practical constraints that operate. Mixes lead to quite diverse approaches toward technology, law and power within particular internet communities and help define significant demarcations between them. Rather than presume an inquiry into the roles of these communities is a wasted effort, deliberations, proposals and actions that construct technological realities and global powers deserve to be carefully surveyed, identified and mapped.

This kind of exploration has its own problems of selectivity and of producing communities as (hopefully, at least interesting) cultural artefacts. Further, because of the well-developed urgency associated with our technological time, which is always about 'here and now' – an instant threatening to vanish into the void of the past – there is the problem of dredging up old, cold debates. But my inquiry is more about the manner of travel – about the journey – than it is about the 'here and now' of the destination. It is primarily about exploring the processes, the understandings of power, historical position and influence related to internet cultures. And in hoping to better understand these communities and their travels, perhaps we may better understand more precisely where we are, here and now.

3

Universal standards and the end of the universe: the IETF, global governance and patents

In 1953 Arthur C. Clarke wrote a short story about the Automatic Sequence Computer.[1] The story draws upon cabbalist beliefs that the Holy Text contains a revelation, hidden in the letters. Because God's name cannot be arbitrary, the correct order and number of the letters is the key to the revelation. If every possible permutation of the Holy Text could be calculated, it is believed that the Holy Name will be pronounced.

In the story, the Automatic Sequence Computer calculates any routine mathematical operation involving up to ten digits. The machine is hired by a Lama, who seeks to convert its number-crunching ability into the calculation of combinations of letters, according to an alphabet the lamasery has developed:

> 'All the many names of the Supreme Being – God, Jehovah, Allah, and so on – they are only man-made labels . . . but somewhere among all the possible combinations of letters which can occur are what one may call the real names of God. By systematic permutation of letters, we have been trying to list them all.'

The lamasery has been working on this task for over three centuries. It was predicted that completing the work would take another fifteen thousand years. But with the new technology, the task might be accomplished in a matter of a hundred days.

Two technicians are sent to the lamasery to assist with the installation and maintenance of the machine. They are bemused by what they see as the folly of the monks and the meaninglessness of the project. But their machine performs well. Their main worry is that the monks will change their mind, ask for a different computation and, in doing so, extend their stay. This fear proves to be unfounded.

Toward the very end of the three months, when the machine reaches its last cycle there is great excitement. The High Lama asks one of the technicians,

George, if he'd ever wondered what they were trying to do. As George later relates to Chuck:

> 'Well, they believe that when they have listed all his names – and they reckon that there are about nine billion of them – God's purpose will be achieved. The human race will have finished what it was created to do, and there won't be any point in carrying on. Indeed the very idea is something like blasphemy.'
>
> 'Then what do they expect us to do? Commit suicide?'
>
> 'There's no need for that. When the list's completed, God steps in and simply winds things up . . . bingo!'

Chuck just sees this as further evidence that the monks are crazy. But George sees it as a cause for real concern:

> 'Yes – but don't you see what may happen? When the list's complete and the last trump doesn't blow – or whatever it is they expect – we may get the blame. It's our machine they've been using. I don't like the situation one little bit.'

It never occurs to the technicians till very late in the day that it might be appropriate for them to inquire into the significance of the project – a project they have helped bring to fruition. They are technicians, not philosophers. Their job is to keep things moving. In the 1950s worrying about the future and about how computers could affect it – create their future and that of others – hadn't rated so highly.

But here in a place a long way from their more familiar Manhattan mountains, the technicians are vulnerable.

They fear that the Lama and his assistants will challenge the reliability of the technology, rather than accept responsibility for spiritual error. To George the best possible outcome is suggested by a childhood recollection of what happened when a local preacher had wrongly predicted the end of the world. Some believers had sold their houses and made rather radical lifestyle changes based upon what had now objectively been proven, an erroneous view. But rather than accept the gravity of their mistake, many simply assumed the preacher had miscalculated the dates. They went right on believing.

> Would the monks smash up the computer in their rage and disappointment?
> Or would they just sit down quietly and begin their calculations all over again?

Chuck and George decide they don't want to stay around and see how those in the lamasery deal with modern scientific truth and unpalatable realities. They decide to leave.

The two make their way down the mountain on horseback toward a runway and an old DC3 aircraft, reassured by the security of a bright, cold, clear sky, that means the weather will not impede the pilot's take off:

'Wonder if the computer's finished its run? It was due about now.'

Chuck didn't reply, so George swung around in his saddle. He could see Chuck's face, a white oval turned toward the sky.

'Look', whispered Chuck, and George lifted his eyes to heaven. (There is always a last time for everything.)

Overhead, without any fuss, the stars were going out.

***

Questions of responsibility

The engineers, logicians, mathematicians, programmers and administrators whose technical productivity powers the internet make decisions in the form of rules, conventions and standards. Whilst this is now commonly recognised in literature about internet governance, the role of these parties as knowledge producers and law-makers, and how they see the question of responsibility associated with their standard-setting, is rarely the object of study.

Conventional wisdom suggests that internet culture could once be read in terms of its origins. The internet was the product of its early engineering environment. This was a male, techie culture that was relatively homogenous informed by the close-knit, personal and relatively casual relations attributed to the Californian engineering communities of the time:

The 'community consensus' idea of the early days of the Internet (1986–1996) was indeed part of a specific culture that developed among the (mostly male) engineers. Like all social groupings, that culture developed its own pecking order and ruling elite, but it also had communitarian, democratic and liberal elements. Democratic in the sense in which the Magna Carta was democratic – peers demanding that their prerogatives not be impinged on by the King. Liberal in that they supported open systems and resisted the state. Communitarian in that there was a strong sense of collective identity and responsibility and because one of the key issues for them was whether you were inside or outside their community.[2]

Though it is never directly stated, current histories of the old days hint at hippie 'spiritual errors' associated with this first community of believers. The implication is that, whilst they saw themselves as relaxed and unauthoritarian, in fact they were dogmatic, somewhat arrogant and naïve. They failed to appreciate the social complexity of the universe they were building or reflect on their ability to rule the horizons just by prescribing social norms.

In any case, these technical communities got too big, the politics too difficult to manage in-house, or to be overseen by any one national government agency. Eventually new specialist global institutions like ICANN (Internet Corporation for Assigned Names and Numbers) emerged to take over some of the management issues. It is not surprising that most of the governance critiques have focused on ICANN. ICANN was perceived as a kind of a prototype for a new technocratic form of world governance – with its experiments in voluntary organisation, registration, voting, supranational regional representation and complex interactions within nation states. ICANN and its experiments with global representation and democracy have borne the brunt of critical attention.[3]

ICANN was established in 1998 to take over the role formerly administered under US government contract by the Internet Assigned Number Authority (IANA), co-ordinating the global assignment of internet domain names, IP address numbers and protocol parameter and port numbers.[4] Former ICANN Chair Esther Dyson has said that the institution 'governs the plumbing, not the people. It has a very limited mandate to administer certain (largely technical) aspects of the Internet infrastructure in general and the Domain Name System in particular.'[5] However deciding a right to a domain name is not simply a technical matter. The right to 'own' names is already governed by established bodies of law.

Developed nation states already had established trade mark and trade practices laws, and associated bureaucracies administering the right to use and own names within their jurisdictions. These laws generally balance competing commercial demands, competition issues, consumer protection and free speech considerations. However even within the common law, Anglo-speaking world, there are significant differences in the applicable legislation.

The expectations of the global rewards from e-commerce were initially extremely high, and profile online 'signage' was recognised as a key component of commercial success.[6] Enterprises keen to set up websites and attract custom commonly experienced threats of litigation from larger organisations with well-known registered trade marks who objected to the 'online upstart' presuming an entitlement to use 'their' name in relation to an internet address. Fan sites and individual personal webpages were also commonly aggressively targeted, with the owners told that if they did not shut down immediately, litigation was imminent. At the time this led to a proliferation of sites dedicated to exposing the intimidation.[7]

It was widely feared that the economic and legal privileges of multinationals would only be further concentrated through the establishment of new global legal institutions managing domain name spaces. The predatory and often misleading massive overstatement of the significance of the trade mark registration, mapped onto claims to thereby have a prior 'right' to a unique internet address, fuelled suspicions about the interests served by 'technical' decisions concerning online addressing systems.

Though not without controversy, the domain name ownership issue was largely defused by ICANN developing a uniform dispute resolution policy. ICANN policy is to essentially maintain authority over cyber-squatting, where the only interest in the name is to profit from it, generally by selling it back to a party with a legitimate need to use it, for example, where the aggrieved party already has a reputation associated with the use of that name. When it comes to the more contentious cases of competing rights to legitimate uses of a name, ICANN defers to the outcome of court litigation between the parties claiming rights to the registration within the relevant jurisdictions. The administration of the registration of names within the various country code areas is generally overseen by specialist agencies set up by national governments and affiliated with ICANN.

Whilst much of the heat has now gone from the trade mark issue, what was learnt from this experience was that the power to make decisions about internet architecture was a significant one. These decisions were key to the development of the global economy, for maintaining the power of nation states and a continuing role for associated bureaucracies and courts in relation to the economy, as well as affecting some possibilities for the free expression of citizens online.

Watchdog organisations like ICANNwatch[8] gave voice to the 'open internet' heritage, expressed as a faith in the virtue of 'free' communications:

> We have no particular viewpoint to push or axes to grind; we will offer commentary and criticism from a wide variety of different perspectives, guided only by our belief in the power of ideas and informed discussion and debate to shape events and institutions . . .

But the earlier casual and relaxed attitude once associated with openness toward decision-making lapsed, replaced by a sense of gravity and solemnity. As the ICANNwatch mission statement announces, 'The consequences of these developments for the Internet's future could not be more profound – David Post.'

It is interesting that whilst the governance model of ICANN has attracted a lot of debate, other large-scale global institutions that share a similar heritage, like IETF (the Internet Engineering Task Force), a body responsible for developing technical standards for the internet, have escaped the same level of scrutiny, at least for now. There is one cynical explanation for this. The more specialised the global organisation and the less openly it discusses its decision-making processes and engages with nation states, the less likely it is that it will be exposed to criticism from outsiders, especially from lawyers.

A new United Nations-endorsed organisation, the World Summit on the Information Society (WSIS),[9] was formed following a resolution of the International Telecommunications Union in 1998 to examine issues concerning the information revolution and its impact on the international community. Though observing that 'the global information society is evolving at breakneck speed',[10] the first summit was not held till December 2003 and a second is scheduled for November 2005. The rather ambitious Declaration of Principles adopted at the first summit by representatives affirmed a:

> . . . common desire and commitment to build a people-centred, inclusive and development-oriented Information Society, where everyone can create, access, utilize and share information and knowledge, enabling individuals, communities and peoples to achieve their full potential in promoting their sustainable development and improving their quality of life, premised on the purposes and principles of the Charter of the United Nations and respecting fully and upholding the Universal Declaration of Human Rights.
>
> Our challenge is to harness the potential of information and communication technology to promote the development goals of the Millennium Declaration, namely the eradication of extreme poverty and hunger; achievement of universal primary education; promotion of gender equality and empowerment of women; reduction of child mortality; improvement of maternal health; to combat HIV/AIDS, malaria and other diseases; ensuring environmental sustainability; and development of global partnerships for development for the attainment of a more peaceful, just and prosperous world.[11]

It is unclear whether this forum will provide more scope for debate about models of global governance.[12] Some hope that the more 'international' orientation and links with the United Nations will permit a shift away from the perceived cultural baggage, as well as the leadership role of the United States, that has marked the early debates. However there is no guarantee that US influence can be so clearly or homogenously identified, and presuming that undue cultural influence can be identified as a problem, that it could be effectively isolated. To date there has been scant analysis and understanding of the intersection of culture and governance in relation to the internet. 'Cultural explanations' have been generally addressed in terms of others creating problems to be later solved, rather than culture being acknowledged as an inevitable part of the governance debate.

As Foucault and others have discussed, the question of governance involves far more than simply establishing the formal apparatus and rules associated with ruling.[13] My concern is that, especially in law circles, short, vague references to 'culture' mask far more complex relationships of power and governance.

Though in both engineering and legal domains Arthur C. Clarke's concerns about responsible computing have been taken to heart, loose sociological explanations and philosophical and psychological profiles have been suggested to explain past attitudes toward issues of responsibility and accountability. Though writers on the early history of the internet are channelling what they see as 'cultural explanations' for the emergence of new forms of governance associated with technological law-making, the tendency is still to individualise origins. 'Pioneers'[14] like Stephen Crocker, Vinton Cerf,[15] Jon Postel[16] and Tim Berners-Lee[17] are treated with fondness and respect, and credited for planting the seeds for what followed.

There is a lack of narrative resources that makes it difficult to relate technology and social theory.[18] To fill the gap we resort to telling the story of the prominent individuals and their association with the development of innovations to anchor the narrative. One consequence of this is that although it is recognised that the development of the internet was collaborative, questions of responsibility are still largely tackled as if it were a matter of locating authorship – of locating significant personal inscriptions ultimately disseminated in the form of important structural decisions about governance and settled as standards and conventions. And perhaps the challenge of governance, especially outside of the United States, is perceived as overcoming the embodiments of those personal, 'cultural' influences, and relocating responsibility for the future to different participants residing elsewhere. But there is no reason to believe that by changing the forum or its leadership this will lead to different or better outcomes for internet governance.

Without agreement over the values served in relation to the practices of governance, there are often claims that the exercise of power is merely coercive. In the absence of supporting rationales for the exercise of power that the membership accedes to, the complaint is often that the rule is really only grounded in compulsion and it is therefore illegitimate.

'Cultural' explanations that act as a rough code for references to 'Californian' political values used to explain the roots of internet governance need to be related to the politics of the institutions in which the values were expressed. Whilst individuals can and do make a difference, what gets lost in the stories about internet pioneers is a more practical and functional focus on the way institutional considerations affect action and technological realities, as such. For example, whilst certain engineers' views about the state and consensus come to be highlighted, the practical reasons for adopting a collaborative approach are de-emphasised. Institutional co-operation and reliance on open standards were important to the development of the internet, not just because of the imposition of personal values and particular cultural norms, or because this accelerated progress or innovation. More simply the task was too big for any one person, team or department. The talent and equipment were never all in one place. It was experimental work. This created a certain level of freedom and opportunity for younger, energetic, obsessive types who could individually contribute components, but these efforts and sub-divisions of labour had to be integrated with those of others, elsewhere.

Though describing the specific example of high energy physics and astrophysics, Peter Galison describes the tendency to conjure a 'pseudo-I' as the speaking voice for large-scale science projects.[19] He notes some aspects of these 'metacollaborative' projects:

- the modes of discourse are quite variable. There are usually notes, technical papers, rapporteur talks, conference presentations. Each of these avenues of publication has its own characteristic content, including forms of review, forms of attribution, which may include anonymity, and intended range of circulation;
- who can speak is also regulated. There can be an authorship committee or equivalent authorising body, as well as determinations about what can be publicly said, where 'public' is itself a variable construct;
- there are controls over who is counted as a participant in a list. There may be temporary participants to masthead mentors, engineers allowed to sign off on technical reports, authors left off and others dissuaded from removing their association.[20]

Galison suggests that the scale of these mega-science projects means that the collective author is always more than the additive sum of many individuals executing the tasks:

The team supplanted the individual not because the individual was just articulating a widespread murmur of the group. No, the team replaced the individual because the individual did not (could not) know the length and breadth of the experimental problem. When the spokesperson spoke she did not necessarily articulate the general consensus, she spoke of things that no-one in particular could ever possibly fully know, but that the group could, in the end, assemble.[21]

... The answer to 'Who is We?' in the context of a two-thousand strong fluid collaboration must always remain unstable, oscillating between the desire to make scientific knowledge the issue of a single consensus mind and the desire to recognise justly the distributed character of the knowledge.

... It may be that experimental knowledge in the age of massive collaborations never comes back to a single center, but rather only to partial overlapping, complicated, inchoately bounded assemblages.[22]

As a functional matter, there is really no point in trying to distinguish the importance of one effort or contribution. Galison argues that that we seek to do so probably relates to the weight of conventional models of attribution in science, and the way efforts are institutionally supported in terms of scientific currency – the conferring of recognition, prestigious appointments, research monies, prizes, salary.[23]

Adapting Galison's observations about the nature of metacollaborative projects to the internet, the description of the demands on participants that affect the form and composition of contributions would apply to both its roots and to the current more mature form. The adoption of informal and 'open' communications and collaboration amongst differently skilled, but like-thinking and committed others, involves more sociological dimensions than it being just the consequence of the mandating of a particular cultural or lifestyle choice by a few. Further, these observations about the nature of metacollaboration lead to difficult questions about the ability to ask anyone to be responsible for the whole, or even for the order of the smaller bits and bytes that are ultimately assembled and continually reassembled.

In discussions of internet governance there is still often a tendency to pretend that the internet can be tackled as a bounded institution developing in accordance with centralised control and along linear notions of time. Whilst no one seriously claims to be on top of all its dimensions, the pretence is that by a process of general oversight through bodies like ICANN, WSIS or other specialist agencies, and practical dissection and distributions of attention to sub-groups of expertise, governance issues and conflicts over direction can be controlled and resolved. Responsibility can be demarcated and attributed to a myriad of 'pseudo-I's'.

The formal constitution and rules of participation in these pseudo-I's will differ. Some may be left relatively alone to continue the tradition of self-governance and 'open' forms of communication. Others will have to acknowledge the ongoing interests of powerful nation states and regional blocs in agenda and policy setting, especially in relation to established areas of government intervention – telecommunications infrastructure, copyright, patent, trade mark law, privacy and e-commerce. 'Self-governing' global communities will have to negotiate these particular political agendas and expectations as well as they can. In each of these pseudo-I's we can expect to find different instincts expressed concerning questions of responsibility, and similar problems of approving the 'I' capable of speaking for the whole collective.

The Internet Engineering Task Force (IETF)

> 'We reject kings, presidents, and voting.
> We believe in rough consensus and running code.'[24]

The IETF was formed in 1986 as a forum for settling short-to-medium-term engineering issues, co-ordinating the efforts of contractors working on development of the internet, which was then known as ARPANET because of the network's association with the US Defense Advanced Research Project Agency (ARPA). The unclassified military traffic had been split off to a separate network, MILNET, in 1984.

IETF's work is linked to that of a number of related organisations, such as the Internet Research Task Force (IRTF). The IRTF focuses on longer-term issues related to internet protocols, applications, architecture and technology. The Internet Architecture Board (IAB) co-ordinates the work of both IETF and IRTF, oversees the process of setting standards and deals with appeals. IANA has responsibility for assigning and managing IP addresses, protocol numbers, RFC numbers and related issues.

The delineations of knowledge and expertise in the IETF are usually described as practical and fluid. The authority structures have developed somewhat organically – in response to perceived needs and demands that are grounded in the experience of trying to get things working, anticipating and identifying problems and developing solutions. Decisions are not made in accordance with a preconceived plan for the whole. Action is taken when justified by proven, specific results, rather than with reference to rank or formal experience. This meant that throughout the 1980s and 1990s structures, priorities and divisions of labour were created and recreated from time to time. However the basic administrative framework related to IETF became more settled in the early 1990s. And there is a more formal hierarchy that has been in place since that time.

In the early 1990s it became apparent that institutional support for the development of this new network, initially provided by the US Department of Defense, Department of Energy, NASA and the National Science Foundation (NSF), would not be endless nor necessarily sufficient. Further the ability to continue to control and co-ordinate standard-setting and related architectural issues would most likely be compromised if there was no overseeing of the commercial development of the internet by people like ISPs. Greater participation from outside of the US in the development of the internet was also to be expected and accounted for. With these concerns in mind the Internet Society (ISOC) was formed in 1992. It was largely made up of people historically associated with the IETF.

ISOC formally describes itself as 'a neutral and internationally recognized body devoted to the support of Internet administrative infrastructures.' More informally the mandate is to 'keep the internet going'.[25] ISOC seeks financial support for the standards process from commercial and institutional sources and provides funds to bodies like IETF.

The IETF mission involves:

- identifying and solving the more pressing operational and technical problems in the Internet;
- specifying the development or usage of protocols and the near-term architecture to solve such technical problems for the Internet;
- making recommendations to the Internet Engineering Steering Group (IESG) regarding the standardization of protocols and protocol usage in the Internet;
- facilitating technology transfer from the Internet Research Task Force (IRTF) to the wider Internet community; and
- providing a forum for the exchange of information within the Internet community between vendors, users, researchers, agency contractors, and network managers.[26]

Membership of IETF is open and it includes network designers, operators, vendors and researchers, all of whom are invited to participate in discussion which largely takes place in working groups devoted to particular technical areas. These groups communicate by online discussion lists, meetings, conferences, technical presentations, network status reports, working group reports, publications of conference proceedings etc. The material is archived and easily accessible.

The Structure of IETF

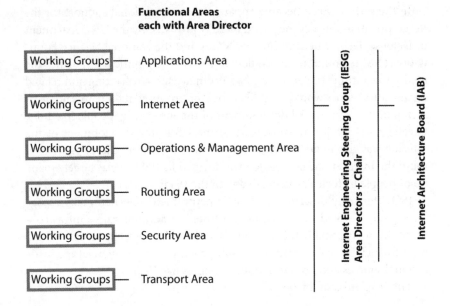

**Functional Areas
each with Area Director**

Working group activities are co-ordinated by Area Directors (ADs) who oversee the work in nominated functional areas e.g.: Applications Area (app); Internet Area (int); Operations & Management Area (ops); Routing Area (rtg); Security Area (sec); Transport Area (tsv). The functional areas and associated working groups are constituted as required. All this activity is overseen within a hierarchical structure.

In explaining the authority of the Area Directors, RFC 3160 states that whilst

> many people look at the ADs as somewhat godlike creatures . . . most ADs are nearly indistinguishable from mere mortals and rarely speak from mountaintops. In fact, when asked for specific technical comments, the ADs may often defer to members at large whom they feel have more knowledge than they do in that area.

Discussions are computer-technical, and disputes within Working Groups (WGs) are sought to be resolved via demonstration of recommended solutions, and subsequent discussions of working models via email.

There are various stages that contribute to the development of RFCs, and there are different types of RFCs – historical, experimental, informational and standards. Another unit related to IETF – the RFC Editor – is responsible for editing, formatting, and publishing Internet Drafts as RFCs, as well as acting as a repository for all kinds of RFCs. Rather than simply deleting a superceded RFC, new standards are simply published as new RFCs. Hence the RFC Editor also serves as a kind of library or archive of all past and current RFC activity.

For an RFC to become a 'standard' there have to have been several independent interoperable implementations of the specification. Whilst the Working Groups run by 'consensus', Internet Drafts have to be approved by a vote of the Internet Engineering Steering Group (IESG). This body is made up of all the Area Directors and the Chair of IETF. Further, two votes against can block a draft from progressing. The reason given for developing voting and veto powers at the IESG is the principle of ruling by consensus:

> . . . one of the main reasons that the IESG might block something that was produced in a WG is that the result did not really gain consensus in the IETF as a whole, that is, among all of the Working Groups in all areas. For instance, the result of one WG might clash with a technology developed in a different Working Group. An important job of the IESG is to watch over the output of all the WGs to help prevent IETF protocols that are at odds with each other.[27]

The Internet Architecture Board hears appeals against IESG actions.

Though there is a formal structure and hierarchy, the figure used to show the organisational relations in IETF emphasises information flows, rather than a monarchical distribution of power. This is because the IETF represents itself as a model of an open, self-governing community. Here 'open' refers to both the capacity for anyone interested to participate in agenda-setting and decision-making in Working Groups, and to the objective of the activity – that is maintaining the interoperability of the internet architecture.

Openness, global sovereignty and autonomy over standard-setting are not something IETF members have taken for granted. As the internet has expanded and administrative overviews have become necessary, and as commercial imperatives have conflicted with openness, the mettle of the organisation has continually been tested. For example, there was an unsuccessful challenge to IETF's role in developing standards by another voluntary, international body – the International Organization for Standardization (ISO).[28] There have been significant disputes about the role and power of the IAB and its relationship with IETF and ISOC. This led to tailor-made innovations regarding qualifications for representation at the IAB. These involve an unusual combination of self-selecting, democratic, random and targeted selection processes.[29] The assertion of intellectual property rights over code associated with standards has also been an ongoing cause of concern and disagreement.

The IETF has strongly resisted the imposition of any top-down or monarchical rule on members. Whilst some concessions have been made, constitutional obstacles have been designed to obstruct any with aristocratic, moneyed or bureaucratic presumptions to rule over the members by easily assuming power or closely directing the members to preconceived outcomes. The complex structures and their interdependency on strong, purpose-driven personal relations, built through the activity centred in the myriad of working groups, defuses attempts to manipulate decisions. There are, of course, still privileged participants. However it has been made difficult for 'outsiders' to assert authority and gain respect and influence without an association with the practical work of standard-setting. The expectation is that those in formal positions of authority will be in close connection with those who play a more active part in the metacollaborative process. Drawing upon Galison's insights, the people with the most influence are those whose expertise is recognised by others, those who are invited to give technical presentations, permitted to moderate or mediate discussions and disputes, or advise on speakers for conferences and publication. Through connecting power with position, personal relations and practical goals, a space is secured for the ongoing expression of the established political culture and technical objective of the organisation. In short, the mechanisms of governance are designed to try to keep those in positions of power non-manipulative and in touch. The constitution of the organisation is an investment in a particular vision of free and open global communications that comes to life in that institutional space.

Rough consensus and the power of ideas

As can be seen from informational RFCs,[30] individual contributions are sometimes recognised. But the tendency is to valorise a selfless contribution made to the common goal, rather than foster a culture of individualism. Ascriptions of individualised genius are commonly supplemented by references to progress based upon the power of the ideas. In selecting what is a valuable contribution, rather than deferring to an historical authority figure, the suggestion is more likely to be that the rather anonymous collective voted with its feet. Responsibility for decisions lies with the community and 'rough consensus'. This can also operate as a code for laissez faire or survival-of-the-fittest idea-competition principles. More recently, more elegant communications theories have been used to assess and legitimate IETF's consensus forms of decision-making.

Michael Froomkin has sought to justify the decision-making processes of the IETF with reference to it meeting Habermas's criteria for a reflexive, communicative practice. In law there is an interest in social theories that can legitimate authority or rule, with reference to more than simply the bare power of a sovereign authority to coerce legal subjects to obey their rules through institutionalised violence. Law as coercion fits ill with modern democratic ideas of governance and citizenship. And because ultimately this idea of power is tied to a sovereign state that is able to enforce its command, it is also of limited value in the context of global law-making. Owen notes that:

> With the emergence of supraterritorial constituencies, extensive multilateralism, the retreat of the welfare state, and transformations in the organization of 'legitimate' violence we now are witnessing a radical reordering of the global political and economic architecture. The traditional territorial state, as Jan Aart Scholte suggests, is losing 'predominance as a site of governance.' If the association between the nation-state and democracy is purely contingent, the dissonance between the notion of state sovereignty and existing power arrangements under globalization demands a revision of our notions of governance and conceptions of the public sphere. Responding to critiques of *The Structural Transformation*, Habermas has since revised his notion of a single authoritative bourgeois realm conceiving a globalized 'postnational' world of numerous debating publics less encumbered by the constraints of material inequality and nationalism.[31]

Habermas suggests that laws, conceived in the form of norms, can be empirically validated by meaningful participation in decision-making in global 'public spheres'.

Froomkin argues that many of the hallmarks of IETF's decision-making conform with Habermas's requirements for an active public sphere. Here human freedom is expressed as the communicative practice of the discourse space. For example, Froomkin says that:

> The Internet Standards process also fits Habermas's basic rules of discourse . . . everyone must agree that:
>
> (1) Everyone who can speak may take part in the discourse. The second rule covers the freedom of discussion . . .

(2) (a) Everyone may problematize any assertion.
   (b) Everyone may introduce any assertion into the discussion.
   (c) Everyone may express his or her attitudes, wishes, and needs . . .
(3) No speaker may be prevented from exercising the rights laid down in
   (1) and (2) by any kind of coercion internal or external to the discourse.

These conditions describe the rules of an IETF working group. Indeed, these rules of discourse accurately describe the conditions for participation in the IETF in general. As Harald Tveit Alverstrand, chair of the IETF, stated in a presentation to INET 2002, the 'requirements for being effective in the IETF' include '[w]illingness to listen, [w]illingness to learn, [w]illingness to be convinced.'[32]

Froomkin's point is not that the IETF has had a secret fixation with a particular brand of post-Frankfurt School social theory that they have managed to put into practice on the global stage. Rather he seeks to show that the discursive practices adopted by IETF demonstrate the practicality of Habermas's ideas of participatory law-making, and that many critiques of the theory are of less significance when the theory is considered as it is meant – as social and political practice. He is also interested in using the IETF as a 'best practice' model for global governance. After showing off the IETF as a successful democratic and authoritative decision-making institution, Froomkin turns his attention to ICANN.

ICANN's shortcomings in Habermasian terms are used to explain that body's failure to gain the confidence of internet communities and the necessary respect needed for its decisions. ICANN is criticised for its lack of openness, its closed forums that selectively deny participation in regard to key issues, with hints of corruption of agendas by commercial interests. In these terms Froomkin considers ICANN to be a comparative failure as a model of global decision-making.

Froomkin is not alone in his negative assessment of ICANN. A popular version of the ICANN story is that various allegiances between national governments and large corporate interests blocked the potential for any meaningful, direct democratic participation by global citizens in ICANN, who, if they are recognised at all, are treated as simply one of a number of other stakeholders. The potential for active citizenry is diminished – reduced to a more passive representation of the interests of internet 'end-users'. This disenfranchises global citizens, constructing them as primarily consumers of agendas generated elsewhere, mainly useful for moderating potentially negative outcomes of decisions that are, for the most part, the proper domain of corporates and governments. The structure and practice of ICANN conferred key power on government/corporate roles because it was assumed that only they can be fully trusted to know and serve the best interests of the internet, conceived of as a key component of the global information economy.

This 'failure' story about ICANN is particularly common in liberal IT law circles where there is a suspicion about the departure from internet self-governance, and a wariness about the ambition of 'modern' nation states asserting a stronger role in relation to new global forms of governance. The development of the global information economy first generated utopian libertarian discourses that were often gleeful about the then apparent limits to the rule of nation states in relation to governing the developing internet infrastructure. For many of these critics, any significant political role played by nation states in relation to ICANN is inherently problematic.

Nonetheless Froomkin and others are right to point out that without full participation by global citizens in decision-making at all the levels of governance ICANN is incapable of generating a coherent institutional rationale that is perceived as democratic and legitimate. All it is seen as representing is the voice of powerful sectional interests, where private ambitions are fronted by vaguer references to representing the good of the internet community as an ill-defined whole. As a forum popularly perceived as 'corrupted' by sectional interests, ICANN cannot generate any grassroots respect for its actions, and those voices, disenfranchised, focus on obstructing and resisting the 'powers that be'. Public criticisms generate stories that further the spread of discontent about the institution within and outside of ICANN forums. In turn, attempts are made to internally manage malcontents, disciplining the more vocal, unruly participants. Managerial 'peer' pressure is backed up with threats and force, embodied in coercive legal forms such as confidentiality agreements dictated to those who are speaking 'at large' for the disenfranchised membership. Because of its failure to generate legitimacy for its rule, ICANN is in perpetual management crisis. It flounders, ultimately unable to serve any of its constituencies well.

Whilst ICANN has clearly proven to be a far less happy experiment in global governance than IETF, there is a key difference between the two constitutions of these bodies that needs to be acknowledged.

Drawing again on Foucault, the comparative success of the IETF in pursuing its goals in producing relatively harmonious social relations within the institution and attracting little criticism from outsiders is not simply a matter of the IETF having a constitution grounded in superior communication rules that are received and acted on in practice by an enthusiastic membership. There is a culture or a kind of 'biopolitics'[33] associated with those communication rules that holds the individuals together as a social body. In Foucaultian terms the biopolitics constructs the whole as an object of rule. The 'culture' of the place is set to anticipate and manage conflict. This means that for the most part, the membership rules without the need for reference to the formal rules of the organisation or to problematise their enforcement.

In terms of the IETF, the biopolitics involves a political commitment to openness and consensus that is hard to separate from its technical objectives. The IETF began, not with a shared political commitment to a Habermasian brand of democratic participation in abstract, but with a 'public' commitment to being an association formed with a view to some good purpose. From the beginning there was a shared identity amongst participants – of class, gender, socialisation, expertise, and most importantly, a strong commitment to the technocratic objective that they all sought to fulfil. Their technical focus and objective tests of viable models provided a common language for all and underpins the production of consensus. The shared purpose, understood as a practical matter, structures IETF discourse and maintains it within known and predictable parameters. Newcomers are invited and are free to speak – but the institutional space mandates that they must abide by communication rules that are both political and technical in nature. With new blood and free exchanges the institution is not static, but the institutional culture is continually renewed – not as a matter of abstract, philosophical or political allegiance, but in terms of the lived experience of happy participants who continue on the IETF traditions and pursue the organisation's ultimate objective.

Conflict is expected. Here Bourdieu's work in relation to mechanisms for mediating conflict and progress in science is useful. He argues:

> As a system of objective relations between positions already won (in previous struggles), the scientific field is the logic of a competitive struggle, in which the specific issue at stake is the monopoly of scientific authority, defined inseparably as technical capacity and social power, or, to put it another way, the monopoly of specific competence, in the sense of a particular agent's socially recognised capacity to speak and act legitimately (ie. in an authorised and authoritative way) in scientific matters.[34]

> The structure of the scientific field at any given moment is defined by the state of power distribution between the protagonists in the struggle (agents or institutions) ie. by the structure of the distribution of specific capital, the result of previous struggles which is objectified in institutions and dispositions and commands the strategies and objective chances of the different agents or institutions in the present struggles.[35]

Though Bourdieu might identify the IETF as merely one player within a field loosely described as computer engineering, because of their professional socialisation those active in the IETF can be expected to draw on similar devices for resolving technical disputes as are used to manage conflict in the broader field. References to progress based on the power of the idea masks the management of conflict within and between working groups where other matters such as experience, history, reputation, prestigious associations, charisma, language fluency and communication competency, institutionalisation etc come into play.

Within the IETF the distributed character of knowledge, authority and activity ensures that competition is relatively localised and well focused. The commitment to 'consensus' across working groups contains disputes to smaller, manageable units where unresolved differences can be attributed to 'subjective' matters – personality, differences in experience, background and expertise. This fragmentation helps deflect questions arising about the politics surrounding the selection of 'winning' contributions. And in the IETF 'losers' are encouraged to channel their energies into proving the superiority of their technical solution amongst their peers. They are free to continue to develop it, or design another one, and keep lobbying for its adoption as they will.

It is true that discourse in the IETF is not 'just technical'. The diverse nature of RFCs bears this out. However the politics of the discourse about the realm of the technical, knowledge about the nature of the discourse space in which discussion of the technical arises – the key rules of engagement – are well known and actively maintained. Though the formal structure of the organisation has been reinvented and this has involved struggle, there has been a long continuity in the institutional culture and its primary objective. And the current constitution is designed so that its culture should have a relatively secure future, and so the dissent is caught, processed and controlled.

ICANN never ever had an established culture, a clear objective or shared purpose that was owned by its membership, in the sense that the point of the exercise was collectively understood or practically capable of expression. The problem was more fundamental than one of a lack of common purpose or objective. ICANN was confounded by the question of who its membership really were, and about whom the institution was properly accountable to. Unlike the IETF it was never confident of its 'public' mission.

A technical legal answer – that ICANN was accountable according to the legal conditions of its corporate registration in the United States – was never sufficient if its claims to account for the global nature of its constituency were to be taken seriously. Attempts to artificially construct regional clusters were ill-conceived, given that there was no obvious way to confidently define any region of the globe – outside of deferring to the banality of a geography that ignores the human face of history, and makes divisions that hold no natural meaning, outside of personal opportunity, to subjects. The recognition of its law-making authority over the domain name system required the enactment of supportive, co-relative legislation by nation states. This inferred a contingent recognition of ICANN's authority, accompanied by the ever-present reality that the localised laws that were essential to the practical implementation of its rule could be changed as national circumstance, political interest, governmental attention and international agreements determined.

ICANN could never afford to distance itself from the demands of nation states, assuming it ever wanted to do this. Unlike the IETF, on a practical level ICANN's work was dependent upon the participation of nation states and nationally constituted domain name licensing bodies, such as auDA,[36] that have their own local agendas, interests and formal accountability. Further, unlike an IETF Working Group, there is no 'metacollaboration' that binds the whole in a practical common enterprise that can develop by 'rough consensus'. The work of ICANN and its 'sub-groups' like auDA are not functionally related as a whole, as in the IETF. Functionally ICANN and its sub-groups are answerable to nation states.

Habermas and Hannah Arendt[37] could dispute the claim that the IETF is a 'public' space because its primary function is arguably a 'private' concern – technocratic management of a particular asset of the global economy. That is, the objective of the activity is related to personal economic advancement. To Habermas the public sphere is 'a site for the production and circulation of discourses that can in principle be critical of the state. The public sphere in Habermas's sense is also conceptually distinct from the official economy; it is not an arena of market relations, but rather one of discursive relations.'[38]

Seeking to differentiate the IETF from ICANN by suggesting the former is motivated by 'public' concerns, whereas the latter is driven by 'private' demands, does involve a misrepresentation. It rarefies some of the political voices in IETF that may more dogmatically cast themselves in a pro-public/anti-private light, related to an open source/anti-proprietary software opposition. These dichotomous representations are themselves highly problematic, and need to be considered in light of the broader discourse generated at grassroots level. Further, RFC 1602, that mandates that proprietary specifications can only be incorporated into standards where ISOC obtains a no-cost license to the code, is not exactly an impetus to develop internet architecture in a non-commercial way. Rather it is in line with elder statesman Vint Cerf's expression of 'core beliefs' about the IETF, that conflate the experience of democracy and freedom with the advancement of private commerce:

Internet is for everyone – but it won't be if it isn't affordable by all that wish to partake of its services, so we must dedicate ourselves to making the Internet as affordable as other infrastructures so critical to our well-being. While we follow Moore's Law to reduce the cost of Internet-enabling equipment, let us also seek to stimulate regulatory policies that take advantage of the power of competition to reduce costs.

Internet is for everyone – but it won't be if Governments restrict access to it, so we must dedicate ourselves to keeping the network unrestricted, unfettered and unregulated. We must have the freedom to speak and the freedom to hear.

Internet is for everyone – but it won't be if it cannot keep up with the explosive demand for its services, so we must dedicate ourselves to continuing its technological evolution and development of the technical standards [that] lie at the heart of the Internet revolution.[39]

Froomkin says:

Participants understand the IETF's mission of enhancing communication via the Internet to be a good in itself, and to be of instrumental value in enhancing both democracy and commerce.[40]

... In short, Cerf asserts a fundamental normative commitment to global, ubiquitous communication as a means of enhancing democracy. Communication tools need to become cheap enough that cost is not a barrier to access, and easy enough to use that neither knowledge nor language are bars to participation. Programmatically, governments need to stay out of the way and eschew censorship or access control to allow everyone the greatest freedom to participate in global discourse.[41]

As Owen notes, 'Deliberative notions of an immanent global public similarly depend on a telos that presents the West as already democratic.'[42] One might add to that, that in the IETF, through the link with commerce and free speech, the possibilities of 'freedom' and 'democracy' have become prescriptively coded. Whilst a natural association of democracy, free speech and commerce may read as 'so true' for those immersed within particular American political traditions, it perplexes some global citizens, especially those schooled outside the US, who sit at the fringes of that political experience. It only raises suspicions and worries about the relation between the internet, the US military-industrial complex, and the ambition behind new global forms of governance. How do we know that this new mode of governance based on consent and civil consensus is not still just a demand for polite acquiescence to similar political objectives to those previously associated with repression and imperialism exercised by developed countries via the authority of nation states and their associated power blocs?[43]

Putting the question of the limited and arguably private economic character of the freedom associated with IETF activity to one side, it could be argued that a multiplicity of public spaces, as opposed to the construction of one public sphere, only attests to the impoverishment of the contemporary political experience and signals a departure from a democratic society. Following Arendt, Habermas's original discussion of the bourgeois public sphere had also cast a single, overarching public arena as desirable.[44] Yet this assessment is grounded in an understanding of the solidity of physical space and linear time, with relatively immobile and fixed social relations. This is precisely what is challenged by the technological character of our time.[45] To the extent that it is accepted that public life is capable of expression online and that freedom can also be experienced 'virtually', thanks to the work of parties like the IETF, it is now possible to create and recreate public spaces, and to tailor communication rules and define public goods, as communities desire them. Though this doesn't mean that the IETF is itself necessarily one of these spaces.

As Fraser puts it, so long as the multiple publics are not merely 'enclaves', even though, through the process of self-selection and cultural privilege they may be rhetorically open but 'involuntarily enclaved', it is not clear why a singular public is essential to democracy, an empowered citizenry and freedom. Further, as Fraser notes, 'The idea of a public sphere as an arena of collective self-determination does not sit well with approaches that would appeal to an outsider perspective to delimit its proper boundaries . . . Only participants themselves can decide what is and what is not of common concern to them.'[46] What citizens consider to be 'public' is more fluid than its abstract, immoveable representation in some political philosophy, and the reality of differences over the notion of what is public and political can be accommodated in spaces made by the use of these technologies.

Denying the political character inherent in new forms of global governance simply forecloses the possibility of the virtual space encapsulating more than a narrow preoccupation with fostering the global economy. It gives away to others sovereignty over too much of contemporary life, and diminishes the moral and ethical dimension of debates about the governing of the economic sphere. It detracts from the voices of those who wish to raise 'public' debate and ask questions about the social power associated with technologies, and supported by laws such as those creating intellectual property rights.

The question remains whether the IETF deserves the accolades that some might attribute to a public space for open and free discourse. Is it predominantly a space for the airing of small technical concerns aimed at

advancing commerce? Are the interests pursued primarily of narrow economic import, to the advantage of already dominant groups and individuals
who work to the disadvantage of subordinates? Or is it a wordly space, where
participation is both a means of individuals expressing their own voices
amongst others, for articulating a public identity, for pursuing the common
good of the public-at-large, even perhaps sensitive to social and cultural
diversity?

Keeping in mind the problems of assuming that an organisation as multi-
focused and specialised as the IETF can be described holistically, it is important to explore how the IETF understands its broader mandate. How does
it respond to issues of commerce and the technocratic demands of corporations and nation states?

The IETF discourse surrounding patents is a good place to start, because
patents are generally seen as a key legal instrument of government economic policy, central to investment in the technological infrastructure. The
government/commerce/private property nexus is expressed in the US constitutional power over intellectual property rights:

> Art. 1, Section 8, Clause 8. The Congress shall have the power . . . to promote
> the progress of science and the useful arts, by securing for limited time to
> authors and inventors the exclusive right to their respective writings and
> discoveries.

Whilst the Australian constitution has no equivalent declaration of the
interest served by the intellectual property power,[47] political discourse in
developed countries rarely disputes a sharing of the same broad objective.
In the context of globalisation, harmonisation of intellectual property laws
has led to protection being extended and strengthened globally, through
the World Intellectual Property Organization (WIPO) treaties, the World
Trade Organization (WTO), Trade Related Aspects of Intellectual Property
(TRIPS) Agreement, and through bi-lateral Free Trade Agreements.[48] In
this context there is some difficulty in separating national from international intellectual property agendas. However developing countries, especially through WIPO, have asserted different economic agendas and stressed
the need for technological transfer of expertise, with varying levels of success
from time to time.[49]

In its dealings with the reality of patents being associated with some of the
technologies suggested in relation to establishing universal standards, how
complicit has the IETF been in serving global commercial agendas? How
narrowly does it see the role of law? And how do patents affect 'consensus'
and assessments of 'the power of the ideas'?

Responsible patenting?

A patent is a limited monopoly right granted in the public interest. It secures public access to a technology by rewarding private investment in innovations that meet legislatively defined criteria. Public benefit is marked in terms of the law providing access to both the patented technology that is then sold and/or licensed in the market, and to the practical knowledge about the working of the invention which, as a condition of the grant, must be disclosed in the patent specification and made available in a publicly accessible database.

The legal requirements for a grant of a patent support the gate-keeping of knowledge. Because conditions of the grant are that the patent is 'novel', that is, the invention has not been previously disclosed to the public, and 'inventive', that is, the invention claimed is not obvious to a skilled worker in the relevant field, it is prudent to keep research related to the development of the invention confidential. Rather than favour co-operation, the law affirms a commercial environment that is guarded and competitive. Success comes from beating competitors to the post. The stakes are winner takes all, because the patent holder's rights relate to the knowledge field itself. A competitor who has independently arrived at the same technical solution is nonetheless prevented from working in a patent area without permission.

The art of drafting a patent specification is one of satisfying the technical legal requirements for full public disclosure of the invention, and at the same time maximising the breadth of the monopoly claimed, in order to extend exclusive control over the knowledge field. Patent portfolios are generally considered as significant technology assets. Aggressive protection of quite expansively defined rights can also hinder the development of related innovations by competitors.

Though the criteria for patenting are designed to secure open access to new knowledge, the law sends ambiguous signals in relation to the requirement for definition of the private property the grant conditionally encloses. As a legal matter there is a requirement of specificity about claims made in relation to the state of the knowledge field, and in relation to the nature of advance claimed, to ensure that there is some public benefit conferred by the monopoly. Given the existing state of knowledge in the field, is the invention claimed an advance on the art in the sense that it is both novel and inventive? However the patent claimed and tested has to be expressed in a form that is capable of being uniformly, bureaucratically classified and assessed in relation to others with consistency and efficiency. In testing patent applications there is a concern not to make the process so stringent and render rewards too unpredictable to discourage investment in patenting 'success'.

Within the legal community there is often suspicion about the veracity and breadth of patent claims. Most patents escape the significant costs associated with the formal, adversarial scrutiny commonly associated with litigation. Litigation is too costly and time consuming for many affected by a patent to embark upon. Outcomes can be uncertain, especially in emerging fields of research where the pace of change often precedes significant academic and professional comment and reflection about the status of the 'art'. In relation to computing technologies, knowledge tends to be fragmented and distributed in line with internet infrastructure. This creates even more difficulties in solidly defining the knowledge field and in retrospectively demarcating what was, at the time of an application, a significant advance on the art, than is the case in more established research areas. The pragmatic preference may be to work around the patent or pay a licensing fee regardless of views about the merits of claims. However once re-examined, many patents are invalidated.

Patents create both open and closed technical communities. Patents presume that knowledge naturally exists in an open community, but this 'commons' is defined somewhat provisionally, sequentially and rather linearly, its legal measure being in relation to existing and past patent claims. The information commons appears in patent law as the state of the knowledge field existing prior to the lodging of an application, against which the application is to be judged. With a successful application, the new knowledge then hangs in a kind of 'open suspension' during the patent term (generally 20 years). During this period there is an accessible record of what will become public, but only conditional rights to use that knowledge respecting the terms of the monopoly granted. Knowledge only emerges fully unrestricted, and thence clearly open and public, after the end of the patent term, ready to feed the cycle of property rights again.

The private controls over the knowledge field created by the system are mediated by the patents administration. However governmental responsibility over the legitimacy of the grant is only conceived in narrow technocratic and managerial terms. The law makes no judgement of the market value of the patent applied for. The patents examiner and a court asked to review a grant or enforce a patent do not inquire into the social utility, market consequences, environmental costs or morality of an invention.[50] The administration of the patents system does not create any space for the airing of broader political or economic considerations and questions of social policy.

Examiners and courts adopt a position similar to that of Arthur C. Clarke's characters, Chuck and George, in regard to broader issues of responsibility for science and technology. The only real concern is for identifying a technical advance. Does the technology work as claimed? Or can the technical specification be re-jigged and tailored so it does meet the set legal criteria? And in terms of litigation, the focus is on the technical legal dispute between the named parties, and involves no address to the broader consequences of enforcing a patent on others sharing the universe. Further, special interest groups usually lack legal standing to raise 'relevant' issues in court raised by patent litigation.[51]

By defining the conflict narrowly and as primarily between the patent office and an applicant or between a patent holder and a private competitor, patent law avoids appreciation of the political import of the patent system and its impact on communities. To the extent that a challenge to a patent is perceived as 'political' in nature, the preference is to redirect discontent to the legislature who may be invited to consider the area as a special case and make separate legislative provision for those circumstances.

The lack of any address to questions of social responsibility or inquiry into the consequences of patenting technology has attracted a great deal of attention and global criticism, especially in relation to the patenting of life-forms, genes, essential life-saving drugs and medical treatments.[52] However in relation to computing and the internet, e-commerce and business process patents, critical attention has tended to focus more on debates about the nature of innovation and technical progress in this particular industry.

Patents are recognised as a relative latecomer to the development of the internet. The historically told story is that:

1. The royalty free (RF) way of working is important for the Web. From an historical perspective, the Web was developed in an RF mode. The ethos was that royalties were not charged, and the initial developers didn't patent anything. When companies later joined in, then those companies didn't ask for royalties either.

2. People like this for lots of good reasons:
   When you have an RF assumption; uptake is very fast and there is a level playing field between established businesses and smaller developers.

   You get more consistent adoption, interoperability. There were many similar systems before the Web. But the technologies in question (HTTP/HTML) spread quickly. If you don't have RF, there may be a greater risk of fragmenting the Web.[53]

In relation to internet architecture, intellectual property claims were relatively late to arrive on the scene. As such they are often presented as a deviation from the established norm of openness and co-operation. Given the pace and degree of 'progress' before IP claims, how can respect for these rights be justified? Why should patents be thought of as valuable or necessary in order to secure investment in these kinds of innovations? The concern is that the guarded and competitive approach supported by patents could conflict with the tao of the internet. On the other hand, many of those who are most highly skilled and eager to contribute useful technology may work for corporations that enforce intellectual property rights. Can an organisation like the IETF afford to ignore these contributions?

Pragmatics of the IETF universe

Section s10 of RFC 2026 sets out the IETF policy on intellectual property rights (IPRs).[54] In brief:

- Any contribution submitted in a meeting, working group, mailing list or other activity associated with the IETF (including the IESG, ISOC, IAB and RFC Editor) is 'copyright-free' in the sense that, if the contribution is to be published, translated or further disseminated in some way, IETF has the relevant rights to do so. So for example, once an email or a computer program has been forwarded to the IETF, an author cannot seek to prevent its ongoing circulation by IETF by asserting their copyright in the text, and so the IETF can publish or disseminate contributions as it sees fit.
- There is an obligation to disclose any proprietary rights that may be related to contributions and the names of contributors and their sponsoring organisation is acknowledged in uses made of the work.
- Contributors are responsible for making others who may have rights associated with contributions they make, such as employers (who usually own the copyright generated by employees) and third parties, aware of IETF terms and conditions regarding IP rights in contributions, and encourages all interested parties to bring to its attention notice of proprietary rights at the earliest possible time.
- In relation to the standards track process, no contributions can be treated as confidential.
- In relation to specifications on the standards track that involve any patent, patent application or other proprietary right, a notice of such rights will be included by the IESG indicating their presence.

- Upon approval by the IESG of an internet standards track specification, the IESG will attempt to obtain written assurance from the owner of proprietary rights associated with the standard, that any party will be able to obtain a license to use the technology under openly specified, reasonable and non-discriminatory terms (RAND license). The IESG may delay approval of a specification in order to secure such assurances.
- The IESG makes no determination about whether the licensing terms established by a proprietor are reasonable in practice, however standards can be reviewed in the ordinary way.

The problem the IETF faces is defined in these terms:

> It will always be better for the Internet to develop standards based on technology which can be used without concern about selective or costly licensing. However, increasingly, choosing a technology which is not impacted by IPR over an alternative that is may produce a weaker Internet. Sometimes there simply isn't any technology in an area that is not IPR-impacted. It is not always the wrong decision to select IPR-impacted technology, if the choice is made knowingly, after considering the alternatives and taking the IPR issues into account.[55]

The reality that the IETF confronts is that many contributions are impacted by intellectual property rights and claims. However this may or may not be apparent from the outset of the standards track process. Clearly the situation is easier to deal with where the full status of every contribution is known, and the policy is designed to solicit this information, where it is known. But it is unrealistic to expect to be able to proceed fully aware of all the potential IPRs that may affect a standard.

Copyright arises with the creation of the work, but is most usually only formally asserted once a commercial opportunity is sniffed out. Likewise a contributor may submit their own code as royalty-free and believing it unaffected by others' claims of rights, but this does not prevent a distant patent owner later arguing that part of that code comes under the ambit of their monopoly. Intellectual property claims are often enforced relative to the commercial activity and strategies of others. To the extent that law favours co-operation, it relies on the detail of contract law and licensing agreements to define the relevant terms and obligations.

The 'openness' of the organisation to accepting contributions from anywhere creates problems for the IETF because it immediately means that the very diverse attitudes to IPRs and related commercialisation practices and strategies appear within the work of the organisation. It is not a simple matter of dividing internet development into pro-patent and anti-patent camps, because large corporations who generally practise royalty-free licensing still often maintain patent portfolios that could be used defensively, if a situation with a competitor strategically requires this.

IETF policy sends very mixed signals to developers about the problem of tying up internet architecture with patents, whether or not the patents are ultimately found to be valid or likely to be regularly enforced. The IETF does not encourage, verify, authorise or disprove patent claims, although the lack of confidentiality, archival activity and personal contacts of the organisation do provide patent-busting raw material that can be useful in litigation contexts. On the other hand, because there is no real inquiry into the details of RAND licensing, there is no way of assessing the fairness of the terms or its impact across the board. In order to maintain a modicum of consensus about minimising the costs of patenting, the policy simply diverts attention away from the more difficult politics of its implementation. For example, is it fair or reasonable that the same terms be offered to a large multinational corporation, a small-medium enterprise, a university, a school, a community organisation or to those in developing countries? Is differentiating 'discriminatory'? Should all organisations be expected to determine these issues the same way? Information concerning the detail of how licensing terms are determined would usually be considered confidential commercial information and not be readily available to inform discussions about the merits of licensing terms.[56] But few organisations needing a RAND license will implicitly trust another organisation, on whom they are technologically and legally dependent, to act with their best interests at heart. Further, IP licensing of internet standards is likely to draw attention from anti-trust and competition law, which increasingly intrudes into the framework of intellectual property monopolies.[57] Many large corporations fear that the anti-trust actions, involving time-consuming and difficult negotiations with the associated government bureaucracies, can be readily initiated by small organisations with little understanding of their organisational complexity and constraints. An associated concern is that patent-impacted standards feed the growth of this developing area of legal practice.

It is a reference to the priority of the practical computer-technical mandate of the organisation that ultimately justifies the IETF IPR position. The concern is that the discussion about patents in relation to standards simply diverts attention away from the main objective: identification of what, at the time, is best available practice.

The IETF IPR stance is useful for defusing conflict that could disrupt the progress of working groups. However it also pretends that simply by disclosing IP interests, the private pressures and interests associated with the assertion of the rights can be mediated so as not to unduly affect collective determinations of what is best. As noted earlier, the 'power of ideas' involves more than evaluation of objectively proven technical value. There is social capital invested in organisations, supporting the market value of technology assets, encoding contributions and affecting positive and negative judgements of worth. The fact that IPRs may be associated with standards raises the stakes for all, and despite attempts to keep law off the agenda, when there are patents involved, which is increasingly the case, it necessarily adds a layer of complication and discontent to be managed. Because of the bottom-up structure, ultimately the policy invests heavily in a faith in the intelligence, trust and goodwill of members to accept differences on this point and to keep focused on the technical task on a case-by-case basis.[58]

The IETF IPR policy is a pragmatic acceptance of legal realities and the power of the nation state to create rights that promote its particular technological agenda:

> The IETF policies are . . . designed to ensure that IETF working groups and participants have as much information about any IPR constraints on a technical proposal as possible. The policies are also intended to benefit the Internet community and the public at large, while respecting the legitimate rights of IPR holders.[59]

But though the belief is that members can sensibly mediate the private power supported by the rights, the greater problem is that patents involve far more than just respecting the established private rights in inventions owned by individuals and corporations. Patents create a subversive power in relation to the openness of the knowledge field, and consequently patents affect IETF autonomy to maintain the openness of the internet over time. Whilst the private right owned is defined, its application in relation to the activities of others is variable. Will a license be sought? From which competitors? At what point? Enforcement of the patent can be very uncertain. This renders the commons – the knowledge base that is otherwise free to all – contingent and insecure, with significant prospective and retrospective implications for the technical heritage of the broader community. Further, in respecting patent-affected technology, the IETF implicitly respects a system that has no time or space for considering issues of responsibility in relation to the broader social context and impacts of the law.

This problematic can be seen in relation to the controversy involved in enforcing the Eolas patent.[60] The Eolas US patent 5,838,906 ('906) is described as a 'Distributed hypermedia method for automatically invoking external application providing interaction and display of embedded objects within a hypermedia document.' Eolas successfully took action against Microsoft, arguing that the Internet Explorer web browser infringed the patent in the way it handles plug-ins and applets. However technology covered by the patent is applicable to web programs involving text, simple graphics, interactive video and audio, plug-ins like Adobe's pdf document reader, and scripting languages like Java – any program that gives web access to data where some of the object's data is located external to the webpage. Other large companies impacted by the decision include Adobe, Apple, Sun, IBM and Macromedia. Thousands of third-party companies that build products around major internet platforms are also likely to be affected.

One of the problems for the web is that whilst Microsoft is now engineering Internet Explorer to work around patent '906, the changes to their browser program will create problems for displaying pages authored under the older technology. Whereas it was once presumed that the internet was the communications medium capable of bringing infinite copies of extraordinarily diverse resources to any computer located anywhere in the globe on demand, the fragility of the data over time and the dependence of access on maintaining stable, reliable open architecture are now painfully apparent.[61]

In seeking to have the decision reviewed, Tim Berners-Lee, as Director of the World Wide Web Consortium (W3C), a member-based standard-setting body, wrote to James Rogan of the US Patent and Trade Marks Office, that the

> impact of the '906 patent reaches far beyond a single vendor and even beyond those who could be alleged to infringe the patent. The existence of the patent and associated licensing demands compels many developers of Web browsers, Web pages, and many other important components of the Web to deviate from the fundamental technical standards that enable the Web to function as a coherent system. In many cases, those who will be forced to incur the cost of modifying Web pages or software applications do not even themselves infringe the patent (assuming it is even valid). Given the interdependence of Web technology, those who wrote Web pages or developed software in reliance on Web standards will now have to retrofit their systems in order to accommodate deviations from standards forced by the '906 patent. These deviations will either reflect individual decisions by developers about how to avoid infringement liability, or will be an effort to be compatible with decisions individual vendors make in the course of their own re-design. What's more, the inevitable fragmentation and re-tooling costs caused by the ability to enforce this patent, which we believe to be invalid, cannot even be remedied by individual parties choosing simply to pay licensing fees to the patent holder.[62]

The uproar concerning a District Court decision enforcing the patent against Microsoft has generated significant interest in the global organisation and dissemination of relevant documentation to demonstrate the prior art and seek to have the patent overturned.[63] This activity was acknowledged by Stephen Kunin, the Deputy Commissioner for Patents Examination, in his order for re-examination:

> A substantial new question of patentability exists with respect to claims 1–3 and 6–8 of the 906 patent in view of prior art acknowledged by the patentee in the 906 patent and the newly cited teachings of Berners-Lee, Raggett I and Raggett II . . . This creates an extraordinary situation for which a director-ordered examination is an appropriate remedy.

However whilst this intervention may be extraordinary, it does not mean that re-examination itself will necessarily take the broader context or impact of such patents on the internet community into account. The level of public discussion and scrutiny will no doubt affect the process indirectly, but re-examination is not a democratic process.

The sky is falling?

The IETF IPR policy demonstrates an appreciation that its work is not *just* about the airing of small technical concerns, and that it is not *just* about advancing commerce and the infrastructure of commerce. However it is also true that whilst individuals can express their own voices amongst others on the subject of patents in the IETF forums, they are not exactly encouraged to develop a public legal identity at the institutional level – with a clear and unambiguous position on innovation, patents, monopolies, law and the power of nation states. Rather, in the name of institutional consensus, they are expected to be sensitive to the diversity of views on the subject. Overall, the preference is to keep the focus small – to picture well-designed technical constellations that appear from time to time, rather than take in the complexity of the whole sky.

What this means is that whilst the IETF understands that it is a law-maker in relation to the internet, and that its standards processes necessarily intersect with the laws of nation states, the organisation casts itself in a passive role in relation to the nation state. Currently the IETF lacks the ability to assert a leadership role as a producer of legal knowledge about intellectual property rights and internet architecture. This is unfortunate because the IETF is capable of significantly and directly impacting upon the import of the patent activity of the state, which is threatened by the global context of internet standard-setting. Were the IETF to enforce a royalty-free mandate, this would change the character of the organisation and perhaps its membership, but it would not necessarily be a less open body or be less committed to open architecture. Arguably it would be more so, especially given the distance of time.

4
Linux is a registered trademark of Linus Torvalds*

'Under the spreading chestnut tree, I sold you and you sold me.'
George Orwell, *1984*

In Orwell's *1984*, the Chestnut Tree Café is the haunt of free spirits – artists and musicians, members of the underground, outcasts, enemies, untouchables. It is a space for human contact and some sense of community, even though it co-exists within the strictures of the repressive state. As a meeting place it still suggests the possibility for open expression.

> There was no law, not even an unwritten law, against frequenting the Chestnut Tree Café, yet the place was somehow ill-omened.[1]

For Orwell, the overwhelming surveillance of Big Brother is supplemented by social controls over language. One of the objectives of Newspeak, the official language of the State of Oceania, is to diminish the range of possible thoughts by cutting down the choice of words to a minimum. Oldspeak, the natural language of the Proles, 'with all its vagueness and useless shades of meaning'[2] is to be destroyed. The communication agenda is not merely a demand for lexical correctness. The aim is also to penetrate history and memory, so that the historical record always confirms the present view. This means that the official versions of the past must be constantly corrected and rewritten:

> Who destroys the past controls the future: who controls the present controls the past.[3]

Manufacturing history on demand is the job of Winston Smith, the main character of the story. And his conscience is troubled by the demands this makes on him.

Winston's defeat at the end of the story – his selling out – involves a betrayal on two levels. He capitulates to the immortal collective brain of the Party and accepts everything – that the past was alterable and that anything could be true. And he tries to save himself from further torture by asking they take his lover Julia, his one meaningful human attachment in the world, instead. When Winston returns at the end of the story to drink and play chess at the Chestnut Tree Café he has accepted the state's language demands on him, and the costs of this. He and Julia acknowledge to each other their mutual betrayals and that it is an event from which the relationship cannot recover. Winston now calls the recollections of time spent as a boy with his mother 'false memories'. Winston's betrayals are linked. In *1984* acquiescence to the communication rules of the state also means his acceptance of complete and absolute social isolation.

What's in a name? What is open source?

To lawyers open source is a reference to copyright licensing arrangements for computer code. However the objective of open source runs counter to a conventional corporate understanding of copyright practice.

Historically copyright has been used to control the circulation of works and maximise income streams through enforcing limited, exclusive private use rights to the code that makes up a computer work. With respect to the copyright in the source code associated with a computer program, the law allows owners to sell access to the program, but to keep the source code hidden.

The social relations associated with this use of law are unequal because the 'run me, but don't touch' aspects of the copyright power make it more difficult for others to develop programs that replace all or part of the owner's program or that interoperate with it. This has obvious advantages for market leaders. The exclusive power to control the circulation of code can be used to frustrate technological developments and improvements, unless they are specifically consented to by the copyright owner. Because the monopoly power conferred by the law is potentially so strong, there are statutory 'balances' or 'exceptions' in copyright laws that permit limited kinds of access to code, without the need to obtain consent from the copyright owner. But if you outstep the parameters of these rules, this conduct will generally involve a copyright infringement. And there is no rule that mandates release of the source code.

Whether the correct terminology for access rights to computer works is 'balance' or 'exception' depends upon the jurisprudential model used. In the US the constitutional power to make intellectual property laws reflects a social policy of promoting the progress of science and the useful arts. This leads to a concern to limit and balance the exclusive rights of owners with the needs of other creators and users. However in other jurisdictions, such as Australia, there is no social policy formally stated in relation to the constitutional power to make intellectual property laws. The copyright legislation only refers to 'acts not constituting infringement'. To some legal positivists who think of law in terms of rules, this suggests that the 'access' provisions are merely exceptions to the regular legal rule of protection of owner's rights, and these are not necessarily related to a broader social purpose of balancing interests in copyright law more generally.

The conventional use of copyright may, in some conditions, help maximise income streams to owners *and* encourage innovative product development. However the social and technological interactions it is modelled on focus on meeting the needs of the private actor and their ownership interest in code, backed up by the state and its disciplinary legal processes. The pre-eminent legal concern is for the owner and their exclusive connection with the code. The law does not mandate the owner's social isolation. Indeed for a profit to be made by the licensing of the software the owner needs to interact with others. However the legal presumption is that all social interactions can be formally demarcated by forward planning, with arrangements consummated in a tailor-made legal agreement that specifies what kind of touching of code is and is not permitted. The legal arrangement anticipates the personal detachment of the parties and the apparent lack of any ongoing connection between them as engineers or as citizens, outside of the specified legal arrangement. Some argue that this is the entire point of a legally enforceable agreement – to grant the freedom to do certain things without having to commit to a personal relationship with others in order to do them. Because there is not a pre-existing trusting relationship nor necessarily a desire for one, what law provides is a 'substitute source of reassurance' for the parties. From this perspective what the law grants is the freedom of personal detachment, under the shadow of the disciplinary state.[4]

Open source uses the same legal power that derives from the right to control the circulation of code, but mandates certain freedoms to access and use code in place of the usual restrictions. This creates a more open programming environment. There are key differences in the license terms used, and to maintain some integrity in the commercial use of the term 'open source', the Open Source Initiative (OSI) has drafted a number of criteria used to certify the licenses it considers as open, designed to meet the needs of the commercial world. The OSI argues that:

The basic idea behind open source is very simple: When programmers can read, redistribute, and modify the source code for a piece of software, the software evolves. People improve it, people adapt it, people fix bugs. And this can happen at a speed that, if one is used to the slow pace of conventional software development, seems astonishing.

We in the open source community have learned that this rapid evolutionary process produces better software than the traditional closed model, in which only a very few programmers can see the source and everybody else must blindly use an opaque block of bits.[5]

An OSI certified license must provide the programmer with source code that is human-readable. There cannot be restrictions on what modifications can be made to the software, on how it can be sold or given away.

Free software, licensed under the GNU General Public License (GPL), and authored by the Free Software Foundation (FSF) refers to four kinds of 'freedom' for the users of the software:

- The freedom to run the program, for any purpose (freedom 0).
- The freedom to study how the program works, and adapt it to your needs (freedom 1). Access to the source code is a precondition for this.
- The freedom to redistribute copies so you can help your neighbor (freedom 2).
- The freedom to improve the program, and release your improvements to the public, so that the whole community benefits (freedom 3). Access to the source code is a precondition for this.

Linux started out as a UNIX-like kernel[6] originally developed by Linus Torvalds in 1991 that was rapidly advanced by contributions from thousands of individual enthusiasts. It is the best-known example of free software licensed under the GPL. The term 'Linux' now comprises a wide range of software including the operating system, web servers, programming languages, databases, desktop environments and office suites.[7]

Linux has been successful in competing with large proprietary organisations like Microsoft and there are many large corporate and government users of free software. In addition to technical judgements about the reliability of the code, the ability given under the GPL to access, use and adapt the code for whatever purpose, with no up-front financial cost attached, is a significant reason for its increasing market penetration.

In addition to tying use of the code to an all-purpose public license protected under copyright law, a trade mark helps distinguish the products which Linus Torvalds is happy to endorse with his reputation. An interviewer describes his controlling interest in these terms:

In a way, Torvalds is less a ruler (or a hood ornament, for that matter) than an ambassador, roaming his virtual world and exerting his influence to prevent technical fights from devolving into sectarian battles. Take the factions that want him to make toppling Microsoft a priority: Create a version of Linux as simple for novices to use as Windows, they reason, and you loosen Redmond's grip on the PC. 'That's the kind of politics you see inside Oracle and Sun,' Torvalds says. 'Once you start thinking more about where you want to be than about making the best product, you're screwed.'

. . . when it comes to weighing the merits of a technology, Torvalds is adept at separating the idea from the person suggesting it. His is a world that works only if the best idea wins; he has no giant marketing budget to compensate for poor technical decisions, no clout in the marketplace to compensate for mediocrity.

. . . Mike Olson is the CEO of a Massachusetts-based database startup called Sleepycat Software and contributed critical components to Linux as a UC Berkeley grad student. He describes Torvalds as 'very, very good – much better than engineers in general – at smoothing out difficulties, building consensus, and building community. He really has only a technical agenda.'

'I spend a lot more time than any person should have to talking with lawyers and thinking about intellectual property issues,' Torvalds says with a sigh.[8]

Though law is used strategically to control the circulation of code, copyright does not establish the exclusively controlled legal relations as used by proprietary companies. Rather law is used to try to create a stable, decentralised, collaborative programming environment. For this reason open source is often described in terms of it founding a 'community'. And though a trade mark is, by its very nature, an exclusive association, what the Linux mark is generally used to signify is the politics of the software production. There has been discussion about whether 'open source' or 'free software' should also be registered trade marks, however the general descriptive nature and the widespread use and misuse of the terms in the industry would prevent any particular trader or organisation from obtaining registration of the terms. The term 'OSI certified' and a logo for open source and OSI certified are registered trade marks of the OSI.[9]

The philosophy surrounding open source and free software has led to a proliferation of many related licensing ventures targeting all kinds of copyrighted content. Some, such as the Creative Commons movement, explain the motivation as a concern for an erosion of use rights in contemporary copyright jurisprudence. Through simple but innovative licensing and global affiliations, the Copyright Commons aims to create more 'cooperative and community-minded . . . voluntary and libertarian' copyright licenses, aimed at freeing access to content such as websites, scholarship, music, film, photography, literature, courseware.[10] Others such as the *The Common Good Public License*[11] cite the authority of the Universal Declaration of Human Rights as part of their cultural heritage.

There is a lot of debate about the appropriate use and misuse of terminology associated with these movements. With regard to software, some emphasise key differences between 'open source' and 'free software'. For example, Richard Stallman of the FSF argues that:

> The Free Software movement and the Open Source movement are today separate movements with different views and goals, although we can and do work together on some practical projects . . .
>
> The fundamental difference between the two movements is in their values, their ways of looking at the world. For the Open Source movement, the issue of whether software should be open source is a practical question, not an ethical one. As one person put it, 'Open source is a development methodology; free software is a social movement.'[12]

He adds:

> The main argument for the term 'open source software' is that 'free software' makes some people uneasy. That's true: talking about freedom, about ethical issues, about responsibilities as well as convenience, is asking people to think about things they might rather ignore. This can trigger discomfort, and some people may reject the idea for that. It does not follow that society would be better off if we stop talking about these things.
>
> Years ago, free software developers noticed this discomfort reaction, and some started exploring an approach for avoiding it. They figured that by keeping quiet about ethics and freedom, and talking only about the immediate practical benefits of certain free software, they might be able to 'sell' the software more effectively to certain users, especially business. The term 'open source' is offered as a way of doing more of this – a way to be 'more acceptable to business'. The views and values of the Open Source movement stem from this decision.[13]

For some American free software advocates lexical correctness matters because of a desire to emphasise the civil rights implications of the free software movement. Stallman describes these in terms of support for '**free** as in **"free speech"**, not **free** as in **"free beer"**.' The philosophy is one of contributing to and building the community, and not just opportunistically taking from it. To put it another way, there is a concern that corporates might take advantage of the tools provided by the open source community, but foster an environment of personal detachment and self-interest. For free software advocates this simply reproduces the alienating social relations of the proprietary world. This is seen as bad for both the programming environment and for society more generally. Precision in use of terms like 'free' and 'open' is essential to the definition of the social movement and to differentiate it from the proprietary status quo.

For other critics discussion of civil rights is less important than open debate about the transformative capacity of the free software movement – its ability to change the mode of production of the capitalist system.[14] Is this a revolutionary movement or just another reinvention of stagnating capitalist relations? In online discussion groups and in related media forums there is often heated discussion about what is radical; what is transformative politics; what is a dangerous development; who poses the latest threat to freedom and openness. Advocates are often very defensive of the movement and ever alert to shifting strategies, new start-ups and alliances that may be made as new opportunities are calculated.

What country are we at war with? Who are 'we'?

There is scant evidence about who really contributes what code and other related expertise to open source and free software projects, and in that sense there is some vagueness in determining who should be considered as members of the related programming environments. Some economists have tried to identify the demographic aspect by studying particular attributions of authorship in a project and identifying regional clusters of activity.[15] Open source is a global activity, even though projects may be identified with particular locations and institutions.

However whatever the empirics of the production of open code, in terms of public profile and discussion of open source, the English-speaking world looks to the United States as the leading knowledge producer about open source. This is most obviously a reflection of the strong presence of the US online. Further, most of the major controversies about open source production that have fuelled debate about the politics of software production have originated in the US. To the extent that open source and free software are seen to enshrine a different approach to intellectual property, it is American initiatives and reactions that have primarily forged the sense of difference.

More recently there has been an emerging interest in trying to gauge the amount of corporate open source development built around pursuing a particular strategic agenda, compared with the more decentered peer-networked production that follows along the lines of the Linux paradigm. Though only a niche study looking at open source production in seventy geoinformation technology projects, Gilberto Camara argues that

> the vast majority of substantial software design and development is still the product of qualified teams operating at a high level of interaction. Developing software in a decentralised manner requires a modular design that is difficult to achieve for most applications, since few software products can be broken into very small parts without a substantial increase in costs.[16]

The implication is that the Linux model of production is an exceptional case and it is not the norm for most open source applications and products.[17]

Corporate analysis of open source production supports the view that the decision to adopt the model is most likely to be strategically rather than politically motivated. As Richard Gabriel and Ron Goldman from Sun Microsystems explain:

> A myth of open source is that by developing software this way, a company can reduce its costs because outsiders will be writing some of the code, and the code will be developed faster because of the increased workforce. In fact, a typical open-source project attracts relatively few outside developers.

But it is argued that there are still good business reasons to adopt the model because:

> Most companies are not large enough to influence the direction of their own markets, and few companies are able to design products that truly serve their customers. Most companies find they need to fine-tune designs and products over a series of releases . . .
>
> [With] the Innovation Happens Elsewhere [IHE] strategy . . . [t]he primary goal . . . is to increase the number of potential customers – that is, the size of the market available to the company. To do this, the IHE company tries to create more products in the market that either are enablers for the products the IHE company sells or form an aftermarket for them. Rather than trying to accomplish this alone, the IHE company tries to encourage other companies or organizations to do this work – but for their own purposes.
>
> Even further, the IHE company, by creating, building, and maintaining a set of communities around these gifts, can engage in serious conversations with outside companies, organizations, and individuals. Such conversations

not only can improve the IHE company's products, designs, and directions, but also provides the IHE company with an opportunity to demonstrate leadership and vision, thereby putting it in a position to strongly influence the direction and structure of the competitive landscape.[18]

Advocating the strategic advantages of open source production and choosing between proprietary and open source licensing based upon assessments of the market for particular technologies, rather than wholly committing to open source, polarises the open source community. To give one example, Sun Microsystems' CEO Scott McNealy's self-promotion that 'Open Source is our Friend'[19] has attracted considerable comment and discontent. As Eric Raymond puts it:

> ... Sun's insistence on continuing tight control of the Java code has damaged Sun's long-term interests by throttling acceptance of the language in the open-source community, ceding the field (and probably the future) to scripting-language competitors like Python and Perl. Once again the choice is between control and ubiquity, and despite your claim that 'open source is our friend' Sun appears to be choosing control.[20]

Sun's Simon Phipps responded to this criticism.[21] In turn Eric Raymond replied:

> Simon Phipps, Sun's Chief Technology Evangelist . . . objects to my having responded to remarks Scott McNealy made to analysts as though they had been addressed to the open-source community. I deduce from his objection that Mr. Phipps thinks his boss has a right to tell conflicting stories to different audiences.
> . . . in public, you'd best expect the open-source community to have an equally public opinion about whether you really are one or not – and not to be shy about expressing that opinion, either, whether it's through me or any one of half-a-dozen other community spokespeople.
> Mr. Phipps then launches into a list of Sun projects that he characterizes as contributions to open source. The proper response to this is to ask: where's the code? Marketing and spin and 'initiatives' are all very well, but what code is Sun issuing under licenses conformant to the Open Source Definition? That, ultimately, is what the community cares about. Show us the code.[22]

Raymond, President of OSI, assumes the role of spokesperson and protector of the community. Instrumental decision-making poses a serious problem for the formation and definition of open source as a community.

When corporates utilise project-to-project assessment to decide whether to use an open source license, inclusion in the community becomes conditional and transitory. It is another business alliance and the friendly associations suggested seem very vulnerable to the shifting calculations, alliances and manipulations that are part of the market dynamic. Regardless of the views of individual employees, from their employer's perspective membership of the community is dictated by convenience. This disrupts the trust relation that is essential to membership in a community. And it makes it much harder to differentiate open source friends from what is characterised as the proprietary norm in terms of kinds of social relationships associated with the movement.

The concept of 'the enemy' – a never-ending threat to the collective – is important to the definition of the open source and free software movements. With ongoing conflicts within communities, it is attacks from hostile forces that most clearly define difference, forge common bonds and a sense of identity as Other.[23] But, unlike in the fictional case of *1984*, here antagonistic relations and conflicts are not contrived by powers within the movement:

> For years, Bill Gates and other top executives at Microsoft railed against the economic philosophy of open-source software with Orwellian fervor, denouncing its communal licensing as a 'cancer' that stifled technological innovation.
>
> Today, Microsoft claims to 'love' the open-source concept, by which software code is made public to encourage improvement and development by outside programmers. Gates himself says Microsoft will gladly disclose its crown jewels – the coveted code behind the Windows operating system – to select customers.[24]

Microsoft's 'love' for open source is treated with scepticism for many reasons.

Microsoft's public commentary on open source has to be read in the context of the corporation's broader ongoing strategies for managing the threat posed by the success of open source and Linux in particular.[25] There is also the corporation's continuing need to allay concern about anticompetitive behaviour and stifling control over segments of the market. Drawing attention to open source achievements can help in this context. Any public comment about open source has to be closely read as marketing spin and part of a broader manoeuvring in the marketplace, against a history of antagonism toward open source. The selectivity and control maintained by Microsoft's version of open source, 'shared source', does not fit with any conventional understanding of 'openness'. It is not an attempt to join the community even in the sense that, for example, Sun Microsystems has.

Microsoft's public embrace of open source has carried with it attacks on Free Software and the GNU GPL. These attacks prompted a joint press release from the open source and free software community that addressed the crude 'divide and conquer' strategy:

> It's the share and share alike feature of the GPL that intimidates Microsoft, because it defeats their Embrace and Extend strategy. Microsoft tries to retain control of the market by taking the result of open projects and standards, and adding incompatible Microsoft-only features in closed-source. Adding an incompatible feature to a server, for example, then requires a similarly-incompatible client, which forces users to 'upgrade'. Microsoft uses this deliberate-incompatibility strategy to force its way through the marketplace. But if Microsoft were to attempt to 'embrace and extend' GPL software, they would be required to make each incompatible 'enhancement' public and available to its competitors. Thus, the GPL threatens the strategy that Microsoft uses to maintain its monopoly.[26]

Further, Microsoft and other proprietary software advocates, under the auspices of groups such as the Initiative for Software Choice (ISC), have continued to lobby against the adoption of open source and free software both nationally and internationally. For example, government information technology procurement policies that require bureaucracies to consider or prioritise open source software have been met with complaints that these policies are 'anti-competitive' and a 'restraint on trade'.[27] It was also reported that proprietary corporate lobbying and pressure from Lois Boland, director of international relations for the US Patent and Trademark Office, was responsible for the cancellation of a meeting about open source to be held by the World Intellectual Property Organization (WIPO). WIPO is an international body that sets intellectual property rights and standards around the globe.

> One lobbyist, Emery Simon with the Business Software Alliance, said his group objected to the suggestion in the proposal that overly broad or restrictive intellectual-property rights might in some cases stunt technological innovation and economic growth.
>
> Lois Boland . . . said that open-source software runs counter to the mission of WIPO, which is to promote intellectual-property rights.
>
> 'To hold a meeting which has as its purpose to disclaim or waive such rights seems to us to be contrary to the goals of WIPO,' she said.[28]

The claim that open source and free software are against the philosophy of intellectual property rights is also echoed in public statements and letters to members of the US Congress by Darl McBride, President of Santa Cruz Operation (SCO). SCO is engaged in litigation against IBM over the UNIX code and is threatening related lawsuits against corporate Linux users. McBride claims that 'the unchecked spread of Open source software, under the GPL . . . [is] a much more serious threat to our capitalist system than U.S. Corporations realize'. The request is to 'solidify the rule of copyright' so that 'the GPL should not be allowed to continue.'[29] Microsoft has been accused of both fund-raising for SCO litigation and of encouraging others to invest in SCO.[30]

'Doubleplusgood' is in the detail

'Doubleplusgood' is part of Orwellian Newspeak – the process of filtering out superfluous words, nuances and the subtleties associated with free expression. Open source and free software can be abstractly defined in relation to simplified political, social or programming objectives, however this focus tells you little about the real complex of reasons behind particular decisions to use open source code or free software. Use of the code, and even contributing to the development of the resource, does not of itself clearly indicate self-identification with any shared values or identity. On the other hand, it is not all that helpful to try to define what these 'communities' share with reference to particular internal disagreements that emerge at any one time over the proper use of the code. And it is even less appropriate to try to define the movement(s) by adopting the current and shifting projections of those who are obviously hostile to it.

A discussion of open source that is pushed forward by turgid analysis of rhetoric or a focus on assertive personalities, personal clashes and dissection of the community into factions sheds little light on the broader structures and connections at work that help define an open source and free software sensibility in relation to the rest of the world. A more focused and practical way of understanding the formation of this 'community' – its distinctions and the achievements of the 'movement' – (if indeed it is to live up to the political expectation inherent in that term) is needed.

Looking at how the desired social relations of open source are pursued through legal relations is useful here. How are legal processes and the disciplinary power of the state negotiated? Do the formal legal relations used by open source and free software sit well with traditional intellectual property jurisprudence and the interpretative mechanisms of the state? More simply, given the critiques of the conservatism and proprietary corporate bias of contemporary copyright law that is often acknowledged in legal circles and in open source and free software communities,[31] how can legal institutions be trusted to found anything other than alienating, self-interested, private social relations? When it comes to legal practices, who or what do open source and free software place trust in?

Language, trust, community and law

Open source and free software positioning in relation to law is double edged. It is founded in a desire to engage intellectual property rights differently to those of proprietary corporations. However it is still dependent upon the manipulation of rights and powers made possible by legislation and enforceable by the courts. Despite disciplinary power being intrinsic to formal drafting of legal relations and tied with law enforcement, the desire is that the licenses will create a more sociable dynamic and invigorate the notion of a sharing programming community which benefits us all.

The licenses endorsed by the OSI and FSF aim to be relatively simple in terms of language and intention. A plain English explanation of what is understood as 'free' and 'not free' commonly accompanies the legal form of words. For example, Debian, the producers of the Debian GNU/Linux system, have published the *Debian Social Contract* and *Debian Free Software Guidelines* to explicitly explain the set of commitments the Debian community agrees to abide by. Obviously identifying with this community entails some knowledge of, and degree of conformity with, the associated social beliefs. Most commonly allegiance is demonstrated by actions – by choices made in relation to programming preferences and legal practices. Debian provides samples of free licenses they consider to be 'free' – GNU GPL, BSD-style licenses, and the Artistic License. This encourages consistent use of legal terms and facilitates the broader entrenching of these forms of software freedom in industry. In their archive Debian separates compatible software into 'contrib.' and 'non-free' categories. This also alerts users to the need to refer to licensing restrictions associated with non-free code, and in the process reinforces awareness of the social and economic virtues of free software.[32]

In the open source and free software movements there is some practical realisation that legal complexity is itself a form of social exclusion. In contracts law jurisprudence, academics have noted '40 years of empirical studies which show that business people make little use of contract law in settling disputes, preferring to rely, instead, on trust and various non-legal sanctions. In fact, these studies show that contract law is often an impediment to good business relations rather than a template around which business people organise their transactions.'[33] The need for recourse to technical legal expertise in order to create and understand basic legal obligations is inconvenient. It generally complicates whatever personal relations exist and fosters a sense of unease and distrust. In the software industry it can also disadvantage smaller enterprises without much experience in accessing legal professionals, and even for the experienced party, recognition of the need for a lawyer can be a disempowering moment.

The educative point of all licensing arrangements is primarily the same, even though the terms of licenses can differ. The motivation is not to teach a sophisticated understanding of ways of structuring legal relations but rather to primarily teach a social lesson – trust in the broad ambitions and practicalities related to sharing access to code. The object is to build up confidence that this environment provides optimal support to individuals and groups for the development of interesting and useful technologies.

Success in spreading open source and free software culture mitigates against the need for recourse to litigation to enforce the license. As legal counsel for the FSF, Eben Moglen explains:

> . . . with respect to the portfolio maintained for the FSF, complaints are on the scale of some 150 a year, of which investigation creates a reasonable likelihood of an infringing activity of one sort or another in half, and of the vast bulk many dozens a year are immediately adjustable on first contact with the infringer.
>
> There are probably somewhere in the neighbourhood of a dozen cases a year that represent something that evolves toward an adversary situation. Of those so far, at least 50% are adjustable given goodwill on both sides or given the leverage which we have as a copyright holder in a system with strong mandatory relief rules, preliminary injunction style. Moreover it is the rare defendant, as I have said in public on many occasions, who actually wants to plead my license and argue that he understands it better than we do about whether he is violating the terms . . .
>
> Adversarility is unlikely in large organizations at the moment because almost all the major players building information technology systems understand the benefits from free software and they face enormous difficulties with vendors, suppliers, workers – for being the people trying to kick over the apple cart. There are SCOs in the world of course.[34]

Norms, social pressure and a fear of facing legal sanction for trouble-making can be very effective. But for these 'informal' mechanisms to work there needs to be a clear, unambiguous communication of the story of community objectives *and* a practical, simple legal expression of the minimum rules of compliance that are compatible with these sensibilities. For this reason keeping some control over the history of the movements, the language and licenses used, and maintaining the profile of the 'hood ornaments' – the importance of those with the authority to confidently speak for the community about acceptable and unacceptable practice – matter. The more muted or confusing the message about the benefits of open and free software, and the harder it is to understand and comply with the minimum legal requirements, the less likely it is that informal regulation will work effectively. The importance of this cannot be underestimated because if recourse to formal legal advice is frequently necessary to understand obligations or force compliance, this makes it much harder to experience and believe in the freedoms the movement itself advocates. It would also blur identification of any significant stated difference in legal practice from the proprietary experience.[35]

The social relations of open source and free software are closer to a trust relation between parties than to a conventional private property relation. A legally enforceable trust relation is not something entirely unknown to law. In legal theory a trust relationship has been characterised as a means of importing a certain idea of community or communal norms into law, in contrast to the arm's length, individualist relationships more familiar to modern common law and exemplified in the legal notion of contract.[36] Trust law recognises that not all human relations fit the formal, rational, individualist mode, and that the social and moral context intrinsic to a trust relation creates different issues of justice for law to deal with. In a trust relation the obligations of the parties are not as clearly defined in advance. The relationship is more open-ended and the goodwill and discretion inherent in the relation create issues of vulnerability – questions of power and dependence that need to be addressed.

In law there are many ways in which a trust relation can arise – through words, intention, conduct or circumstances. But generally in law a trust involves recognition of conditions that have created a special property relation between parties, where one party (the trustee) is taken to have agreed to act for, on behalf of, the interests of another person (the beneficiary). The trustee, through having legal title to the property, has a special opportunity to exercise that power to the detriment of the beneficiary. But the law will step in to hold trustees to their duty to exercise their power or discretion in the interests of the person(s) to whom the duty is owed. In a sense what the law enforces is the social or moral obligation owed to the other, at the expense of the trustee's pursuit of self-interest. Cotterrell argues that:

> Trusting is a way of coping with the impossibility of gaining sufficient knowledge of all the complex circumstances. In trusting, one takes the risk one's expectations will be defeated.
>
> Where law effectively and comprehensively guarantees the trustee's personal obligations to the trust beneficiary it reverses, to some significant extent, the balance of power and dependence in the trusting relationship ... A person who is morally dependent on the goodwill of another who he or she trusts is converted into an (equitable) property owner able to call upon law to control the trustee so as to ensure protection of the beneficiary's assets.[37]

An open source or free software license is not normally characterised as a trust relation, however there is an Australian case that acknowledges the cultural inadequacy of copyright only recognising individualised, exclusive property rights.[38] The property relation at the heart of copyright is not very well developed conceptually.[39] As James Boyle observes, 'right now, we have no politics of intellectual property – in the way we have a politics of the environment or of tax reform. We lack a conceptual map of issues.'[40]

More generally, the need to invigorate the private property model and depart from its simple organising idea of ownership and control has long been acknowledged in property law theory.[41] And as Cotterrell also recognises, 'The trust increasingly appears as a business enterprise shifting and developing its operations to maintain and enhance its capital value and income producing capacity.'[42] There is nothing especially remarkable or anti-capitalist in viewing open source or free software copyright in legal terms of trust. Rather conceptualising free software in terms of trust is arguably compatible with previous innovations that stabilise the legal environment to support new forms of capital accumulation, such as the regulation of the quasi-public corporation.[43]

Trust law suggests some interesting possibilities for the development of new legal policy arguments to support free software and open source. Trust law can be read as intervening in social relations involving trust so as to stabilise expectations of otherwise power-deficient group beneficiaries. Historically equity has functioned innovatively in the creation of legal relations appropriate to economic and social conditions. Further, group beneficiaries as distinct from individual persons – corporate or natural – do pose problems for law, whether considered as subjects of property or contract.[44] For these reasons there is much to be said for developing a rationale for open source and free software with reference to equitable models, especially so in jurisdictions where broader constitutional arguments in support of the ambitions of the licenses are thin.

Who destroys the past controls the future

The main advantage in developing the trust concept to help understand and interpret free software licensing is to distance the movement from jurisprudence that affirms the connection between copyright and the language of exclusive control founded in a private property claim. Eben Moglen explains the validity of the licenses in terms of this power, founded in 'pure copyright':

> The goal of the GPL [GNU Public License] and secondarily the L-GPL [Linux-GNU Public License] is to use pure copyright, in a minimum tool-set guaranteed to exist by the Berne Convention . . . The goal of that license is to use only copyright principles and only that that Berne must provide, where it is providing anything at all. So, my assumption is that any Berne member system contains the principle that as to software, in order to copy, make derivative works and redistribute, modify or unmodify software you must have a license of some kind.
>
> I'm assuming in other words that it is always infringing conduct everywhere to make permanent tangible copies, modify and create derivative works, and to distribute. And I always will have distribution before enforceability.
>
> So all that I do is bring an infringement action. It is the defendant's responsibility to prove license and the only credible license for the defendant to plead is my license, because code is not otherwise available except under that license.[45]

There is something discordant in using this kind of expression of power and control given the aims and philosophy of the movement, even though the need to invoke the power is in the 'exceptional' case. It still echoes of an authoritarian, permission-based system.

And perhaps this is the crux of the problem – it is hard to have faith in law making a space for private relations to operate differently to the proprietary norm. This is especially the case in Australia where we lack a clear and unqualified articulation of the social promise suggested by the US constitutional power.

Even in relation to American jurisprudence, there is room to doubt that law can be trusted. For example, in the *Eldred* case,[46] concerning a constitutional challenge to legislation extension of the copyright term, Justice Ginsburg said:

The 'constitutional command' we have recognised, is that Congress, to the extent that it enacts copyright at all, create a 'system' that 'promote[s] the Progress of science'[47] . . . it is generally for Congress, not the courts, to decide how to best pursue the Copyright clause's objectives.[48]

But in a note she added:

As we have explained, '[t]he economic philosophy behind the [Copyright] [C]lause . . . is the conviction that encouragement of individual effort by personal gain is the best way to advance public welfare through the talents of authors and inventors.' Accordingly, 'copyright law celebrates the profit motive, recognizing that the incentive to profit from the exploitation of copyrights will rebound to the public benefit by resulting in the proliferation of knowledge . . . The profit motive is the engine that ensures the progress of science.' Rewarding authors for their creative labor and 'promot[ing] . . . Progress' are thus complementary; as James Madison observed, in copyright '*[t]he public good fully coincides . . . with the claims of individuals.*' (my emphasis)[49]

Here there is both a recognition of politics – where different opinions may surface – and a denial of that reality. Congress is the external source competent to determine the objective of copyright where there are difficult choices to be made. However the contemporary choices that Congress makes are then stripped of that particular context and associated antagonisms by judicial reference to a singular, reductive reading of legal history and philosophy. Copyright is characterised as an essentialist, eternal pursuit of a private power to exploit or reward individual owners, and by securing the jurisprudence as respect for this particular reading of the ownership right, the Court fudges the shifting and complex politics behind the law's recent 'advance' under both the *Digital Millennium Copyright Act* and the *Copyright Term Extension Act*. Further, legally endorsing the profit motive in this abstract manner simply shifts the power balance to private owners to determine any limits to the right without any requirement of a formal consideration of the reality of 'balance'. The suggestion that copyright history can emphatically be called upon in exclusive support of the private claims of individuals is a form of Newspeak. It cuts down history, embodied in a complex of decisions, to a simplistic slogan in order to authorise a very contemporary political choice. Further, it is still Newspeak when history is likewise flattened by the other side, to authorise contemporary demands to support creativity.[50]

Attempts will continue to be made to overcome the politicised origins of particular legal values by self-serving references to constitutional and common law doctrine from all sides. However the artificiality and pretence behind this enterprise are quite difficult for anyone, particularly for those with any knowledge of the messiness of copyright's history, to suppress. Yet to the extent that we need to ground our laws in narratives that make sense beyond their explanation as a response to immediate political demands made on the state, the attraction of reinventing an historical source of authority for our laws will remain.

For those of us beyond the US, contributions linked to US constitutionalism have peripheral import value for a global legal culture. The extent to which the development of critical jurisprudence is tied to external validations in the US constitution, the less easily these ideas are able to travel. Other avenues are needed for the development of a global legal culture.

Newoldspeak: private power, public good

The reordering of the global information economy is expressed, everywhere, in creative reworking of legal notions of property and right. Whether through developing notions of equity or constitutional jurisprudence, it seems that the security of open source and free software licensing relies upon the tradition of legal respect for the private autonomy of owners to distribute their property as they see fit. It is indisputable in copyright law jurisprudence everywhere in the developed world that private power per se is a public good. Thus it is through legal respect for the exercise of individual free choice associated with the private ownership that this jurisprudence can advance and the social and economic practices associated with the licenses will continue to develop.

Accordingly there is cause to treat with caution current rhetoric surrounding the notion of copyright founding a 'commons'.

Larry Lessig describes the commons this way:

> Open source, or free software, is a commons: the source code of Linux, for example, lies available for anyone to take, to use, to improve, to advance. No permission is necessary; no authorization may be required.
>
> These are commons because they are within the reach of members of the relevant community without the permission of anyone else. . . . The point is not that no control is present, but rather that the kind of control is different from the control we grant to property.[51]

In their book *Empire*, Michael Hardt and Antonio Negri argue that:

It seems to us, in fact, that today we participate in a more radical and profound commonality than has ever been experienced in the history of capitalism. The fact is that we participate in a productive world made up of communication and social networks, interactive services, and common languages. Our economic and social reality is defined less by the material objects that are made and consumed than by co-produced services and relationships. Producing increasingly means constructing cooperation and communicative commonalities.

The concept of private property itself, understood as the exclusive right . . . becomes increasingly nonsensical in this new situation. There are ever fewer goods that can be possessed and used exclusively in this framework; it is the community that produces and that, while producing is reproduced and redefined. The foundation of the classic modern notion of private property is thus to a certain extent dissolved in the postmodern mode of production.

. . . Private property, despite its juridical powers, cannot help becoming an ever more abstract and transcendental concept and thus ever more detached from reality.

A new notion of the 'commons' will have to emerge on this terrain . . .[52]

Whatever alternate or liberationist cultures that free software, open source and the cultural commons movements seek to establish, these cultures are legally dependent upon an exercise of a private property power. There is a new sociality of sharing that is celebrated by the movements. A culture of a 'commons' is made possible through creative use of the law. However in celebrating that potential it needs to be remembered that it is linked to the flexing of autonomy grounded in a private property power. The Commons movement has not to date secured any fundamental departure from that power. And in that regard the law only creates a space for open source, free software and free culture that is analogous to the freedom celebrated in the Chestnut Tree Café.

5
In a world without fences who needs Gates?

–T-shirt slogan

In *Internet Dreams*, Mark Stefik ponders metaphors for the information infrastructure. He says the metaphor of the electronic marketplace speaks to 'the trader within us, the archetype that prepares us for action and commerce. Because of its general role in getting things done, this archetype is also related to the older and more traditional archetypes of people who go out into the world to make a living . . .'.[1] He then notes that 'in nomadic hunting cultures the dominant archetype in stories about action in the world is the shaman-hunter-trickster.'[2] And that 'the trickster is known in the myths of many cultures.'[3]

In Italo Calvino's story 'The Argentine Ant',[4] a couple and their young child, encouraged by the recommendation of their uncle that life is easier and jobs not too hard to find, decide to settle in a seaside town. At first glance the town seems to live up to his promise. It seems relaxed, peaceful and friendly enough. The nephew muses that it is easy to notice why Uncle Augusto would be happy in this contented world, even if the couple were a little uncertain about how they can find work and build a future in this place.

But then they discover the ants. They are on the walls, the faucet, the baby, in his basket, the food – a thin black surface coating the milk. They are in the garden and on all the trees. And then they find out that the neighbours on both sides are engrossed in efforts at ant control. Dealing with the ants seems to be the main work activity of the town. Neighbours offer bemused advice – suggesting various technologies and processes they think are worth trying and expressing scepticism about other methods.

The whole town, it seems, battles with these ants, without much success. And everyone blames the problem on the treatment offered by the Argentine Ant Control Corporation. A company representative, the ant man, arrives regularly to put down poisoned molasses all over the town –

> 'They've been putting that stuff down for twenty years, and every year the ants multiply.'[5]
>
>   . . .

I went up to the women and heard Senora Brauni holding forth to the accompaniment of angular gestures.

'He's come to give the ants a tonic, that man has; a tonic, not poison at all!'

Signora Reginaudo now chimed in, rather mellifluously: 'What will the employees of the Corporation do when there are no more ants? So what can you expect of them, my dear Signora?'[6]

After struggling to locate and then remove an ant from the distressed baby's ear, and egged on by the town's indignant women, a small posse assemble. Led by his wife, the group set out to accost the ant man.

However the husband observes all these town women drop out of the party as they pass by their own homes. They remain voicing outrage, but stand back, watching and waiting for the ensuing spectacle. When he and his wife arrive at the door of the Ant Corporation warehouse the support group is gone, though the women can still be seen peering from chicken coops and gardens, calling, gesturing and inciting her to take action. His wife needs little encouragement. She is furious. She screams accusations of this conspiracy inflicted on the town, tormenting her and her child. The ant man plays to the watching crowd – she's crazy, a nutter he suggests. They all return to their wretched lives with the ants.

The story closes with the couple resigned never to complain again, trying to reconcile themselves to this place, the future they had chosen, and trying to share their son's innocent wonder at the world. Life goes on.

It's official: everybody hates Microsoft
Iowa farm girl, last holdout; gives in
after talk with preacher

Sixteen-year-old high school sophomore Becky Atherton, believed to be the last remaining American who did not hate Microsoft, announced today that she was 'tired of being different' and would now hate Microsoft just like everyone else.

. . . 'We are just so proud of our little Becky,' said her mother, Marian Atherton, who has hated Microsoft since reading a newspaper article about the company 1998. 'We were so worried about her being the last one – you know how teenagers are; they just want to be so darn different. But we prayed on it, and our prayers were answered.'[7]

Few corporations are the subject of popular debate, suspicion and derision in the way that Microsoft is. The late 1990s generated a glut of Microsoft hate and culture jamming websites – Why I hate Microsoft, Microsuck, antibill collections. Of course there are also 'support' organisations like the 'Committee for the Moral Defense of Microsoft' and the Ayn Rand Institute 'Microsoft Defense Site'. Many of these sites are still actively maintained and renewed. There are few who don't have an opinion about Microsoft.

When I ask law students to rank the world's biggest companies, invariably Microsoft is always listed at the top of the rank of IT firms, and expected to be within the top ten of all companies. Likewise students seem to know a lot about Bill Gates – his personal wealth, self-made image, that he is a university drop-out and his recent philanthropy. There is usually quite an enthusiastic response, and the class quickly divides into those with Micro-conspiracies and scandals to share that exemplify the trickster spirit of the company, and the one or two brave programmers, immediately branded by the rest as nerds, who clearly find the anti-Microsoft enthusiasm tiresome or undeserved, and say so.

If you ask these students how they know these things about Microsoft, and what do they know about the other leading IT companies and executives, or if they could name any other Microsoft executives, the discussion usually falters. They know companies – IBM, Sun Microsystems, Intel, Apple, Novell, and the name of Microsoft co-founder Paul Allen is usually mentioned, but these names are thrown into the discussion with little detail or emotion. There is not much interest there.

When you point to the *Forbes* magazine's yearly 'World's Biggest Companies' and 'World's Richest People' lists, that provides hard data for comparison, many are surprised.[8] Sure Bill Gates is mind-bogglingly rich – rank 1 with a personal wealth listing in 2004 of US $46.6 billion, but his corporation is only one of a large number of leviathans. In terms of sales, profits, assets, market value and employees Microsoft ranked at 31, behind IBM at 16, and Verizon Communications at 26 in 2004.

Does that matter? Does this mean we should be paying more attention to what the other corporations and their executives are doing as well? What does a biggest/wealthiest ranking mean? You ask more questions – what operating system do you use? What browser do you use? Who wrote the operating system for your mobile phone? What about the processor for your digital camera?

If pushed to consider this, the students agree that the other corporations are important too. But they don't have the same profile because they haven't generated the notoriety that Microsoft has. The interest is not really in size, or market success in moving large amounts of product, or simply in profit. What attracts interest is the exercise of power, and how it is wielded in relation to these things. The other leviathans are just not as distinctive or interesting in terms of power relations as Microsoft is.

It's not just a question of where the corporation is at today, compared to others. It's as the marketing says, a matter of where you want to go, and the Microsoft promise that it will be the one to take you there. Microsoft is about the future of the new economy.

Especially in law circles, Microsoft is usually discussed with reference to anti-trust law monopolies, abuses of market power and the question of government and court interference in the technology market.[9] The focus quickly moves to details of particular business dealings, the difficulties of evidence in the anti-trust case, and economic discourse on the significance of 'lock-in' and 'network effects' in high technology markets. Are Microsoft's market leadership and control deserved? Are other innovators unfairly blocked? Can anything be done about it anyway? Should law interfere in the market – to what end? At what cost? On whose advice?

The problem with this kind of analysis of Microsoft is that it is far too narrow. It focuses on Microsoft as primarily a source of product, and disregards its role as a knowledge producer. In selling us information commodities, we are sold on a vision of the information economy, and it is almost impossible to separate the two. Microsoft through its business practices, marketing and the profile of Bill Gates has a distinctive culture all of its own. The corporation, personified in Bill Gates, is an archetype of new economy success. Its strategy for success has been central to the development of many internet cultures – some of which have been fashioned in resistance to it and its role in the US economy and social life.

What Microsoft typifies is a broader way of thinking about the information economy, about technology markets and innovation. It is the 'typical' ideological aspects of Microsoft – its generation of knowledge about the information economy – that anti-trust law, and law more generally, struggles to manage. Whilst the 'atypical' features of Microsoft – its control over the PC architecture – causes discontent, fear of disrupting the generation of the knowledge economy complicates acting upon those complaints. And in failing to manage Microsoft's leading role as a knowledge producer we can see the limits or failings of our existing legal institutions in dealing with the ideological aspects of the information economy.

This chapter explores Microsoft as an archetype of the information economy – a model of action and commerce, and a trickster that generates demands for legal institutions to better manage innovation, wealth creation and global information markets. The controversy surrounding this corporation is considered as symbolic of far broader anxieties about innovation, US power and the development of the global economy. And the limits and ambivalence confronting the legal order in regulating the corporation reveal something of the way that Microsoft, as knowledge producer, advances the development of global markets.

The information future is here and here again

In discussing Microsoft culture I draw first on the writing of Bill Gates. His books and his testimony before Committee hearings are striking in style. Gates speaks not just for his own interests but as a Captain of the Information Industry, with Microsoft's success, failings and future explained in terms of the significance of the global economy and its potential. Gates often assumes an advocacy role, selling an idea of the information future and, in responding to critics, normalising Microsoft's place in that universe.

In *The Road Ahead*, Gates explains that:

> The global information market will combine all the various ways human goods, services and ideas are exchanged. On a practical level, this will give you broader choices about most things, including how you earn and invest, what you buy and how much you pay for it, who your friends are and how you spend your time with them, and where and how securely you and your family live. Your workplace and your idea of what it means to be 'educated' will be transformed, perhaps almost beyond recognition. Your sense of identity, of who you are and where you belong, may open up considerably. In short, just about everything will be done differently.[10]

In *Business @ the Speed of Thought* he engages more directly with the role of high-speed communications in reshaping the economy. This is important because:

> A digital nervous system is the corporate, digital equivalent of the human nervous system, providing a well integrated flow of information to the right point of the organization at the right time. A digital nervous system consists of the digital processes that enable a company to perceive and react to its environment, to sense competitor challenges and customer needs, and to organize timely responses . . . it's distinguished from a mere network of computers by the accuracy, immediacy and richness of the information it brings to knowledge workers and the insight and collaboration made possible by the information.[11]

This is different from a 'General Motors' economy. It is now possible to gather facts about changes to technology and markets on a global scale and react to ensure a competitive advantage. Employees are knowledge workers because rather than making and consuming things, they produce and consume information. It is that task or knowledge capacity, made possible by global communications networks, that brings commercial advantage and powers the economy.

With his emphasis on the importance of decentralised global information flows and the capacity to respond quickly to the various kinds of data gathered to maximise competitive advantage, Gates' description is not all that different to others' explanations of globalisation and the network economy.[12] His emphasis on the empowering potential of information technology for individuals also fits alongside the earlier utopian cyberculture literature of the 1990s,[13] although cyberculture's preference for a libertarian expressive citizenship forged through the wires is described by Gates as an identity as wired employee and online shopper. He describes the internet as 'a shopper's heaven',[14] with every internet buyer knowing every seller's price and vice versa so everyone in the market would be able to make fully informed decisions and society's resources would be distributed efficiently. With such market efficiency he thinks 'Adam Smith would be pleased.'[15]

Where his analysis fundamentally differs from this earlier literature is in his account of success in negotiating the knowledge economy and his explanation of Microsoft's powerful position in determining that future. Gates argues that:

> No segment of the world economy is more dynamic than the computer software industry . . .
>
> . . . In the computer industry, product life cycles are short – just twelve to eighteen months typically as software producers race to introduce new products at an even faster pace. The rate of innovation continues to accelerate as microprocessors become more powerful and new software products are developed to take advantage of that increased power.[16]

In the computer industry rapid change in unpredictable directions constantly creates new market opportunities and threatens the position of existing competitors. The position of a product, no matter how popular, is never secure because it is impossible to know when the next new idea will come along that could render the entire product category less important or even obsolete.

This analysis draws on the insights of Intel co-founder Gordon Moore. In 1965 he suggested that the number of microcomponents that could be placed in an integrated circuit of the lowest manufacturing cost was doubling every year and that this trend would likely continue into the future.[17] This means that the potential power of a computer continually increases, and that new computing capacity drives the development of new and enhanced products.

In this environment it is claimed that a company is driven, as Bill Gates says, to 'Innovate or die!'[18] Inventive activity is thus a by-product of market forces. The market has established its own rules and cycles. It heralds constant change and creates seemingly endless technological possibilities. If you don't keep innovating, other newcomers will steal the advantage. Consumers in the marketplace are assumed to be fickle when it comes to product or corporate loyalty, and demand for new, cheaper, enhanced product is treated as voracious and seemingly insatiable.

Here technology shapes culture and the economy. Technology producers invest in progress or obsolescence (depending upon one's point of view) and market technology at a price that ensures its mass take up. Demand goes up and down. Nonetheless faster computing power must also continue to develop in order for producers to remain globally competitive. In this technological cycle it is dangerous to legislate and forestall the possible development of some new and unforeseen 'good' by regulating the market. It is assumed that the market and ultimately consumer interest will determine what in fact works and is 'good'.

In his books Gates suggests that success comes from a manager's understanding of these market processes and cycles, and the capacity to identify and negotiate the next big trend. His books do not stress the importance of *creating* new knowledge and innovative products per se. What makes the difference is the ability to *identify* market trends early and managerial action on that knowledge in the workplace – making whatever changes in structure, personnel and priority are deemed necessary to capitalise on the development. Of course Microsoft infrastructure will assist with that process.

The Road Ahead posits that the key to delivering the potential of the information technology and in becoming a market leader stems from engaging young, smart, savvy, committed individual collaborators in the first place. These are true believers in particular technical desires, capable of reading and adapting to change and dedicated to seizing opportunities. Gates explains IBM's failure to appreciate the importance of embracing the right culture or attitude in managing technology as a counterpoint to Microsoft's success:

'IBM wasn't paying enough attention to the trends and technologies that ended up being important.'[19]

Success or failure in the IT business depends ultimately on managerial skills and corporate culture – reading the technological cycle and perpetuating it.

In *Business @ the Speed of Thought* Gates says:

> The impetus for Microsoft's response to the internet didn't come from me or from other senior executives. It came from a small number of dedicated employees who saw events unfolding ... smart people anywhere in the company should have the power to drive initiative. It's an obvious, commonsense policy for Information Age companies, where all the knowledge workers should be part of setting the strategy. We could not pull off such a policy without the technology we use.[20]

Again he stresses that it is the culture and information technology of the organisation that matter most here – a culture where there are ongoing decentralised flows of information, with the network and the culture – the employees and the technology – working seamlessly together, well co-ordinated by management as one system.

This is a system of cyborgs. However recognition of that deal is displaced by language that stresses the natural evolutionary development of the market and the culture created by management. Managers and markets are presented as the dynamic forces. And the metaphors carry with them the suggestion of freedom – an energetic, self-correcting and self-perpetuating balanced system.

So how does law fit into that?

Law as cyborg

Law is a discipline that houses the collective expression of variable national, and in some cases international, social, cultural and economic interests. It is a site for political struggle and disagreement.

Law in this full sense does not fit into the Microsoft picture. Law's messiness – its distinctive histories, the multiple objectives – potentially threatens the pursuit of this particular technological freedom. More particularly the capacity of law to stabilise and control markets and managers, or for society to want to express choices beyond supporting or ditching that particular technological product, is precluded. Regulation of managerial prerogative is presumed a dangerous and unnecessary intervention in optimal cycles of innovation:

'Bill's thought was that once we accept even self-imposed regulation, the culture of the company would change in bad ways,' a former Microsoft executive explains. 'It would crush our competitive spirit.'

Gates said flatly: 'The minute we start worrying too much about antitrust we become IBM.'[21]

Intellectual property law and licensing agreements are however anticipated as part of the picture.

From the perspective of law this appears to present a contradiction. Government is seen as neutral in its provision and enforcement of intellectual property rights where these rights help the corporation, but wrongly interventionist in questioning the effect of the grants of these monopoly rights. The legal writer James Boyle relates this to the 'Chicago School of Economics' wisdom that 'the greater the monopoly . . . the greater the incentive to other firms to find some way to circumvent it. If a monopoly continues it is a sign that the market is working, not failing.'[22] Monopoly power then is a healthy creation of the marketplace, and not an incident of the state creation of the monopoly rights, in the first instance. Defining property rights is cast as a neutral activity, as if there were no choices to be made in the state creating and enforcing them. Boyle argues: 'In the information economy, where power is likely to be measured in intellectual property rights, the idea that the state is not somehow making choices and picking winners is particularly obtuse.'

But from the perspective of Gates there is no contradiction. Law is fine – so long as it supports that cybernetic promise of the market. That is the measure of appropriate governmental action. Here IP rights are not treated as encompassing a complicated and somewhat confusing jurisprudence combining an assortment of interests: incentives provided to owners to encourage investment in the dissemination of innovation, the information needs of competitors and downstream developers, and the interests of society and culture as a whole. IP rights are treated as simply part of the information tools and assets good managers naturally use to strategic advantage.

IP and industry debates about innovation in high technology industries, and how or whether private rights support or stifle the market, are irrelevant. The political and philosophical content of law that leads to discourse about limits to ownership has no place in his world view. Law is simply a matter of calculating commercial advantage. This is most clearly demonstrated in strategic responses to software piracy that tie-in users to Microsoft:

One of the reasons we wanted to sell to computer companies rather than consumers was software piracy. We wanted to get paid for our work, and when companies bundled our software with their computers, they included our royalty in their price.[23]

Likewise, when it was disclosed in 1995 that the national telephone company of Uruguay, Antel, had pirated software worth US $100,000 the Business Software Alliance, the anti-piracy lobby heavily funded by Microsoft, 'abruptly dropped the suit in the fall of 1997 . . . And, according to Antel's information technology manager, Ricardo Tascenho, the company settled the matter by signing a 'special agreement' with Microsoft to replace all of its software with Microsoft products.[24] There are different strategic advantages in using copyright, patents, and confidential information laws to protect and license access to code, ideas, systems or know-how. But there is nothing particular of interest that distinguishes these various rights in his analysis, perhaps apart from the capacity to demarcate the relevant protected data or information assets owned under each category of law. That different intellectual property rights may have distinctive legal rationalities and associated qualifications attached to the grant of the private right, and therefore suggest different limits to ownership and implications for the market and innovation, is ignored. The reality that strong IP rights are clearly not supported by an incontrovertible industry or broader cultural view of 'right',[25] and that government might want to take this diversity of views and interests into account, is sidestepped. There is no interest in acknowledging any contextual view of these laws, their histories, politics or costs. Whilst this itself is not at all surprising from a business perspective, the question is whether ultimately the courts reinstate a broader and more balanced view. Does this Captain of Industry's view of law influence how judges and lawyers determine the scope of their responsibility? Does law activate its political capacities or perpetuate a reductionist view, where profit maximisation is conceived as the only concern of law?

In explaining the technology market that is here now and tomorrow, Gates naturalises the cyborg within us and assumes a servile, cybernetic role for law. The language he uses – digital nervous system, flows, cycles, unfolding events – mixes natural and mechanistic metaphors. The virtue of mixing these associations is that he plays to those attracted to the utopian promise of information technology and to those believers in the naturalness of self-interested economic actors and market forces. And both of these interests are also connected with the idea of a natural role for law in fulfilling these particular desires.

What is also suggested by implication here is the unnaturalness of law in actively considering, let alone pursuing other broader agendas or interests. Such interest could stifle growth and pervert the information economy. The proper role for law is to support the development of global networks, and never question the politics of the ownership of the information, code or data associated with these flows. Natural growth precludes this debate.

To some however, ownership is inherently political. And a large and noticeable growth in the marketplace is a source of suspicion. It may not be healthy – a cancer or some other form of infestation.

What the critics claim

Much of the criticism of Microsoft directly addresses the culture of the organisation, which has itself become an object of study:

> The company is self-contained and thinks of itself as separate from the rest of the industry . . . **Microsoft is like the military**. I don't mean . . . that it is a rampaging force bent on world domination. I mean that in many small aspects of daily life and in large questions of long-term strategy the organization resembles a big, successful military establishment.[26]

Microsoft is often presented, not so much as having a distinctive culture, as being a cult. It is described as an organisation of like-thinking, highly trained, logo-wearing devotees, defensive of their organisation and boss, excessively fat or thin, smugly bound together by lucrative share options in boom times; internally competitive and suspicious of each other in down times. Presented as mentally and physically separated from the rest of the world at the Microsoft 'campus' in Seattle, and doggedly furthering organisational imperatives, the implication is that there is no space for reflection on the company, Microsoft's relation to the broader community and industry, and the individual's responsibility in relation to those things.

Microsoft is hardly a unique organisation in not fostering internal critique, but this is overlooked. Microsoft, we are told, is not 'typical'. There is a strong desire to discount any perception that Microsoft's market 'success' is natural or morally deserved. And if success is not ethically and morally deserved, then the culture of the organisation is, by implication, corrupt and corrupting. Government must act to stop the infestation further consolidating and continuing to spread.

A point of comparison is often not so much other corporations as it is with Microsoft exemplifying a 'proprietary environment' versus free software and open source environments. Open source and free software are presented as offering a more genuine marketplace freedom that maximises social utility. Without copyrights and patents controlling the pace of development, competition is far more intense and the winner more likely to be the best technical offering. Take up of a technology truly represents the product best serving needs at that moment in time. The openness of these producers to healthy competition is contrasted to the stagnating situation of Microsoft, where insularity and the single-mindedness of the company foreclose many development possibilities. Comparatively Microsoft lacks innovation and profits from appropriating the technological gains developed by other truly innovative people. Thus by developing derivative products Microsoft also diverts earnings away from those who truly deserve them. The corporation stifles the development of better-executed products. Intellectual property laws underpin discontent because it is these rights that create Microsoft's capacity for market control in the first place. Rather than supporting innovation, Microsoft's use of intellectual property law simply privatises what might otherwise be free technological progress belonging to humanity, and proprietary code can be insulated from more vigorous competition in the marketplace.

This process is enabled by Microsoft having captured the market in the first instance through its control over the PC operating system and deals with original equipment manufacturers. It is argued that Microsoft can use its operating system monopoly to force users to continually upgrade to their suites of buggy, bloated new products. Not permitting backward compatibility means that users have little choice but to comply. Control over the source code, enabled by copyright law, frustrates those who wish to develop new or different products leading to reduced choices and poor service. This is no level playing field. Code is shared with Microsoft's chosen developers, but not with others outside the circle. Further by counting on its reputation as a market maker and buster, Microsoft can undermine investment in new products simply by announcing a Microsoft competitive version is coming soon – 'vaporware' that never arrives. Sucking up to Microsoft and not publicly criticising the corporation or its products is thereby encouraged if you want to get ahead too.

In short the complaint is that the corporation's profitability rests on opportunism, intimidation and the stifling of potential technological threats to its power.[27] The perception of danger in speaking out – fear of reprisal – only breeds further discontent and anger about the hypocrisy in Gates marketing fictions about Microsoft's success being well deserved and innovation-based.

So what enabled Microsoft's rise to success?

In a sense Gates' description of his success is truthful. Innovation is not simply a matter of technological merit, and profiting from innovation is really a consequence of management.

The key to Microsoft's rise is generally attributed to two bad decisions made by competitors:[28]

- Apple refused to license its code AND
- IBM with 70% of the PC market decided to outsource two vital components – microprocessors and operating system software.

In a short period of time Intel had captured 85% of the chip market, and Microsoft Windows was the operating system of 90% of PCs. IBM was no longer the leviathan it had been and was unable to call the shots.

Moore's law worked to the advantage of both companies. Bit-intensive software applications demand greater processing power and hardware upgrades; high-end chips depend on ever expanding software functionality (word processing comes with dictionaries, grammar checking, thesaurus). Whereas according to Moore's law the price of processing power should halve every 18 months, by adding new features prices were kept stable for quite a time.

However critics claim that soon the US $2000 PC market was saturated. New upstart companies like Dell, Gateway and Compaq developed low-profit systems (sub-US $1000). In response to the perceived threat the corporations diversified – Intel into multimedia for the Pentium platform, Microsoft applied the operating system to a greater range of products including web browsers, and began to make deals with content owners (like Disney, Time Warner and Dow Jones), and email services like Hotmail.

Even with these initiatives, it was claimed that Microsoft was unable to rival Netscape Navigator – superior product, downloaded by users for free and used primarily to access free online content. It was argued that the Microsoft Network was not competitively priced nor its proprietary services comprehensive enough to attract sufficient custom. There was also a threat posed by the development of Sun Microsystems' Java technologies. So Microsoft denied access to Windows 95 unless it came bundled with Internet Explorer, and set about securing agreements with PC makers including IBM, Apple and Compaq to install the Microsoft operating system and browser as standard. Eventually Netscape lost it market share and companies working on alternate browsers, like Compaq, reluctantly dropped development of alternate browsers. Those who entered into deals with Microsoft quietly complained, leading to the Department of Justice review in 1997.[29]

In journalistic accounts of Microsoft's history the pace of the technological cycle is driven by Moore's law – except that there are natural limits to the market for cutting edge products. Profits can be threatened by lower targets in terms of product enhancements and price cutting. The market does not necessarily want the latest and greatest, as Gates implies:

> They need to make you unhappy with what you have and make you want something else. Isn't this wonderful: An industry whose business model is based upon the need to make their customers unhappy.[30]

There is a good market for 'lesser product'. But selling the lesser product is cast as unwelcome competition by Microsoft and as an affront to the ideology of the innovation/market cycle. There is also 'good' market for new enhanced product, but this poses a threat to existing market share, because whilst success can be copied, there can be advantages in being the first mover.[31] Managing innovation is not simply a matter of sponsoring, recognising or distributing new product. The relevant managerial skill also encompasses maintaining existing market share by blocking alternatives that could develop the top, sides and the bottom ends of the market, and incorporating good technical developments into the Microsoft universe.

Technology is taken up because it is innovative as with Netscape, but also dropped, as with Netscape – not out of consumer choice per se but because consumer choice is directed to specific products and away from others. Netscape made a mistake in assuming that innovation alone would make them a winner. Whilst it is true that you innovate or die, and that innovation brings with it market advantages, relations are more complex than that mantra 'Innovate or Die!' suggests. To economists this territory is ripe for further exploration. But to Microsoft critics it is clear that technological innovation alone will not make you a winner. Consumer choice will not necessarily rule either. The industry significance of the producer of the technology will affect how, why and on what terms the innovation is recognised. Who your friends are in the industry, and who they aren't matters a lot. The losers in this equation are presented as the vulnerable, truly innovative but relatively powerless individuals and corporations, and consumers whose access to the excellent product is frustrated, whilst they are sold on a poorer imitation of it. Where innovators can challenge the mega corporation for a while, in a relatively short time from when the threat first comes to notice, strategies are drawn up to 'manage' change and prevent damage to ongoing profit forecasts and loss of market share. You need friends in government, if you are going to survive.

Regulation then, through competition law, is seen as putting to rights what should be won by the market's 'true' innovator, whose product would be freely chosen by consumers, in a 'properly' functioning marketplace. Anti-trust law is seen as the most appropriate legal avenue to challenge abuse of power, where 'abuse' is hoped by many to encompass quite broad complaints about corporate behaviour. It was anticipated that law would set new standards of corporate responsibility in the information economy, sensitive to the unique aspects of that environment.

How economists debate technology choices: network effects, path dependence and lock-in

We are told that in a market system innovation is rewarded and the best product will win in the marketplace. But with regard to Microsoft the accusation is that this is not the case. In exploring this discord some economists explore the possibility of 'network effects' and 'path dependencies', which 'lock-in' consumers to particular technologies:

> When there are benefits to compatibility, or conformity, or certain other kinds of interaction that can be categorised as network effects, a single product would tend to dominate in the market. Moreover this product would enjoy its privileged position whether or not it was best available.[32]
>
> . . . A particular kind of network effect occurs as technology develops. As more firms or households use a technology, there is a greater pool of knowledge for users to draw upon. As we gain experience and confidence in a technology, the expected payoff to someone who adopts it may become greater . . . Working knowledge of a technology, availability of appropriate equipment and supplies, and more widespread availability of expertise all make a well-worked technology more useful to businesses and consumers.[33]

In economic terms, it may be more efficient for everyone to choose a particular product, which in turn can quickly become the industry standard. If this is the case, the monopoly in that product is the consequence of rational market behaviour driven by consumer choice. Though a product may be temporarily entrenched, in technologically dynamic markets the need to innovate constantly threatens market position. There is no market failure that requires intervention, because it is assumed the innovation cycle will regularly redistribute players into winner and loser camps.

Others argue that this process can lock-in consumers to inferior product because the switching costs from an entrenched product to a superior one come to be too high. There are also concerns about the innovations that 'could have been', if consumers were not already tied to particular code.

The development of the internet is recognised as an instructive case. Throughout the 1980s and early 1990s Microsoft's business strategies had led it to dominate the PC operating system market and locked-in consumers:

> for the data of one product to be freely moved into that of another, each must abide by an increasingly complex set of agreements and internal standards . . . Meanwhile the business arguments force deliberate obsolescence of products. Whether or not the customers are happy with the earlier software is of little concern; unless they upgrade to the new standards, they will soon find that their information structures are incompatible with those of their co-workers. It is a never-ending cycle in which users are trapped.[34]

Independent developers are similarly trapped. However the internet provided the possibility of moving outside of this circle because the transfer of information was not dependent upon what operating system was being used. Middleware technology like Netscape Navigator exposed 'application programming interfaces' (APIs) that made it easier to port from one operating system to another. Sun's Java technologies enabled applications to run on a variety of platforms with minimal porting. These innovations, coupled with a steep rise in internet usage, created the possibility of a widespread take up of new platforms and applications. Innovation thereby threatened the existing market for Windows and hindered the acceptance of Internet Explorer as the browser standard.

Judge Jackson's findings[35]

In the US legal proceedings Judge Jackson determined that Microsoft did enjoy monopoly power because of its large and stable share of the market for Intel-compatible PC operating systems. He found that a market share of 95% of the operating system market for PCs excluding the Apple Mac, and well above 80% including it, acts as a high barrier to entry, the consequence being that customers lack commercially viable alternatives to the Microsoft operating system.

Judge Jackson found that the main driver of network effects was the established size of the market for the operating system. Because of the market share, independent software vendors (ISVs) feel obliged to develop product that runs on that platform as a priority, thereby contributing an ever larger body of applications that continue to support it. And having such a large body of applications provided by ISVs further augments Microsoft's dominant market position:

> What for Microsoft is a positive feedback loop is for would-be competitors a vicious cycle. For just as Microsoft's large market share creates incentives for ISVs to develop applications first and foremost for Windows, the small or non-existent market share of an aspiring competitor makes it prohibitively expensive for the aspirant to develop its PC operating system into an acceptable substitute for Windows. To provide a viable substitute for Windows, another PC operating system would need a large and varied enough base of compatible applications to reassure consumers that their interests in variety, choice, and currency would be met to more-or-less the same extent as if they chose Windows. Even if the contender attracted several thousand compatible applications, it would still look like a gamble from the consumer's perspective next to Windows, which supports over 70,000 applications. The amount it would cost an operating system vendor to create that many applications is prohibitively large.[36]

Microsoft never had to confront a 'highly penetrated market dominated by a single competitor' and could rely upon what Judge Jackson calls 'the applications barrier to entry' to maintain its dominance.[37] Though Microsoft still invests in research and development, and Judge Jackson acknowledged that the company cannot stave off 'paradigm shifts through innovation, it can thwart some and delay others by improving its own products to the greater satisfaction of consumers.'[38]

In relation to Netscape, Judge Jackson notes that by December 1994 Netscape Navigator was the browser market leader and that Microsoft did not believe that simply by improving their inferior browser they would get most people to switch away from Netscape.[39] Navigator and Java were perceived as distinct and related threats that could diminish the applications barrier to entry.[40] Judge Jackson quotes a memorandum from Bill Gates describing Netscape as a new competitor pursuing a multi-platform strategy that could 'commoditize the underlying operating system.' But of course Netscape would need to release a version of Navigator compatible with the release of Windows 95:

> If Navigator written for Windows 95 relied on Microsoft's Internet-related APIs instead of exposing its own, developing for Navigator would not mean developing cross-platform.[41]

The Judge found that:

> Microsoft representatives made it clear . . . that Microsoft would be marketing its own browser for Windows 95, and that this product would rely on Microsoft's platform-level Internet technologies. If Netscape marketed browsing software for Windows 95 based on different technologies, then Microsoft would view Netscape as a competitor, not a partner.[42]
>
> Microsoft knew that Netscape needed certain critical technical information and assistance in order to complete its Windows 95 version of Navigator in time for the retail release of Windows 95 . . . the Microsoft representatives at the meeting had responded that the haste with which Netscape received the desired technical information would depend on whether Netscape entered the so-called 'special relationship' with Microsoft.[43]

Delays in releasing the technical information to Netscape led to a much-improved version of Explorer being the only Windows 95-compatible browser on the market for some time. However Judge Jackson speculates that had Netscape accepted a special partnership with Microsoft:

> Microsoft quickly would have gained such control over the extensions and standards that network-centric applications (including Web sites) employ as to make it all but impossible for any future browser rival to lure appreciable developer interest away from Microsoft's platform.[44]

Further, he doubts that had Netscape accepted such conditions on access to essential Windows 95 code it would have left the firm with the ability to survive as an independent business.

He describes Netscape's experience with Microsoft as similar to that of others in the industry, discussing tense relations designed to halt or redirect product developments with Intel, Apple, RealNeworks, and IBM.

Incentives to increase Explorer's market share included giving it away for free and giving firms promoting it other things of value:

> While Microsoft might have bundled Internet Explorer with Windows at no additional charge even absent its determination to preserve the applications barrier to entry, that determination was the main force driving its decision to price the product at zero.[45]

However Judge Jackson found that Microsoft executives still did not consider these moves were sufficient to undermine Navigator's existing market share, which is why they sought to constrict Netscape's access to distribution channels by licensing arrangements with original equipment manufacturers and internet access providers.[46] Impediments were both contractual and technical:

> As its internal contemporaneous documents and licensing practices reveal, Microsoft decided to bind Internet Explorer to Windows in order to prevent Navigator from weakening the applications barrier to entry, rather than for any pro-competitive purpose.[47]
>
> Microsoft placed many of the routines that are used by Internet Explorer, including browsing-specific routines, into the same files that support the 32-bit Windows APIs . . . by entering individual files and selectively deleting routines used only for Web browsing, licensees of Microsoft software were, and are, contractually prohibited from reverse engineering, decompiling, or disassembling any software files. Even if this were not so, it is prohibitively difficult for anyone who does not have access to the original, human-readable source code to change the placement of routines into files, or otherwise to alter the internal configuration of software files, while still preserving the software's overall functionality.[48]

Deals ensured PCs came from suppliers with Explorer pre-installed. With Windows 98 Microsoft removed the ability to uninstall Internet Explorer and created impediments in choosing a different default browser. Judge Jackson found that the decisions had no technical justification and they harmed consumer choice, as well as increasing the likelihood of browser and system crashes.[49] Deals were made with AOL to distribute Explorer 'to the virtual exclusion of Navigator' despite consumer demand for the alternative.[50] Similar arrangements were then secured with AT & T WorldNet, Prodigy and CompuServe.[51]

The Judge found that Navigator's share of browser usage fell from above 70% to below 50%, while Explorer's share rose from 5% to 50%. In 1998, though the number of new users was rising rapidly, Navigator's share had fallen below 40%, compared to Explorer's share of above 60%.[52]

In his findings of law Judge Jackson described Microsoft's campaign to forestall the development for Netscape Navigator and Java technology as anticompetitive conduct.[53] The attempts to run down the market for Netscape, once it became clear that Navigator would be further developed as a substantial platform for applications development were part of a larger campaign to quash innovation that threatened its monopoly position. The exercise of rights under copyright law did not excuse anticompetitive behaviour.[54] The freedom to control access to code using copyright ends, where the reason for imposing a licensing restriction is anticompetitive:

if Microsoft was truly inspired by a genuine concern for maximizing consumer satisfaction, as well as preserving its substantial investment in a worthy product, then it would have relied more on the power of the very competitive PC market, and less on its own market power, to prevent OEMs (original equipment manufacturers) from making modifications that consumers did not want.[55]

Microsoft could not convince the Court that there was any pro-competitive justification for its dealings. In relation to conduct as a whole the Judge concludes:

In essence, Microsoft mounted a deliberate assault upon entrepreneurial efforts that, left to rise or fall on their own merits, could well have enabled the introduction of competition into the market for Intel-compatible PC operating systems. While the evidence does not prove that they would have succeeded absent Microsoft's actions, it does reveal that Microsoft placed an oppressive thumb on the scale of competitive fortune, thereby effectively guaranteeing its continued dominance in the relevant market. More broadly, Microsoft's anti-competitive actions trammeled the competitive process through which the computer software industry generally stimulates innovation and conduces to the optimum benefit of consumers.[56]

Accordingly he ruled that Microsoft had (1) maintained a monopoly in the market for Intel-compatible PC operating systems; (2) attempted to gain a monopoly in the market for browsers and (3) illegally tied two purportedly separate products, Windows and Explorer. This conduct constituted violations of ss1 and 2 the *Sherman Act* and the remedy required Microsoft to submit a proposed plan of divestiture, with the company to be split into an operating systems business and an applications business.[57]

The District Circuit appeal

On appeal the Court affirmed the first ruling, but rejected the second. It was:

far too speculative to establish that competing browsers would be unable to enter the market, or that Microsoft would have the power to raise the price of its browser above, or reduce the quality of its browser below, the competitive level. Moreover, it is ambiguous insofar as it appears to focus on Microsoft's response to the perceived platform threat rather than the browser market.[58]

The Court noted that the Department of Justice had not offered a sufficient definition of 'browser'. So what was the browser market that Microsoft
had attempted to control? Whilst the theoretical explanation that 'network
effects' conferred monopoly power in relation to a browser market, the evidence was simply not there to support a conclusion of attempted monopolisation.

The third ruling on 'tying' was sent back for retrial. The facts of the
case did not readily fit previous law that involved the tying of 'separate
products'. Newly integrated software products were unlike any the Supreme
Court had considered.[59] Further the practice of bundling was also common amongst firms without market power, hence there may be efficiencies
in tying in technologically dynamic markets that do not apply in other
kinds of markets. More empirical evidence of the effect of the practice was
desirable to demonstrate tying unreasonably restrained competition in this
case.

The remedial order for divestiture was vacated because of an issue
of procedural fairness – the hearing of evidence concerning the splitting of Microsoft was insufficient and factual disputes should be resolved
through evidentiary hearings. Further there was inadequate explanation
of the relief ordered and given the different conclusions on liability the
remedies needed reconsideration. This hearing was to be by a different
judge.

The Appellate Court was not troubled by the notion of law intervening
in high technology markets in theory, however was circumspect in practice:

> What is somewhat problematic, however, is that just over six years have passed
> since Microsoft engaged in the first conduct plaintiffs allege to be anticom-
> petitive. As the record in this case indicates, six years seems like an eternity in
> the computer industry. By the time a court can assess liability, firms, products,
> and the marketplace are likely to have changed dramatically. This, in turn,
> threatens enormous practical difficulties for courts considering the appro-
> priate measure of relief in equitable enforcement actions, both in crafting
> injunctive remedies in the first instance and reviewing those remedies in the
> second. Conduct remedies may be unavailing in such cases, because inno-
> vation to a large degree has already rendered the anticompetitive conduct
> obsolete (although by no means harmless).[60]

The difficulty was exacerbated where academia was undecided about
the relevance of 'old economy' notions of monopolisation given 'network
effects':

there is no consensus among commentators on the question of whether, and to what extent, current monopolization doctrine should be amended to account for competition in technologically dynamic markets characterized by network effects.[61]

Naturalising ideological agendas: a 'technologically dynamic market'

The assumption is that because of the unusually rapid pace of innovation, law struggles to both define and respond to suspect conduct. But what does it mean to suggest that innovation is the cause and possible remedy to this difficulty? As discussed above, the meaning of innovation is complex and discerning innovative developments, distinct from 'innovative' management of an information asset, is difficult.

With information products it is the manager, overseeing technological development and marketing, who creates and asserts limits to the information asset. Intellectual property laws also indicate some limits, but only vaguely. For example, copyright defines the protected computer work, treated as a special form of 'literary work' but only at a very high level of abstraction. The main objective is to limit the protected expression from the unprotected idea. For example under Australian law a 'computer program' means a set of statements or instructions to be used directly or indirectly in a computer in order to bring about a certain result.[62] Clearly the definition does little to constrain the innovative manager determining which combinations of instruction sets are protected. It simply requires that there is more than a single command to qualify for protection.[63]

With old-economy products, such as books, the cultural artefact and tangible product bought and sold could still be relied upon to define the publishing market, notwithstanding that as a matter of legal rights the chattel property (a book) and the intangible copyright (the reproductive rights) are distinct legal interests. But with digital products there is no such tangible or cultural referent that makes sense. The distinction between hardware and software is considered outmoded. As computer buyers we may tend to think in terms of the commonly marketed products and peripherals. We are familiar with computers in terms of how they are purchased, with choices to be made about hardware such as monitors, hard drives, disc burners, modems, mouse, printer and various storage mediums; and specific software such as the (pre-installed) system software and various other applications often included in 'whole package' deals targeting particular kinds of users.

Superficially this suggests computers are made up of a lot of separately defined bits with programmed-in boundaries. But in operating terms the way the components interact is a lot more fluid, and depends on the functions being performed, given the capabilities of the particular configuration. In this environment defining a digital product or market, that suggests obvious, stable boundaries around the related data, is precarious.

Defining the operating system market is not problematic, since Microsoft has primarily been the reference point for this for such a long time. But a corollary of the ability to define such a thing as an operating system market over time is that we should be more than suspicious of that circumstance. That we are now able to confidently define that is itself suggestive of illegal conduct.

Netscape, as an 'early mover', quickly established a common-sense expectation of what could be comprised in a 'browser' product/market. But we know that successful software is always no more than an iteration. The innovation cycle, pushed by both the need to upgrade key components to accommodate new versions of the operating system and the incorporation of other successful ideas that justify a new consumer expenditure to maintain essentially the same basic functionality, means that we think in terms of fast evolution, and optimistically – progress. We think of computer technology in terms of ambitions, not limits and secure market boundaries.

With this apparent state of flux, perhaps recourse to more evidence before embarking on remedial action for anticompetitive conduct is a judicious move. However, realistically, what evidence is there? Where is the evidence going to come from? How tainted will it be by personal histories, particular industry allegiances and frustrated expectations? Evidence, assuming it is forthcoming, simply exposes more detailed conjecture about what the state of play in development was at a particular point in time, and speculation about the potential to profit from that assuming competitors and the markets had behaved as innovation theory anticipates. The only constant measure to which all evidence is related here is the ideological assumption about the proper behaviour of high technology markets. And whilst the claim is that evidence can shed light on the truth of 'abuse' and 'network effects', the reality is that if anticipated developments have not progressed, blame will be shifted home to Microsoft. Liebowitz and Margolis note: 'It is not clear that current anti-trust law addresses such concerns . . . Obviously, no one can empirically disprove the claim that products that might have been created would have been better than currently existing products.'[64]

From a legal perspective:

The integrity of the legal process required court to adhere to a standard of proof which although not expressed in terms of statistical probability was an attempt to capture that probability in a non-mathematical form. However imprecise these legal formulations might be, they still required something more solid than speculation. Conflation of the probable and the possible was a deductive vice to which both sides were equally prone and for which both were equally chided.[65]

But it also could be argued that the emphasis on the need for evidence has the convenient effect of whittling down the extent of the grievance that law has to confront here. The blame is shifted back to the Department of Justice and Judge Jackson for failing to discover and act on sufficient evidence, rather than law itself being seen as incapable of ascertaining the required level of evidence in a 'technologically dynamic market'.

The term 'technologically dynamic market' as it appears throughout the Microsoft litigation is simply a code word for globalisation: the assumed public good in furthering the profitable development of information networks and assets. It is, by nature, expansionary and diffuse.[66] The discourse on evidence distracts from confronting the regulatory confines of a cybernetic law that serves globalisation, without debating the politics of its social relations. In this context the Court view and Gates' views of the appropriate functional domain of law[67] concur. The Court prefers 'a tunnel like focus on information, self-evident and free of context'[68] rather than engaging or encouraging debate about the social networks that inform information and its production – a social inquiry into relations in the industry and their economic and cultural effects.

The Appellate Court was clearly disturbed by Judge Jackson disclosing his personal opinions about Gates and Microsoft to journalists, which though embargoed, were conducted before and after final judgement was entered and published in *The New York Times* and *The New Yorker*:

Reports of the interviews have the District Judge describing Microsoft's conduct, with particular emphasis on what he regarded as the company's prevarication, hubris, and impenitence . . .

He told reporters that Bill Gates' 'testimony is inherently without credibility' and '[i]f you can't believe this guy, who else can you believe . . .?':

As for the company's other witnesses, the Judge is reported as saying that there 'were times when I became impatient with Microsoft witnesses who were giving speeches.' '[T]hey were telling me things I just flatly could not credit.' . . .

The Judge told a college audience that 'Bill Gates is an ingenious engineer, but I don't think he is that adept at business ethics' . . .

Characterizing Gates' and his company's 'crime' as hubris, the Judge stated that '[i]f I were able to propose a remedy of my devising, I'd require Mr. Gates to write a book report' on Napoleon Bonaparte, '[b]ecause I think [Gates] has a Napoleonic concept of himself and his company, an arrogance that derives from power and unalloyed success, with no leavening hard experience, no reverses.' . . .

The District Judge likened Microsoft's writing of incriminating documents to drug traffickers who 'never figure out that they shouldn't be saying certain things on the phone.' He invoked the drug trafficker analogy again to denounce Microsoft's protestations of innocence, this time with a reference to the notorious Newton Street Crew that terrorized parts of Washington, D.C. . . .

The District Judge also secretly divulged to reporters his views on the remedy for Microsoft's antitrust violations . . . In February 2000, four months before his final order splitting the company in two, the District Judge reportedly told *New York Times* reporters that he was 'not at all comfortable with restructuring the company,' because he was unsure whether he was 'competent to do that.'[69]

To the Appellate Court and most lawyers this candidness is judicial misconduct that endangers the perception of judicial impartiality and violates Judicial Codes of Conduct:

Public confidence in the integrity and impartiality of the judiciary is seriously jeopardized when judges secretly share their thoughts about the merits of pending cases with the press. Judges who covet publicity, or convey the appearance that they do, lead any objective observer to wonder whether their judgments are being influenced by the prospect of favorable coverage in the media . . . Judge Learned Hand spoke of 'this America of ours where the passion for publicity is a disease, and where swarms of foolish, tawdry moths dash with rapture into its consuming fire . . .' LEARNED HAND, THE SPIRIT OF LIBERTY 132–33 (2nd ed. 1953). Judges are obligated to resist this passion.[70]

Nonetheless not speaking to the media and 'keeping up appearances' of impartiality are also a form of court image management. It suggests that by maintaining distance, legal determinations are untainted by public opinion, and that this best serves justice.

Fear and trembling in Silicon Valley[71]

Heilemann's writing about the Microsoft litigation[72] plots the difficulties the Department of Justice (DOJ) faced in soliciting evidence relevant to the litigation. He demonstrates the importance of the personalities involved and shows how individual loyalties and personal circumstances can affect legal practice:

> If the DOJ were going to pursue severe sanctions against Microsoft, he [sic] would need the backing of Silicon Valley's leaders. Not backing for himself, but for serious remedies. And not subtle, clandestine, backstage support, but up-front, vocal, public support. The kind that shapes media coverage and editorial opinion; the kind that gets through to the man in the street; the kind that changes minds, and moves votes, in Congress. [The DOJ's] Klein knew that the remedy phase of the trial would be intensely political. He needed the Valley to make some noise.
> What he got instead was a thundering silence.[73]

Whilst played for dramatic effect, Heilemann shows how all the bit and leading players' personalities, personal histories, grievances and fears influence what comes to legal attention. They affect decisions made by both teams of counsel to allow witnesses to appear and opinions being recorded in court.

Heilemann suggests that after the Findings of Fact were handed down, Judge Jackson used the threat of divestiture to pressure Microsoft into reaching a settlement, and that he entered that decision because negotiations completely collapsed. A settlement would have avoided the evidentiary hurdles the case continually presented. With court direction, a settlement was reached in November 2002.[74]

Law is peculiarly vulnerable to the subjective factors and whims of personalities identified by Heilemann, because as the District Circuit Court itself stressed, it is dependent upon access to the personal knowledge and insights of industry players for evidence to prosecute and fashion an appropriate remedy. What this means is that law can't regulate well with an industry culture suspicious of law's efficacy. If the marketplace constrains the free speech of Microsoft's rivals, competitors and dependants, law is impotent to 'correct' that power imbalance. Here we see that the US constitutional framework does not necessarily or emphatically address all free speech needs. The conditions of free speech about Microsoft are determined by the market here, where the market is anything but free. It creates a difficult legal obstacle, if not an impasse.

One institutional weakness of law is the pretence that all the important relevant information will be forthcoming, subjected to testing with judicial oversight, contemplated and then acted upon in accordance with the rules. The pretence is that the institution of law generates such respect that it has authority over the social sphere so as to compel the solicitation of the required information. The appearance of impartiality and neutrality is considered essential to maintaining such respect and authority. But so is a belief in law's practical efficacy.

In endangering 'appearances' of justice, Judge Jackson crossed what the law sees as an essential delineation between the disciplinary realm of law and the freedom of the social and economic sphere. While he has explained his conduct in terms of wanting to 'give some sense of who I am and what I have done',[75] a more subversive reading of this publicity-seeking behaviour suggests that there is more to this than a matter of personal aggrandisement and ego. Given quite rational reservations and fears about the ability and willingness of law to take Microsoft on or apart, the significance of a court determination making a difference correspondingly diminishes. In any case, law itself wants to let the market sort it out itself, wherever possible. In this environment the media becomes a far more important institution for redressing grievances and executing a result or remedy.

Negative publicity – in the form of gratuitous, inflammatory, attention-seeking comments – is a valuable tool for influencing opinion and behaviour in the marketplace. Simply announcing from the bench that Microsoft has a monopoly in the operating system business isn't telling the public anything new. That doesn't change behaviour or encourage different consumption choices. But scandal-mongering and pandering to celebrity character assassination are more interesting. Reaffirming the corporate trickster archetype, and feeding the whispering from the chicken coops and yards, is more likely to help redress the perceived harm, if there is a choice available. And in the global village the media has a longer reach than any particular court.

The argument here is not that the legal settlement was irrelevant. The settlement focused on ending Microsoft restrictions on 'middleware'.[76] OEMs must be free to install and display icons and short cuts for competing software which can be selected as the default by OEMs and end users. Likewise, they are free to remove Explorer. Microsoft is barred from retaliating against OEMs and ISVs for distributing and developing software that competes with the Microsoft platform. Microsoft is required to disclose interfaces and technical information used by middleware to interoperate with its operating system and license any communication protocol used to interoperate or communicate with its server operating product. The license is to be provided on reasonable and non-discriminatory (RAND) terms. Microsoft is also obliged to file six-monthly status reports on compliance, and complaints are investigated. This process has led to pressure to simplify licensing terms and provide more complete documentation to licensees.

The settlement has some capacity to increase competition by removing some of the perceived restrictions on innovation. However for different outcomes to eventuate it is equally important to solicit different choices by consumers. Public shaming of the trickster, unsympathetic media coverage of the corporation, can encourage the delivery of the desired result. And whether or not it was intended by Judge Jackson, the fourth estate serves an important quasi-judicial function here, especially given the self-imposed limits the Court adopts when it comes to interfering directly in 'technologically dynamic markets'.

Why the legal resolution doesn't allay anxieties

The European Commission investigation into Microsoft found that the corporation had violated European Union competition law by levering its near monopoly in the operating system market for PCs onto markets for work group server operating systems and for media players. As well as the imposition of a fine of approximately US $610 million, Microsoft was ordered to disclose interfaces required to interoperate with Windows and offer a version of Windows without Windows Media Player to PC manufacturers.[77] An appeal is now proceeding. In response to the decision US Senate Majority Leader Bill Frist complained that:

> In imposing this anti-consumer, anti-innovation penalty, the Commission has blatantly undercut the settlement that was so carefully and painstakingly crafted with Microsoft by the US Department of Justice and several state antitrust authorities. There can be no question that the US Government was entitled to take the lead in this matter – Microsoft is a US company, many if not all of the complaining companies in the EU case are American, and all of the relevant design decisions took place here. Had the Commission been cognizant of America's legitimate interests in this matter, it would have

acted in a manner that complemented the US settlement. Needless to say, the Commission instead selected a path that places its resolution of this case in direct conflict with ours – and threatens the vitality of America's IT industry in the process.[78]

Another commentator noted that: 'It threatens the ability of multinationals to operate seamlessly around he world', says Russell Roberts, economics professor at George Mason University. 'It is disturbing.'[79]

Here the European anti-Microsoft decision is framed as a 'US' versus the 'rest of the world' concern. The clear presumption is that 'what is good for Microsoft, is good for the US' and 'what is good for the US, is good for the globe'. Such overt allegiance between a particular corporate interest and national and international politics only confirms for many deeper suspicion about fundamental institutional corruption related to the advance of globalisation. It is common in anti-globalisation protests to combine being anti-WTO, anti-IMF, anti-World Bank, anti-Bush, anti-Coke, anti-Nike, anti-Pepsi, anti-war on Iraq, with being anti-Microsoft and against US hegemony. More recently demonstrators are also pro-Linux, which is seemingly liberated from any particular American politics.[80] Microsoft is taken to symbolise an American way of thinking about the information economy, technology markets and innovation. But what the corporation stands for generates deep anxieties about who the beneficiaries of globalisation are and what the future may be.

Moving the village

In a lecture on global labour standards, Cornell University professor of economics Kaushik Basu retold the following tale:

> Several years ago in Delhi, I called a pest control firm to treat our Mayur Vihar apartment for termites.
>
> A South Indian gentleman with a pleasing smile arrived with canisters of chemicals and a large syringe. He went about his task meticulously and, every time he sprayed, a mist settled on everything.
>
> I asked him if all this would really work. Breaking into a comforting grin, he said, 'Sir, have no worry whatsoever. This is very strong stuff. It is totally banned in the United States.'
>
> I edged out of the room, as he reared the syringe for another round of dousing.[81]

One of the logics of globalisation is the avoidance of unwanted state oversight so that corporations gain more unfettered freedom of action. Communications networks facilitate that objective:

> Networked business processes substantially increased management's ability to disperse both the object and subject of labor – jobs and workers – so as to maximise profits.[82]
>
> As **permissive** technologies that are built to facilitate centralized control over far-flung corporate operations, networks permit transnational companies to elevate footloose profit hunger into what they seek to dignify with the term globalization. The result is to pit individual localities, states and entire nations against one another in a competition to attract investment, and this rivalry, predictably produces a 'race to the bottom'.[83]

Developed countries are familiar with the movement of low-skilled jobs, in the manufacturing sector and services, such as data input and call centres, offshore. A recent case study conducted by the Hass School of Business, University of California, notes that California accounts for more than 20% of US employment in computer and electronic equipment manufacturing, and more than 25% of software publishing. Whilst there has been a growth in sales and employment in the sector in the past decade, computer-related manufacturing experienced a decline.[84]

With regard to OEMs, over half of US and Canadian firms outsource at least part of production abroad.[85] Further the share of imported inputs used in manufacturing in the US has continued to increase.[86] The Hass study concludes that the US trade deficit in high-tech hardware expanded over the past decade, and that US multinationals are now responsible for more than two-thirds of all imports of high-tech intermediate inputs into the US.[87] Between 1990 and 2002 the US lost more than 150,000 high-tech manufacturing jobs, despite strong growth in sales. Foreign outsourcing was responsible for one-third to one-half of the increase in relative inequality between blue collar and white collar workers in California. Further, some forms of outsourcing seem to have accelerated during the post-2000 downturn in the technology industry.[88]

To date it has been the 'routine' jobs that have gone overseas. However:

> Recent global expansion of the outsourcing service activities, such as software production to India, Russia and China, raises the prospect that a significant share of California's high-tech service sector employment may be lost to foreign outsourcing, following the same pattern as the earlier loss of high-tech manufacturing jobs.[89]

Table 9 *Proportion of US private labor force in unions 1950–2000*

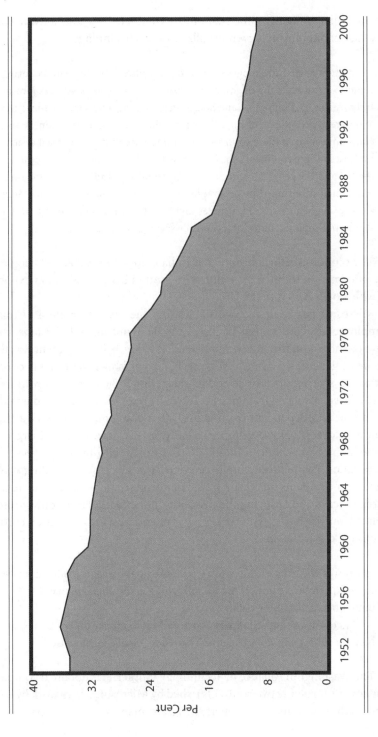

Reference: Robert Brenner, *The Boom and the Bubble: The US in the World Economy* (Verso, 2003), p. 53

An earlier study the same economists conducted suggests a 'New Wave of Outsourcing', involving white collar work, is beginning:

In addition to cost advantages similar to those offered by the manufacturing centers of east Asia, the ongoing of outsourcing of business services jobs to India, Malaysia, Philippines and South Africa among others is also due to the widespread acceptance of English as a medium of education, business and communication in these countries; a common accounting and legal system (at least in some countries), the latter based on the common law structure of the UK and US; general institutional compatibility and adaptability; the time differential determined by geographical location leading to 24/7 capability and overnight turnaround; simpler logistics than in manufacturing, and a steady and copious supply of technically savvy graduates.[90]

The economists further note that India employs over 200,000 people in the information technology sector, with around US $2.3 billion in exports, of which over 70% is to the US.

Microsoft has been accused of 'leading the way to create a virtually "employee-less corporation"', a jigsaw puzzle of outsourced divisions, contract factories and freelance employees.[91] Previously the argument was that a core of generously treated 'Microserfs . . . coltishly loyal to their corporation, its soaring stock price and its staggering 51% operating profit margin . . .' were insulated from market forces by reserves of temps and workers signed on as independent contractors, often doing the same work as full-time employees.[92] However more recently protests have been reported over an erosion of working conditions of Microsoft's full-time employees. The corporation has reduced employee benefits to cut costs, including introducing co-payments on certain brand name prescription drugs, shortening parental leave and reducing the discount on the market price of Microsoft shares from 15% to 10%. Worker surveys and posts to websites recorded employee dissatisfaction:

'Microsoft's benefits used to somewhat make up for what is a difficult place to work,' wrote one poster. 'Are we now going in the direction that it will be both difficult and unrewarding?'

'Microsoft continues to make more and more money every quarter, yet they are cutting employee benefits? That doesn't make much sense.'[93]

The Washington Alliance of Technology Workers has obtained company documents involving two contracts issued by Microsoft where work by software architects, senior developers, program managers and testers will be performed in the US and India by workers employed by Indian technology companies Satyam Computer Services and Infosys Technologies, with different pay rates for 'on-site' and 'offshore' work:

> Nothing in either agreement suggests that Satyam or Infosys workers were used to replace US workers. But when Microsoft's Valentine framed the company's strategy in his 'Think India' 2002 presentation as 'two heads for the price of one,' he implied a corporate strategy of doing just that.[94]

Microsoft is clearly not alone in outsourcing. More than 300 of the Fortune 500 firms use IT services in India to run data and call centres. Some research estimates that the number of US computer-related jobs going overseas will grow from 27,000 in 2000 to 472,000 in 2015.[95] US legislators are trying to restrict the use of offshore contractors by state and local governments and the US Senate recently approved an amendment that excludes certain government contractors from offshore work.[96] However in some cases work contracted to US firms is subsequently subcontracted offshore[97] – a practice it is difficult to police.

Many of the foreign skilled employees attractive to multinationals have tertiary education provided by institutions in the US, Canada, Australia and the UK. Further, many graduates, if they can find employment, choose to stay on, rather than returning to poorer working conditions in their country of origin. These benefits to local economies are often overlooked in what is a heated debate about labour and globalisation.

Pro-globalisation studies argue that the more a developing country integrates into the world economy the greater the reduction of poverty and the more living standards improve. This does not mean, of course, that all developing countries are well situated to attract multinational interest.[98] It also does not mean that there is not, in regulatory terms, a race to the bottom.

US-based criticism of outsourcing in the public and private sector is gathering momentum, with protests more common. The 'freedom' of being a wired employee in the ICT sector in the US is for many also a cause for insecurity. These concerns may refresh debates about the relevance of place, location and national identity in the global economy and lead to more nuanced debates about America, corporate life, innovation and the global economy.

The Microsoft archetype assumes that the consumer and 'citizen' live disembodied and separate lives, and that feelings of disempowerment as a citizen of the information economy will not cross over to affect consumption or employment choices. Those alienated by this new economy are assumed to retreat, sit back and allow the trickster to continue to abuse the trust of the community, returning again and again to offer technical solutions which experience shows do not necessarily serve the environment well. However the information flows and global circulation of opinions, particularly amplified through the media, can provide a competing source of influence or authority over our buying, thinking and acting.[99] Part of the mainstream interest in free software and open source stems from a desire to forge a different sense of action and commerce. And in making legal arrangements more transparent, this suggests a model of commerce with less room for a trickster to manoeuvre. In such a universe the failings of law to manage the environment, and better control the information and its flows, or address the social life of information, might matter far less.

Patrick Broderick, *MP3s = Communism*

6
Telling tales: digital piracy and the law[1]

'Dostoevsky once wrote that "in the end they will lay their freedom at our feet and say to us, 'Make us your slaves, but feed us.'" His prophecy is relevant when examining the modern Information Age – a dark, corporate-controlled society predicted by such artistic legends as Bruce Sterling, George Lucas, Ridley Scott, and William Gibson.'[2]

The MP3=Communism joke captures the spirit of the debate that unfolded over the last six or so years surrounding peer-to-peer file sharing technology and piracy. I have heard several lawyers, journalists and students speak of the MP3 'propaganda' with some amusement, perhaps without ever seeing it. What is odd, however, is that more often than not the informant is uncertain if this is or isn't a genuine RIAA anti-piracy message. What does this bemused confusion tell us about the digital copyright debate?

One of the recurring themes in this debate is a fear of enslavement at the hands of ever fewer global media empires and an accusation that law is swiftly delivering us to that fate. In order to better evaluate the persuasiveness of this prevalent view, we should more fully investigate the popular culture of piracy that law, in the form of legislation, litigation and corporate legal strategy, engages.

We should be suspicious of these pessimistic tales. And not just because of the already familiar position that places faith in counter-cultural anarchic technologies resisting, outsmarting and eluding capture by the corporations and law. My story is more optimistic than that, and less about playing law as a game. What I question is the ability of digital copyright law to grant that level of control over technology and culture to the 'dark' corporate forces of the sci-fi and cyberpunk visionaries.

The topic of copyright has become *the* legal issue that has set the agenda for over a decade in discussion about the future of the internet. Copyright seems to be the point of reference for questions about the internet's infrastructure and communications. To date the digital piracy debate has been predominantly engaged as a question about cultural production. This is a matter we are all assumed to have an interest in and an opinion about, if we are to be considered as engaged with our culture.

On the one hand we have Time Warner CEO Richard Parsons telling us that peer-to-peer:

> . . . isn't just about a bunch of kids stealing music. It's about an assault on everything that constitutes the cultural expression of our society. If we fail to protect and preserve our intellectual property system, the culture will atrophy. And corporations won't be the only ones hurt. Artists will have no incentive to create. Worst case scenario: The country will end up in a sort of cultural Dark Ages.[3]

From the other camp, we are warned that:

> . . . as we rush to embrace the latest and greatest gadgetry or high-tech service and satisfy our techno-craving, we become further dependent on these products and their manufacturers – so dependent that when something breaks, crashes, or is attacked, our ability to function is reduced or eliminated. Given the frequent problems associated with the Information Age – losing internet connections, breaking personal digital assistants, malicious software incidents, or suffering any number of recurring problems with software or hardware products, we should take a minute to consider whether we're really more or less independent – or empowered – today than we think, knowing that how we act during such stressful periods is similar to a heroin junkie's actions during withdrawal.[4]

The technological promise of freedom, a 'high-tech heroin' that many have dreamed of – and perhaps even experienced prior to the arrival of digital copyright laws – has been rudely shoved out of reach:

> To make things worse, government practically has outsourced the oversight and definition of technology-based expression and community interaction to for-profit corporations and secretive industry-specific cartels (e.g., the MPAA, RIAA, SIA, BSA, ICANN) who have wasted no time in rewriting the rules for how they want our information-based society to operate according to their interests, not ours. At times, you might even say we've voluntarily imprisoned ourselves under the control of profit-seeking wardens who have little if any real oversight or accountability for their actions. Our high-tech heroin dealers are not only promoting and profiting from their product but developing the laws and methods to govern and regulate its use while protecting themselves from any negative side-effects and ensuring their revenue stream.[5]

Lawrence Lessig has argued that 'the future of ideas' is at stake. In *The Future of Ideas: The Fate of the Commons in a Connected World*[6] and *Free Culture: How Big Media uses Technology and the Law to Lock Down Culture and Control Creativity*[7] he considers the state of innovation and creativity in these 'reactionary' times. Lessig analyses the subtext of the advertisements from Apple Computer urging that consumers should 'Rip, mix, burn', because 'After all, it's your music'. He seeks to explain the power of this commercial:

> Apple, of course, wants to sell computers. Yet its ad touches an ideal that runs very deep in our history. For the technology that they (and of course others) sell could enable this generation to do with our culture what generations have done from the very beginning of human society: to take what is our culture; to 'rip' it – meaning to copy it; to 'mix' it – meaning to reform it however the user wants; and finally, and most important, 'burn' it – to publish it in a way that others can see and hear. Digital technology could enable an extraordinary range of ordinary people to become part of a creative process.[8]

However, Lessig seizes on the irony that the very same machines that Apple sets to 'rip, mix, [and] burn' music are programmed to make it impossible for ordinary users to 'rip, mix, [and] burn' Hollywood's movies.[9] The problem is that software protects this content, and Apple's machine protects this code. Furthermore, Lessig considers the backlash against the notion that consumers should be able to 'Rip, mix, burn'. He observes:

> But just as the cusp of this future, at the same time that we are being pushed to the world where anyone can 'rip, mix, [and] burn,' a counter-movement is raging all around. To ordinary people, this slogan from Apple seems benign enough; to lawyers in the content industry, it is high treason. To lawyers who prosecute the laws of copyright, the very idea that the music on 'your' CD is 'your music' is absurd . . .[10]
>
> You have no 'right' to rip it, or to mix it, or especially to burn it. You may have, the lawyers will insist, permission to do these things. But don't confuse Hollywood's grace with your rights. These parts of our culture, these lawyers will tell you, are the property of the few.[11]

Lessig and other critics of digital copyright laws are right. We are living in reactionary times. However the problem is, so far most of the analysis has been preoccupied with draconian laws that enable corporate control over production and distribution of digital content. What has been missing from discussion so far is a consideration of *how this legal control over production and distribution fits with the consumption practices that support the development of new digital products and services.*

Copyright law, with its roots in liberal political economic theory, is relatively disinterested in consumption practices. The assumption is that the market processes information about people's needs more effectively than other types of institutions, particularly political institutions, with choices indicated by willingness to buy.[12] The private powers copyright creates are assumed to direct the marketing possibilities of copyright material, by defining what income streams can be created. And where they meaningfully exist, fair use rights and the first sale doctrine[13] can modify those expectations. But how copyrighted culture is actually consumed is not something the law ordinarily considers. It is presumed that demand is satisfied by consumer behaviour that follows the law, and that if it does not, concerned rights owners can litigate to force compliance. It is only where consumption practices are wildly at odds with corporate anticipation, as is the case with widespread piracy, where understanding behaviour that appears to be lawless and deviant becomes a matter for legal re-evaluation.

Whether the behaviour is in fact lawless or legitimate, and how defiance is to be addressed, is a matter clarified by legislative reform. However to date critics have overwhelmingly presumed that it follows from this that the primary site of battle over digital technologies and the law is the legislatures, global law-making bodies and the courts. It is presumed that the outcomes in these places will actually determine what our access to technology and content will be tomorrow or even next year.

We pretend that the public matters because what is at stake will affect them directly, but really only take the public into account as an object of legal regulation – as really little more than slaves to structures determined elsewhere. And we fear that the public will probably embrace the new restrictive technological goods and services, even though we also know that a few noble and some dishonourable but skilled die-hards will continue to provide tools to resist the spirit of the new legal enterprise. As lawyers needing to respond to ongoing proposals for digital copyright law reform we have been drawn into pondering the significance of legal institutions and their deliberations, with too little contemplation of the developing global social relations of the law. In haste to respond to the 'law on the books' academia has run with a kind of – often unrecognised – legal and technological determinism that infects many of the discussions and most of the books about the legal environment of the digital future.

Even though there may be an attempt to accommodate social complexity and limits to predictability of social behaviours, I think debate is legally determinist where the emotional content of the text is an unexamined fear that legal subjects are going to obey these bad laws anyway. A fear of legal obedience – that there will be a crossing over from widespread non-compliance to social acceptance of the 'Say Yes to Copyright' message is the current subtext of much writing. There may be a suggestion that, in the future, consumers will have no choice but compliance. Perhaps the next generations will be won over by copyright education and propaganda. Perhaps non-compliance will become too inconvenient for the time poor or technologically challenged to engage in. Non-compliance might be rationally judged as too risky or expensive for the middle class to pursue. This all may also eventuate, but if it does, to me there is more to the WHY of this than just pointing the finger at the legislature and Big Business grinding down resistance to the laws and pushing restrictive, inefficient technologies,[14] as a sufficient explanation of the social and legal transformation taking place.

According to writers like Bauman,[15] Foucault,[16] Donzelot,[17] amongst others, the construction of Modernity involved the development of new forms of social or cultural regulation that operated at state level in terms of welfare delivery, and also in terms of a reconstruction and intervention at the community level, down to family. Whatever term you want to use to describe the global condition we are now in – postmodernism, information capitalism, the network economy, Empire – what are the cultural mechanisms or forms of social control that support this state of Being?

Communications technologies are clearly one of the current forms of social and cultural regulation, but we should take care not to be technologically determinist here. Copyright owners cannot determine the digital marketplace and global society simply by effecting copyright laws that enhance control over distribution from their end, even with ISPs in tow.

In terms of a 'marketplace' view of the world there are conflicts between content owners and appliance makers. There are conflicts within multinational media conglomerates between the various related enterprises. There is no simple synchronicity in ambition between established American and Japanese technology makers, and even more complication when you consider the Korean, Indian, Malaysian and Chinese technology businesses.

A more careful look at how technologies function as agents of social control – and how the networks and appliances mesh with new technologically inscribed forms of identity – is essential. However this is not just a question about the 'marketplace' view of the world.

The marketplace view is limited by its adopting the perspective of the rational economic actor and his self-calculating behaviour:

> Although economic man is perfectly rational with respect to knowledge of his own subjective well-being, he is at the same time utterly incapable of empathetic knowledge regarding the subjective well-being of others . . . Thus, one way . . . to describe economic man is that he is both peculiarly **capable** and peculiarly **disabled**: he knows everything there is to know about his own subjective life, and nothing whatsoever about the subjective lives of others.[18]

In the digital piracy context, a marketplace view avoids consideration of the very questions that need to be asked about our identities as cultural consumers, and how this impacts on the law.

Our behaviour in the marketplace is not just based on 'rational choices' about desirable products and services. It may well also reflect attitudes toward copyright law and cultural commodification, and it is significantly impacted by marketing practices. Our chosen 'connections' are not just rational private decisions. Consumption choices also build our identity in relation to others. And to understand this more fully, we should pay more attention to the stories being told.

Contemporary marketing practices forge emotional connections that help define 'who we are' in the world. Our behaviour and our identity are influenced by advertising narratives:

> Advertising is not simply an adjunct to the system of objects: it cannot be detached therefrom, nor can it be restricted to its 'proper' function (there is no such thing as advertising strictly confined to the supplying of information).[19]

Rather than being just rational economic actors:

> How people act in the world on the basis of beliefs and desires, how they strive to achieve particular goals, how they meet and overcome obstacles – all this, set in a discreetly structured sequence in time, is conveyed by narrative. And it is through narrative that they are subject to influence. Surely, then, it makes sense to ask: What are the stories and storytelling tools people typically use to organize their experience and memory of human events?[20]
>
> Being part of a community means that we perceive or interpret events in overlapping ways using shared cognitive and cultural tools and materials.[21]

Though some of us are perhaps postmodern, and through communications technologies less tied to the original creator as the source of authority over the meaning of the narrative:

> I think what they (Derrida and Lyotard) are noticing is that we cannot but narrate . . . but there are also problems. . . . (I)n a narrative, as you proceed along the narrative, the narrative takes on its own impetus as it were, so that one begins to see reality as non-narrated. One begins to say that it's not a narrative, it's the way things are.[22]

Another layer of complication here is, as Richard Sherwin explores in his book, *When Law Goes Pop*,[23] that:

> The communicative practices of law, both inside the courtroom and in the court of public opinion, are increasingly going the way of contemporary political discourse – law too is succumbing to the influence of public relations, mass advertising, and fabricated media events. An increasing reliance upon public relations campaigns in the court of public opinion as an adjunct to litigation is part and parcel of this trend.[24]

It is our over-exposure to the marketing of ideas and promotion of legal messages that contributes to a sense of uncertainty about how to correctly read the MP3=Communism sign.

Marketing practices in relation to digital goods and services, and as used by legal actors, need to be taken into account in assessing our behaviour as citizens and consumers of digital culture. This is essential for understanding how copyright law functions as a social practice.

In my view the problem with selling the digital piracy message, and in having law direct our access to new technologies and digital services, lies with the history of consumption of popular culture and consumer expectations of digital technologies. We have been sold on a story of a clean, seamless aesthetic – one that facilitates integration and co-ordination of appliances and lifestyle. As consumers of that fantasy, we place limitations on the development of the technology market, on what is believable as consumer education, and on the ability of law to sell us a structure of 'control'. The longstanding practice of technology marketing has confirmed consumer expectations of sleeker, faster, enhanced products. This story will frustrate the establishment of a different culture based on technological regulation and control. Given our established consumer expectations about what the internet, and what digitisation brings, I think it is now extraordinarily hard to sell the copyright anti-piracy message as part of the sale of new products and services that, in the consumer's eyes, will actually deliver less.

Peer-to-peer: anarchy versus oligarchy?

Interviewer: You've called Freenet 'a near perfect form of anarchy'. Given how enormous the Internet has become, is online anarchy such a good idea?

Ian Clarke: By 'perfect' I mean a well-planned, decentralized system. There are a lot of people now who have a stake in trying to control the Internet, so it's important to build systems that have no central control. If you look at Napster, for example, there are people who have central control, which means legal action can be taken against them. The owners of Napster could be bribed into selling it to the music industry. In order to make Freenet immune to that, I designed it so that it doesn't depend on any one person or computer. I don't control it. If somebody put a gun to my head and said: 'Shut down the system,' I'd be unable to do it.[25]

The legal battle over the development, dissemination and use of peer-to-peer technology[26] is a subject of popular culture. Historical explanations for its development point to the internet's militaristic origins – the desire to create a decentralised communications network for a post-apocalyptic world where any localised failure can be overcome by removing reliance on an intermediary server.[27] More current sociological explanations of peer-to-peer's popularity point to frustration at the way PC use has come to be controlled by plodding IT nerds at work, at universities and via ISPs. These IT experts decide the terms of your engagement with technology and other users, motivated by their own interest in an easy life and pleasing the CEO with the stability and security of their unadventurous IT systems.[28] Peer-to-peer can cut such intermediaries out of the technological loop.

The legal interest in peer-to-peer revolves around a question of law's service to economics – old commerce and e-commerce. But the battle began here in the early 1990s, not as one over peer-to-peer itself, but about accessing content on the internet more generally. Then expectations of the internet as a 'new frontier' were high. The popular slogan was that 'Information wants to be free'.

This began as an argument really directed to the anachronism of maintaining strong property rights in content when there was an enthusiastic take-up of a technology that freed up new ways of accessing and using works, and at a time when postmodern and poststructuralist arguments about the death of the author were also current. The 'Information wants to be free' slogan is most often associated with John Perry Barlow and his early 90s' discussion of what your rights should be on the 'electronic frontier'.[29] In particular Barlow objected to the operation of intellectual property rights in cyberspace because he considered that these laws solidified the fluid character of internet relations and destroyed the life inherent in the online medium and media. In his view, intellectual property laws were designed for a different time and space:

> Copyright worked well because, Gutenberg notwithstanding, it was hard to make a book. Furthermore, books froze their contents into a condition that was as challenging to alter as it was to reproduce.[30]

Intellectual property laws protected distribution rights in tangible goods in order to reward 'the ability to deliver (ideas) into reality. For all practical purposes, the value was in the conveyance and not the thought conveyed.'[31]

Prior to digital technology it made sense to attribute works to a particular person:

> Cultural production, literary or otherwise, has traditionally been a slow, labour-intensive process . . . The time lapse between production and distribution can seem unbearably long . . . Before electronic technology became dominant, cultural perspectives developed in a manner that more clearly defined texts as individual works. Cultural fragments appeared in their own right as discrete units, since their influence moved slowly enough to allow the orderly evolution of an argument or aesthetic. Boundaries could be maintained between disciplines and schools of thought. Knowledge was considered finite, and was therefore easier to control.[32]

However:

> Environments like the Net tend to grow organically. They expand not according to any one person's conscious design, but because the Net is by nature a collection of individuals all making contributions to it. The growth is at an exponential rate, though not as much in terms of size as in terms of features and feature sets . . . Today's Web will be unrecognizable in five years.
>
> One of the biggest misperceptions about content is that it's an asset that endures, that has value, like catalogs, libraries, film records, music records, or written archives. However, as Esther Dyson points out, the time value of information on the Net is extremely short.[33]

Hence Howard Rheingold's claim:

> The concept of 'content' is so poorly defined. One, there's the myth that
> content is king . . . content is not what drives a business. It's the story. It's the
> emotion. It's the way that the information is packaged and programmed.
>   . . . Magazine publishers and newspaper publishers looked at the internet
> as being an ancillary revenue stream. They would repackage their content and
> make it available on CD-ROM, then put it on the Web or America Online.
> That's proven not to work, because this medium demands more. Content
> is not the end-product. Content is the activator of the conversation and the
> community.[34]

Media and cultural theory have explored the way new technologies can
disrupt established habits of communication and transform economies.
Marshall McLuhan explored how the typewriter 'carried the Gutenberg
technology into every nook and cranny of our culture and economy'.[35]
Tom Standage describes the telegraph as the Victorian internet, shrinking
distance, revolutionising business practice and global communications.[36]
Bernard Edelman described the challenge photography and film posed for
a marketplace that originally did not consider the labour involved as creative enough to sustain a copyright. In the 1990s writers such as Martha
Woodmansee,[37] Peter Jaszi,[38] Rosemary Coombe,[39] and Jane Gaines[40] considered the role of copyright from postmodern perspectives, giving rise to
a reappraisal of the relationship between copyright and culture more generally. And Celia Lury[41] and Ronald Bettig[42] linked the history of copyright
law to technological development and legal reconceptualisations that foster
commodification and capitalist accumulation.

Cyberlibertarian writing did not draw directly on postmodern or Marxist
critiques of copyright such as these, but they did adopt a similar sceptical
questioning of the role of copyright in the economy, of the relation between
law and power, and of how laws allocate spoils. In any case, since the 1970s
there has been familiarity with the concept of technology creating new social
challenges and forging social change.[43] The idea that law might play a significant role in fostering or forestalling change is also not a recent, nor
revolutionary one.[44]

Fears for the digital future are well expressed in a 1997 Nebula award-
winning science fiction story by Paul Levinson.[45] In 'The Copyright Notice
Case'[46] forensic detective Dr D'Amato is called upon to investigate the unex-
plained death of a computer programmer. The programmer was working
on a human genome project, exploring some 'odd material' found on 8% of
the X-chromosomes studied. The material does not contain any expressive

or behavioural trait. It appears to be a protein code that is capable of some kind of binary transformation. A way has been found to translate it to words on the computer screen. It says that some intelligent species leave their marks in stone or other stable media. This species used genetically engineered DNA as a means of leaving messages for future generations. It said, 'Anyone who reads these words, who possesses our codes, is free to use them as allowed under our Copyright Notice.' Dr D'Amato finds out that another programmer has also died whilst studying the message. Why?

After some experimentation he discovers that merely decrypting and reading a DNA message is not fatal. But making a digital copy of the words by for example, saving to a hard drive, somehow triggers a massive burst of serotonin in the person sitting in front of the computer. Serotonin is a natural chemical found in the brain. Normally it contributes to a sense of wide awakeness, and raises blood pressure, but a huge overdose of serotonin causes lethally high blood pressure, heart attacks and general organ failure. As Dr D'Amato says, the deaths were caused by 'A primordial copy protection scheme. A copy protection technique from Hell.'

In the digital copyright debate a recurring theme is that law's homage to the right of intellectual property owners involves, not just a legal intervention, but also a cultural intervention. The strategy is designed to slow the development of digital technologies to disrupt the establishment of the new hegemony and the birth of a new age. It is about slowing, if not stopping the information flows, unless or until they are adequately copy protected. A slower pace of change is not only more familiar to the old media owners; it is conducive to a fuller consideration of technological developments so that strategies allowing for profit maximisation can be implemented. In this context, digital copyright law becomes inextricably linked to arguments about controlling or freeing up technological, economic and cultural possibilities.

Vaidhyanathan argues that:

This is a story of clashing ideologies and dizzying technologies . . . They are among the oldest ideologies still around: anarchy and oligarchy. Anarchy is a governing system that eschews authority. Oligarchy governs from, through, and for authorities . . . Oligarchy justifies itself through 'moral panics' over the potential effects of perceived or imagined anarchy. Anarchy justifies itself by reacting to alarming trends toward oligarchy . . .[47]

Those who seek to restrict the flow of information use two rhetorical strategies when campaigning for the techno-fundamentalist changes that would empower them. First, they argue for treating information as property or contraband. An appeal to 'property' removes information policy discussions from the domain of the public interest and an appeal to 'contraband' nudges the public to surrender freedom for the sake of imagined security . . .[48]

He goes on historicising anarchy as a tradition of modern western political philosophy, and loosely places peer-to-peer within a tradition of cultural anarchy:

Peer-to-peer technology spreads cultural anarchy when it encourages both 'inconspicuous consumption' and 'conspicuous production', or, more accurately, conspicuous recombinant reproduction. Peer-to-peer systems, including the Internet itself, are remarkable not because millions of people take millions of files from them but because millions of people compose, copy, place, and distribute millions of files on them.[49]

He argues that cultural anarchy rubs up against a competing ideology – property talk and market fundamentalism:

This ideology rests on the widely held assumption that unfettered private control of resources not only produces the most efficient distribution of these resources but enables some larger public good, such as a proliferation of products and services heretofore unimagined.[50]

One of the reasons the debate about digital piracy fixates on copyright law is because it is through copyright protection devices like digital rights management that 'inconspicuous consumption' becomes observable, managed, and commodified. It becomes possible to monitor micro-uses of cultural works and extract fees. Further the micro-transactions feed into the commodity cycle by providing feedback on the particular user, creating individual consumer profiles, enabling more finely tuned marketing and consequential production.

It is digital copyright law that turns the cultural experience of engaging with works into an individualised, passive one. Personal uses of the web for experiencing, commenting and circulating music, films and texts to others, places that individual in a social context and define them in relation to others. Through copyright this social relation is severely restricted. Digital copyright laws remove personal use/fair use rights where they exist and the material is protected by copy protection codes. It is an offence to circumvent the protection. This leaves the defining cultural experience anticipated by digital copyright law as a peculiarly limited property-fee extraction relation. This takes priority over all other social relations and is unable to be detached from those.

In relation to postmodern identity Brendan Edgeworth has argued that:

> The re-characterisation of the legal subject from citizen to consumer, to citizen as consumer, also represents a shift in emphasis in the substantive content of citizenship rights . . . the new arrangements give priority to particularistic and individualistic rights to purchase goods and services for the satisfaction of preferences in the package of rights expressive of citizenship.[51]

Edgeworth is primarily referring to changes in the management of the welfare state and to the servicing of material needs. However his comment that citizens are now conceived of as consumers could equally be applied to the contemporary conception of our cultural needs as citizens.

Moral panics and copyright law

Moral panics serve a useful purpose in relation to regulating new technologies. In copyright law the capacity for disorder is great, as the law struggles to accommodate legal demands that have accompanied the development of different technologies. Where the old legal category does not really fit the new situation, as Maureen Cain suggests, lawyers must work imaginatively and 'invent relationships' to serve their clients' needs.[52]

New cultural forms, such as the internet, suggest the arrival of new sources of capital anxious for deployment in furtherance of our cultural 'needs'. If only copyright would protect digital goods 'appropriately'. Here capital is presented as pre-existing legal relations, as if it were already out there, an endangered species, slipping away because of legal inattention. The legislature is expected to engage this capital.

Part of the confusion that arises surrounding the MP3=Communism joke rests with the cultural investment in ideas about the primacy of private property rights. This is not a new discourse in relation to copyright, even though it is often recognised as not the only interest at stake. For example, in relation to the limited literary property right accorded by the law, the romantic artist Robert Southey argued in 1817:

> The question is simply this: upon which principle, with what justice, or under what pretext of public good, are men of letters deprived of a perpetual property in the produce of their own labours, when all other persons enjoy it as their indefeasible right – a right beyond the power of any earthly authority to take away? Is it because their labour is so light, – the endowments which it requires so common, – the attainments so cheaply and easily acquired, and the present remuneration so adequate, so ample and so certain?[53]

Whilst the copyright term was soon extended in recognition that a short term disproportionately values works for popular tastes at the expense of the more challenging, original titles, it remained limited in time, in consideration of the social interest in accessing works at competitive prices and in fostering a strong cultural heritage that could meaningfully be claimed as belonging to all.[54]

At the end of the 19th century there was a copyright-like claim made in relation to news items sent to the Australian colonies over telegraph wires. It was suggested by one newspaper that:

> To deny them the very brief copyright asked for would be precisely the equivalent to the withdrawal of the protection of the law to any other form of property. It would be tantamount to a declaration that any man should be free to walk into his neighbour's house and make use of his furniture, to enter his stables and borrow his saddle-horse, or to trespass upon his garden and carry away his fruits and flowers without let or hindrance.[55]

Legal historian Lionel Bently notes:

> In the most startling of such assertions, it was said that if the law failed to protect labour and investment in obtaining the news, then it was only a matter of time before all private property rights, traditionally being seen as rights protecting labour expended or things purchased, would be under threat. . . . it was argued, failure to afford legal protection to news sent by telegram would set in process an unstoppable drift to anarchy.

The *Sydney Morning Herald* called those associated with another publication, the *Empire*, 'communists' for opposition to telegraphic copyright, and for a short time, some of the colonies did create a short-term monopoly in current news transmitted over wires from abroad.[56]

Why are hyperbolic claims about the threat posed to civilisation by communism, piracy and/or anarchy common in copyright debates surrounding 'new' technologies and new markets?

An understanding of the role of narrative in legal argument would suggest that the purpose is, as Vaidhyanathan says, to create anxiety. Such cultural references tap into fears and insecurities, and this serves to foreclose consideration of alternate stories and sensitivity to different fears. The piracy story creates a mythic victim. It suggests chaos. It cries out for a particular authoritative narrative solution.[57] This focus makes it far more difficult to identify with other perspectives. With piracy the legal choice to be made comes to encapsulate an eternal human struggle between good and evil.

Napster, Grokster and more

In the Napster litigation the complaint drew upon references to piracy and the anarchy of the bazaar:

> Napster is a commercial enterprise that enables and encourages Internet users to connect to Napster's computer servers in order to make copies of plaintiff's copyrighted sound recordings available to other Napster users for unlawful copying and distribution. Napster has thus misused and is misusing the **remarkable potential** of the Internet, essentially running an **online bazaar** devoted to the pirating of music.
>
> Napster is not developing a business around legitimate MP3 music files, but has chosen to build its business on large-scale **piracy**. Napster seeks to profit by encouraging and facilitating the distribution and reproduction of millions of infringing MP3 files. Moreover, by deliberately **refusing** to maintain any information about its users in order to make copyright enforcement next to impossible, Napster has created a **virtual sanctuary** where music piracy can and does flourish on a monumental scale.[58]

The bazaar as a foreign, 'eastern', unknowable and hence potentially dangerous creation, is contrasted with the potential of the 'remarkable' internet. But what exactly is remarkable about an entity whose future seems to have been already fully mapped? It seems the internet will have commercial music markets for MP3 downloads, developed in consultation with existing recording companies and their artists and available on their licensing terms. This future is apparently so close to being here that only a 'virtual sanctuary' stands in the way. Here 'virtual' refers to both Internet space and Napster's business practices such as the wilful 'refusing to maintain' data the competitors desire. Law's role is cast as making the virtual concrete – making what we already know about the internet fully arrive, forcing the competitor to conform in its business practices to those of the 'real world' and transforming a mere market projection into something more secure. Were law to act otherwise, law would be conspiring in an 'illegitimate' future, in the sense that it would constitute misuse of an established nexus between capital and copyright law.

In the Napster decision, Justice Patel adopts the narrative spun by the complainant. For example, the complaint:

> Plaintiffs have invested and continue to invest substantial sums of money, as well as time, effort, and creative talent, to discover and develop recording artists . . .[59]

is reproduced in the judgement as:

> The record company plaintiff's sound recordings also result from a substantial investment of money, time, manpower, and creativity . . . In contrast, defendant invests nothing in the content of the music which means that, compared with plaintiffs, it incurs virtually no costs in providing a wide array of music to satisfy consumer demand.

And

> The record company plaintiffs have invested substantial time, effort, and funds in actual or planned entry into the digital downloading market. [60]

The defendant had sought to 'take over, or at least threaten, plaintiff's role in the promotion and distribution of music.'[61] Napster has raised 'barriers to plaintiff's entry into the market for the digital downloading of music.'[62] Napster's own investment in digital download technologies and distribution models is completely discounted as a relevant contribution to the music industry. It was not the 'right kind' of contribution, presumably because it is not closely enough related to the production of 'content'. Law is a conservative force not only because of its ties with established power, but also because legal power contests change. Law redefines contemporary developments in 'its' own terms. And here the judicial view is that copyright law should serve a particular culture of expectation: protecting the established industry's structure and plans for development of the market. Interference with these private 'plans' is piracy.[63]

The recent pro-peer-to-peer decision *MGM v Grokster*[64] provides an interesting point of contrast. Here the piracy narrative is foreclosed by an alternate story. The judgement begins:

> From the advent of the player piano, every new means of reproducing sound has struck a **dissonant chord** with musical copyright owners, often resulting in federal litigation. This appeal is the latest reprise of that recurring conflict, and one of a continuing series of lawsuits between the recording industry and distributors of file-sharing computer software.[65] (my emphasis)

The subtext here is oligarchy. In place of piracy is a narrative about technological change and resistance to market disruption by established stakeholders. The copyright owners claimed that over 90% of the files exchanged through peer-to-peer software offered by the defendants involve copyrighted material, 70% of which they own. The technology should be stopped.

Judge Thomas then relates facts about peer-to-peer architecture, to legal tests for contributory and vicarious copyright infringement. He differentiated the Gnutella/StreamCast and Kazaa/Grokster technology to the Napster case where discussion concerned centralized indexing software where files were maintained on Napster's own servers. In response to the claim that the defendants were liable for contributory copyright infringement, he determined based on the *Betamax*[66] and *Napster* decisions, that the key was whether the technology was capable of substantial or commercially significant non-infringing uses. If it was **not** capable of a substantial or commercially significant non-infringing use, the plaintiff need only show that the defendant had constructive knowledge of infringement. This means the defendant could be liable on the basis of having a suspicion that the software was probably being used for infringing file sharing and then failing to prevent such infringing acts:

> On the other hand, if the product at issue **is** capable of substantial or commercially significant noninfringing uses, then the copyright owner must demonstrate that the defendant had reasonable knowledge of specific infringing files and failed to act on that knowledge to prevent infringement.[67]

It was found that the software was capable of substantial non-infringing uses:

> One striking example provided by the Software Distributors is the popular band Wilco, whose record company had declined to release one of its albums on the basis that it had no commercial potential. Wilco repurchased the work from the record company and made the album available for free downloading, both from its own website and through the software user networks. The result sparked widespread interest and, as a result, Wilco received another recording contract... In addition to music, the software has been used to share thousands of public domain literary works made available through Project Gutenberg as well as historic public domain films released by the Prelinger Archive...
>
> The Copyright Owners submitted no evidence that could contradict these declarations.[68]

In response to the claim that the vast majority of software **is** used for infringing purposes, Judge Thomas replied that the owners had to show that the software distributors had reasonable knowledge of specific infringement, and had then failed to act:

In the context of this case, the software design is of great import . . . Indeed, at present, neither StreamCast nor Grokster maintains control over index files. As the district court observed, even if the Software Distributors 'closed their doors and deactivated all computers within their control, users of their products could continue sharing files with little or no interruption.'[69]

. . . the Software Distributors do not provide the 'site and facilities' for infringement, and do not otherwise materially contribute to direct infringement. Infringing messages or file indices do not reside on defendants' computers, nor do defendants have the ability to suspend user accounts.[70]

Rather, it is the users of the software who, by connecting to each other over the internet, create the network and provide the access. 'Failure' to alter software located on another's computer is simply not akin to the failure to delete a filename from one's own computer, to the failure to cancel the registration name and password of a particular user from one's user list, or to the failure to make modifications to software on one's own computer.[71]

While Grokster and StreamCast in particular may seek to be the 'next Napster' . . . [t]he technology has numerous other uses, significantly reducing the distribution costs of public domain and permissively shared art and speech, as well as reducing the centralized control of that distribution.[72]

In relation to the complaint of vicarious copyright infringement he found that because of the decentralised design there was no evidence that the defendants were technically able to block access to individual users, and as the material did not pass through the defendants' computers, files could not be filtered or searched by them.[73]

The owner's resort to the moral sense of an aphorism – that the defendants 'turned a blind eye' to infringement – was correctly identified for its rhetorical import. Whilst a pirate may have a patch over one eye, the allusion did not fit well within this particular narrative of anarchic design. Accordingly it was cast as irrelevant to applying the precise legal tests for infringement in light of the District Court findings of fact about how the technology operated.[74]

Similarly 'public policy' arguments were dismissed as steps that:

would satisfy the Copyright Owners' immediate economic aims . . . However . . . we live in a quicksilver technological environment with courts ill-suited to fix the flow of internet innovation. The introduction of new technology is always disruptive to old markets, and particularly to those copyright owners whose works are sold through well established distribution mechanisms. Yet, history has shown that time and market forces often provide equilibrium in balancing interests, whether the new technology be a player piano, a copier, a tape recorder, a video recorder, a personal computer, a karaoke machine, or an MP3 player. Thus, it is prudent for courts to exercise caution before restructuring liability theories for the purpose of addressing specific market abuses, despite their apparent present magnitude.[75]

Here more unease is expressed about oligarchy, as well as a familiar reluctance to make practically unenforceable decrees affecting 'private' conduct.

But is this really a case of law supporting, in Vaidhyanathan's terms, an anarchic eschewing of authority? There is a recognition of the anarchic mode of distribution made possible by peer-to-peer. However the reluctance for having law 'interfere' in the market for innovation is consistent with the discourse and deference to the market in the Microsoft case.[76] This is simply substituting a public source of authority about the information products, services and markets – legislation and courts – for private power to foster the new ages' commodity culture. It is worth remembering that piracy itself was a practice sanctioned by government in the aggressive, expansionist pursuit of resources related to earlier forms of imperialism.[77] Perhaps post *Grokster II* we should think of peer-to-peer devotees not as buccaneers, but as privateers – the patriots of the information age.[78]

Standing before the law

Before the Law stands a doorkeeper. To this doorkeeper comes a man from the country who begs for admittance to the Law. But the doorkeeper says that he cannot admit the man at the moment. The man, on reflection, asks if he will be allowed, then, to enter later. 'It is possible,' answers the doorkeeper, 'but not at this moment.' Since the door leading into the Law stands open as usual and the doorkeeper steps to one side, the man bends down to peer through the entrance. When the doorkeeper sees that, he laughs and says: 'If you are so strongly tempted, try and get in without my permission. But note that I am powerful. And I am only the lowest doorkeeper. From hall to hall, keepers stand at every door, one more powerful than the other. And the sight of the third man is already more than even I can stand.'

. . . The doorkeeper often engages him in brief conversation, asking him about his home and about other matters, but the questions are put quite impersonally, as great men put questions, and always conclude with the statement that the man cannot be allowed to enter yet.[79]

With peer-to-peer, copyright owners, as self-appointed doorkeepers to the internet, have, for the most part, had law on side. But what the recent decision shows is a capacity for law to admit a different story that is respectful of the 'peculiarities' of the information flows in the technology marketplace. Law is not necessarily insecure in admitting the other case. However whatever legitimacy for peer-to-peer generated by this recent decision, it could also be easily undone. The US Supreme Court has agreed to review this pro peer-to-peer decision. Further, the *Inducing Infringements of Copyright Acts*[80] is a current US proposal designed to overturn the Sony Betamax decision and punish technology makers, like Apple for the iPod, because the technology could 'induce' or encourage users to infringe owner's rights.

A replay of the US case is also currently before the Australian Federal Court.[81]

Is there any end to this game? Haven't the familiar polarities of piracy/freedom, oligarchy/anarchy been exhausted as a tool for throwing light on the situation? Aren't there other stories to be told?

As with my conclusion to the Microsoft discussion, I want to return to a consideration of that 'large region of everyday life: the flow of information and opinion that surround the acts of consumption and opinion formation and the feedback loops that compete for influence and authority over our buying and thinking.'[82] It is time for Law to go beyond impersonal inquiries into our behaviour and situation. Rather than have the man seek admittance to the Law, it is time for the Law to better engage with the consumer's place in this world. What feeds our techno-cravings, our dependency and desire for these products?

Technology marketing

Information capitalism is associated with businesses maintaining flexible production techniques, linked to increased cycles of information flowing from producers to consumers and back, feeding very short product cycles and life spans. It is a state some have called 'perpetual innovation'.[83] Associated with this there is a shift from physical to experiential commodities:

> a shift towards goods 'either used up during the act of consumption, or, alternatively, based upon the consumption of time, as opposed to a material artefact.'[84]

This is supported by the development of new technologies and appliances – the DVD, MP3, cell phones – devices capable of freeing 'previously dead time and empty space' into 'purchasable experience'.[85] As already noted these commodities are not just useful objects or new tools. The objects cannot be consumed, dissociated from their advertising.

That being said, it would be an oversimplification to assume that the form, content and marketing of all cultural products is now standardised, and that the issues surrounding piracy are necessarily the same as for films, artworks, broadcasts and novels. There may be similarities in 'technological mediation' created by digitisation and the internet, however there are also differences that need to be reflected upon. Despite media, technology and entertainment industry company convergences and consolidations, the various cultural industries' practices are still affected by their heritage. They have separate histories – the establishment of different creative practices and relations with artists, differing geographical connections and reaches, distinctive models of financing and marketing, technological modes of reception, and practices of consumption. These differences still need to be considered before conclusions about selling an anti-piracy message in music can readily be transposed to the case of the other cultural industries and their consuming publics.[86]

Nonetheless, with respect to digital music consumption this is a system of manufacturing desire where the style and brand of the Walkman, the MP3 player and better still, the iPod, are a key to communicating identity to others. Such is the level of recognition of the white iPod headphones that they have become an important sign in a different economy – rendering wearers to risk of mugging, and leading to police warnings to remove or cover them up.[87] But it is difficult for police to sell this advice. It is not necessarily enough to consume digital music as a private experience in this economy. It is not simply about the convenience of purchasing a portable music service and consuming that service. The ephemera associated with the gadget, the symbolism, the cultural meaning of the experience – its fashionableness – matters too.

This is the secret of the iTunes/iPod success and an explanation of the relative failure of other legitimate music streaming or download services.[88] iTunes is both software that organises MP3 files copied to a drive, allows converting from CD format to MP3 and other formats, and also allows you to play and create audio CDs from those files. It is also an internet radio tuner that also allows you to share files across a network with other people using iTunes. There is also an iTunes download store that allows for the purchase of digital music. Though in conjunction with the music store it can be used in accordance with copyright law, the iPod is extremely popular in places like Australia, even though there is no access to a local music download service for iTunes, music cannot be purchased from the overseas sites, there is no significant advertising of legitimate Australian download services, and there is no relevant personal use or fair use right that might arguably permit copying music files to a hard drive. The device sells well and is heavily advertised in Australia on advertising billboards and the like, and it is promoted through radio giveaways, TV show prizes and with text messaging competitions encouraging phone service and confectionery sales to children.

But even the iPod, which has only been on the market since July 2002, has already appeared in various guises. There are different versions and price points, and its fourth generation was released in July 2004. According to Apple it is:

> A musical dream come true, the fourth-generation iPod offers huge capacity, letting you easily slip up to 10,000 songs into your pocket. And enjoy it wherever you go. In the car. On the treadmill. At the office. Around the house.[89]

Part of the attraction of the iPod is that it is both a well-integrated device that makes it easy to use and to share music, as well as fitting our expectations of a small, infinitely portable, wearable gadget. Whilst it is currently a very desirable commodity, given the fluidity of these identities we construct within a perpetual innovation cycle, there is an ongoing need for us to reinvest in new purchases, to refresh our identities and aesthetic experiences, in response to the new trends. As experienced, affluent consumers we know the game element of this. We understand the functional obsolescence of the technologies and the disposability of the associated signs and devices.

But the iPod is not as disposable as popular music.[90] With an emphasis on hits, discovering new talent, celebrity, appropriating different cultural styles and reworking of old genres pop music is especially affected by a short shelf-life. This is music designed by business enterprises for mass consumption and once pushed through new media like radio, cassette-singles and video hits. Simply selling the same music by a different delivery mechanism – adding choices of streaming media or per pay downloads – is not all that groundbreaking an experience for consumers, inured to the flux of product cycles associated with both the music industry and with entertainment technologies. Without the music sale being associated with the marketing of an exciting high-tech lifestyle, it is not a dynamic story with instant appeal.

Don't steal music

> We take our craft – whether it be the music, the lyrics, or the photos and artwork – very seriously, as do most artists. It is therefore sickening to know that our art is being traded like a commodity rather than the art that it is.

From a business standpoint, this is about piracy – a/k/a taking something that doesn't belong to you; and that is morally and legally wrong. The trading of such information – whether it's music, videos, photos, or whatever – is, in effect, trafficking in stolen goods. *Lars Ulrich, Metallica, Press Release, 2000*

Would you go into a CD store and steal a CD? It's the same thing, people going into the computers and logging on and stealing our music. It's the exact same thing, so why do it? *Britney Spears, 'What the Artists and Songwriters have to say', Musicunited.org, 2003*

The use of celebrity to sell anti-piracy messages is an excellent example of the vanishing line between law and popular culture. The legal story yields to the compelling visual logic of film and TV images and the market forces that fuel their production:

... techniques of mass communication fold disparate meaning-making processes into the homogenous stories and images of popular culture.[91]

However so far as the message goes, this legal story is a rehashing of an old-economy message. It articulates the modern social relations of authorship that date from the late 18th and the 19th centuries. This is an idea that, in relation to texts, Roland Barthes described as:

The author is reputed the father and owner of his work: literary science teaches respect for the manuscript and the author's declared intentions, while society asserts the legality of the relation of author to work (the droit d'auteur or copyright).[92]

The recording industry's 'Don't steal music' message suggests the primary commodity experience is the social relation between the artist and the fan. It focuses on music as an artefact divorced from the current technological modes of its consumption.[93] And it completely ignores postmodern, post-structuralist and related globalisation analyses of cultural production, that stress the importance of cultural play and forging an identity by utilising the internet, digital tools and appliances.

Reasserting a modern author relation is a strategy that the Recording Industry Association of America thinks does 'make a difference', especially in regard to lobbying politicians:

When an artist comes to the nation's capital, we encourage them to make the trip enjoyable and meaningful by meeting with policy-makers. The artist is the best person to tell a legislator about the inspiration, perspiration, and commitment it takes to bring a creative idea to life. The artist can speak from experience and from the heart and express why copyright protection is important or free speech is essential. Such informal meetings are often much more informative and effective than an intense lobbying campaign. Artists can make a difference, by getting involved on Capitol Hill, but also in a huge range of causes and issues where their voices can effect change.

That is the point of our new public service campaign, 'Don't Just Make Music. Make a Difference.' Many artists have been 'making a difference' for many years on a variety of issues.[94]

And it is understandable that politicians would fear alienating the fans of these artists and media owners by publicly defying their demands to support the call for stronger copyright laws. Getting behind the cause can also be popularly characterised as political leadership resisting the 'anarchic' spread of MP3 culture. This conservatism taps into older narratives about youth culture, deviancy and the pop music industry. Here music downloaders are characterised as having too much leisure time, questionable tastes and overly generous parents, institutions or employers subsidising their technology and culture fixes. From this perspective, enacting legislation against the file sharers is for their own good, and for the well-being of the economy and the country.[95]

The connection made between contemporary music, file sharing, and deviancy has to date been strong enough to block the mainstream development of more positive, bankable pictures of online music consumers and markets. This is a future that policy-makers and legislators may otherwise well become interested in exploring, for the same reasons as the *Grokster II* court. In view of this the digital commons/cultural commons movement is an important development. It asserts respectable property law-abiding relations alongside the culture of sharing. This could dislodge the 'undesirable' cultural associations between music, new technology and anarchy that have circulated relatively unchallenged to date.

However sympathetic legislature and court aside, there is still a big problem in selling the message that copyright is primarily about saving an important creative and property relation between an artist and their consuming public. Whilst many do value a connection with the creative artist a great deal, who is it that believes a music conglomerate resolutely acts in the best interest of the artists?

Fans have a common-sense appreciation of commodity cycles and an understanding of the control that music consortiums exercise globally over artists and their music. Lots of major and minor artists have told their fans about the disputes they have had with their labels. The industry has always exercised control over creative content through contracts, often related to unfair conditions, anticompetitive practices, and sharp management practices.[96] This knowledge of the industry interferes with any simple message the RIAA pushes that the industry protects the creativity of the artist and supports product innovation. In any case, the industry itself panders to this knowledge in its bad boy/girl, rebel image marketing of artists with an Attitude.

So why is the anti-piracy message and the laws it has informed assumed to be a potent force?

The anti-piracy message tries to disembed the consumption of music from the full range of signs and mix of meanings associated with that practice. The legal campaign valorises a simple relation with chosen artists in an attempt to obliterate other meanings and associations suggested by the experience of music consumption. But I don't see how this one relation is able to obliterate other meanings and associations suggested by the contemporary experience of music consumption. It is simply not possible to suppress the social meaning of the technological delivery mechanism that is part of the choice so many of us make through consuming particular music. To succeed the RIAA would have to put an end to the fluidity of identity and the flux associated with production and consumption of those identities forged through the communications technologies we have become accustomed to. In my view we are too used to information capitalism, and the affluent are too sophisticated and demanding as consumers, to adopt a piracy message that tries to capture one particular meaning in isolation from other messages, and sell that en masse, or even to a few, for long.

We are used to the marketing of signs:

> What fascinates everyone is the debauchery of signs, that reality, everywhere and always, is debauched by signs. This is the interesting game, and this is what happens in media, in fashion, in publicity and more generally, in the spectacle of politics, technology and science.[97]

Law signs are not immune to this process. What will prevent the anti-piracy message from being another kind of distinctive information branding – another part of the mix of related consumption choices – discarded in its time, alongside other fashions?

On a more practical note, there is also the problem of limited income, ever increasing disparities in wealth in our communities, and the realities of consumption choice that will interfere with the selling of a reduced music experience. For example, one of the most consistent findings in market surveys of youth is the high level of cell phone penetration and the cost burden on youth budgets.[98] This is an environment of multiple, competing, discretionary, price-sensitive communications expenditures.

Of course the response to this 'optimistic' reading is to return to a focus on law – that the music industry is so powerful, conniving and strong globally that it will be able to control access to technologies that offer 'more' than a service constrained by strong copyright that inhibits the consumer experience. The suggestion is that it can drive the Korean appliance makers into copyright compliance, regardless of the demand for their unshackled communications products. And there are certainly attempts to do this. For example, LG, the world's third-biggest cell phone-maker, is currently battling with the Korean equivalent of the RIAA, the Korea Association of Phonogram Producers (KAPP) over the sale of a phone model that permits saving 16 tracks at a time:

> 'LG Telecom's MP3 cellular phone provides no protection against playing free copies of copyrighted songs, which is a threat not only to the music industry but to the mobile content industry as a whole,' said a legal advisor working for the KAPP yesterday.
>
> Around 80,000 units of the LG-LP3000 model have been sold through this month, making it one of the hottest items on the telecom market.[99]

Vertical integration of communications and content networks will also continue. The year 2003/4 has seen more media mergers with Sony/BMG reducing the Big Five to the Big Four. There is a buy-out by Time Warner and Microsoft of ContentGuard, which produces digital rights management software used to 'hardwire' anti-piracy messages into digital content.[100] This is technology already licensed by groups such as Sony. It suggests the push for digital rights management that limits the way we deal with works is far from dead, despite less than enthusiastic responses from consumers. Further oversight by competition regulators in the US, Australia and the EU of these developments does not seem to have impeded the general direction of the trend.

But on the up-side, there is already a certain degree of cynicism amongst consumers over a felt gap between the glossy promises of new technology, and what might actually be experienced on delivery. This is especially the case with 'protected technologies'. As one journalist tells his story, unable to play his music in a kid-free lounge room, the other option was to play his new CD on an old portable Discman. But the Discman won't play this CD. Copy protection, he assumes. He has a new Peugeot 307 – a $35,000 stereo on wheels. It doesn't play there either. Having recently upgraded his computer to Windows XP, he puts the music CD in the drive:

> And guess what? It will play it. But it will do much more than that. Windows Media Player actually let me load the songs to the hard drive. A warning screen popped up: a little message that told me the disc was copy-protected and suggested that if I ignored that copy protection, I would be responsible for what happened to the content. OK, I said recklessly, I'll take that responsibility. Then it copied the songs. No more questions.

There is no right to copy songs this way under Australian law. He concludes:

> the record industry, in its wisdom, has given us copy control software that is preventing new CDs from being played in the devices they should be played in, but not actually controlling copying. Indeed, in a weird way, the fact that these discs won't play in so many devices has made it more necessary to copy them. Go ahead, untangle that logic if you can.[101]

These are apocryphal tales.

In an industry traditionally associated with a premium on hype and freshness, operating in tandem with a culture of technology that traditionally sells by offering new enhanced experiences, there remains a problem that media owners have to face. What is going to drive demand for these sad, shackled products? Who is going to want to buy them?

This is not a 'have faith in a free market and be exuberant about the social or creative potential inherent in product innovation' argument. Rather my analysis is sceptical of that politics. But it is driven by a belief that manufacturing desire has a history for us. It has a meaning for us as experienced consumers. And it is not that easy to overcome this history by embarking on a different kind of marketing. The current practices are a part of who we understand we are and what our role is, as consumers in an information economy. And because of that it is hard for any player in the information economy, no matter how large or well connected to law-making bodies, to simply compartmentalise that depth of experience and seek to smother unwelcome parts of it by old legal stories about creativity and the evils of piracy and anarchy, and successfully set off in another marketing direction.

So perversely, my claim is that the success of the mechanisms that drive the information economy at this point in time creates cause enough to doubt that digital copyright reform is really worth the overwhelming attention it has been receiving from IP critics. It is an interesting battle where the nexus of law and economic power is patently exposed. But arguably it is equally the smaller and seemingly less dramatic changes to things like trade marks law that entrench the global power of the well-known brand, that will ultimately have much impact on social life, creativity and our experience of consumption. The protection now awarded to well-known marks has served advertising in the global economy very well:

> The packaged food we buy or eat, the clothes we wear, the products we use at home or at work, all carry trademarks. I need only mention 'Coca-Cola', 'Levis', 'IBM', 'Microsoft', 'Nike', or 'Seiko', and wherever I am in the world, and whatever other language people speak there, those words will be understood. McDonald's has succeeded where Esperanto has failed, in creating a world language . . .[102]

Here the changes are often presented as the law simply 'updating' its logic to global economic realities.[103] However as with copyright, there is no natural, optimal association or trajectory that connects IP laws and the development of capitalism. What needs to be explored are the conflicting political choices about economy, society and law that are made and will continue to be made. And these are choices not just made by government and courts to extend or wind back regulatory reach. They are also made by individuals.

The digital commons movement

It used to be argued that the shift to technological forms of copyright control combined with 'clickwrap' contracts were a threat to the copyright balance established in legislative provisions and potentially a dangerous erosion of sovereignty.[104] It was feared that private power would be extended globally and penetrate more deeply via distribution of works over the internet, where it is possible to control and terminate access in ways impossible to do with hard copies of works. However the current loss of faith in government and legislation as protectors of the public interest in a 'balanced' copyright regime has led to a significant reappraisal of the role of private law in the information economy.

Digital commons, information commons, creative commons, free for education, public knowledge groups have all sprung up. As Lessig describes the creative commons it:

> is a nonprofit corporation established in Massachusetts, but with its home at Stanford University. Its aim is to build a layer of reasonable copyright on top of the extremes that now reign. It does this by making it easy for people to build upon other people's work, by making it simple for creators to express the freedom for others to take and build upon their work. Simple tags, tied to human-readable descriptions, tied to bulletproof licenses, make this possible.[105]
>
> Creative Commons is not the only organization pursuing such freedoms. But the point that distinguishes the Creative Commons from many is that we are not interested only in talking about a public domain or in getting legislators to help build a public domain. Our aim is to build a movement of consumers and producers of content ('content conducers', as attorney Mia Garlick calls them) who help build the public domain and, by their work, demonstrate the importance of the public domain to other creativity. The aim is not to fight the 'All Rights Reserved' sorts. The aim is to complement them. . . . New rules – with different freedoms, expressed in ways so that humans without lawyers can use them – are needed. Creative Commons gives people a way effectively to begin to build those rules.[106]

It could be argued that the creative commons story, whilst told in anticipation of causing real social effects, is also the public performance of a different tune to legislators and courts alike – raising the profile of a different legal story about copyright creators and users. There is a conscious break with the connotation of anarchy and lawlessness that has previously dominated discussion of digital technology and sharing.

Building upon the free software and open source programming traditions, 'restoring' the copyright balance now includes working within the established legal framework but advocating the use of public-spirited copyright licenses for content in order to construct a digital commons of information. The actual terms vary and owners can demarcate license terms as specifically as the law allows all owners to. It need not be an 'all rights or none' arrangement. Though initiated in the US, this is a global movement. In Australia we have seen the launch of a 'Free for Education' license[107] which gives creators and users of educational content a range of options including free and non-free usage, and the introduction of a new 'Creative Commons' Australian licence,[108] which copies the model developed in the US.[109]

Marc Freedman, *You can share if you want to*

There is some attraction in lawyers using private power to found a new global 'sharing' sensibility and in them advocating the importance of creativity to the economy and society. However what is here described and justified as an 'international' social movement and the foundation of an important freedom is also an extension of legal power and juridification of a communicative sphere that many once embraced as 'free', as meaning outside of effective legal practice. As already discussed, the 'information wants to be free' slogan of the 1990s was in part a celebration of the impotence of formal law and regulation on the internet. For many the anarchic 'free' movement of information was part of the attraction of the internet, and especially of peer-to-peer.

Is attaching a creative commons license actually necessary to establish communicative freedom? Legally it is not, and traditionally it was argued that as a matter of law there was an implied license to use works made available via websites for free – free as in free beer.[110] Has the 'piracy' message changed our culture so much that the legal presumption is now that any 'copyright-unbranded' works available online are all to be feared as potentially infringing copies? To rebut a presumption of illegality do we now need to formally affirm our status as lawful proprietors of the copies? The 'civility' of the commons is that of the respectable property holder, graciously consenting to specified free or less restrictive uses, so long as the prescribed notice stays attached.

It is not surprising that it is the sciences, libraries and academia that are most interested in the new licensing regime. Here researchers are already immersed in an institutional and bureaucratic culture. Adding another layer of paperwork, checking consents and documenting permissions comes more naturally here, though often grudgingly and without sufficient administrative support. But compare for example the response of a non-lawyer, Geert Lovink:

> But the digital commons as such should, in my view, not be limited to legal issues (implicitly always those of US law). Creativity may end in legal battles, but that's not its source. It is good to have lawyers defending your case in court, but should they appear in every aspect of life? Even those who reject copyright altogether will in the near future be forced to 'metatag' their work with a legal document. Like wearing seatbelts, licensing may become compulsory, irrespective of your opinion on 'intellectual property rights'. Before the licensing rage kicks off, perhaps it is time to point at the specific US elements in the Creative Commons project and design variations of the CC licenses that are beyond 'localisation', tailored for specific countries, languages, regions and cultures. In the meanwhile, we should be realistic and demand the impossible: 'A license-free world is possible'.[111]

To a copyright lawyer this attitude seems strange or naïve. Artists act in legal ignorance to their peril, and art schools and organisations stress that legal awareness is an important part of professional practice. Lessig is himself critical of lawyers, and advocates a future where content owners can act without need for formal recourse to legal advice.[112] However there is more to this concern about the prominence of intellectual property issues than simply tiredness, apathy, naïvete or ignorance. Lovink's response is an intuitive resistance to juridification, because previously it was possible to express a creative practice without 'rights awareness' assuming such a priority. No doubt how comfortable one is with a rights-based consciousness (commonly associated with US civics) is culturally variable. In any case, the spread of intellectual property rights globally is not intrinsically a good thing,[113] even where the license purports to be on the side of the angels.

To return to the feminist critique of 'economic man', an identity that also encompasses a juridical persona:

Critical-legal-studies critiques of economic man often proceed on the unnecessarily limiting assumption that while we are not motivationally unidimensional as the economists insist, we are 'dual-motivational'; that is, we possess altruistic, other-focused communitarian needs and desires as well as egoistic, self-serving, individualistic desires. The complexity of literary women reminds us, however, that this too is a false duality. We have many kinds of needs, desires, and motivations, not just one as the legal economists insist, and not just two like the communitarian critics sometimes imply. Unlike economic man, literary woman is indeed at times altruistic . . . but she is also at times masochistic, automatic, submissive, selfish, oppressive, and perhaps sadistic . . . Her character is multimotivational, which is why it is worth exploring, and she does not know herself – her own subjectivity – as well as she might.[114]

As an intervention into the popular culture that law engages, the commons movement has much to contribute. However as a matter of practical social relations, the attraction of commons/public domain licensing depends very much on who one is, and where one stands, and in which communities. As well as involving issues of wanting to assume a particular legal and social identity as creator, poverty issues already significantly impact on arts practice in places like Australia,[115] and this also obviously affects consumption of both legitimate and illegitimate product, here and overseas.[116] Further, as indigenous communities in Australia have been telling copyright lawyers for decades, there are far more complex socially embedded ownership relations that must be considered than a communal/private ownership binary allows, however sensitively that line is to be delineated in licensing.[117]

Legal signs, fads and fashions

Intellectual property lawyers have fashioned their own signs, and forged distinctive attitudes in relation to current developments. Academia itself is becoming branded and there is pressure on us all as copyright lawyers, to display the latest fashionable wardrobe. But in responding to current initiatives there is a need to relate the critical insights of other disciplines and take on board suspicions about the hip-ness of identifying too strongly with legal culture(s) at all.

This is the mistake made in the anti-piracy campaign of the RIAA and its strategists. There is a presumption that the only form of power that counts is power conceived of in formal and bureaucratic terms. The idea is that if you get the right laws in place, all of us, societies of consumers, will just fall into the slots they make. But this is not what the information economy is all about, and the more diffuse expressions of identity and social power should not be so readily ignored. The notion that individuals will simply obey a legal command is problematic in terms of criminal law. It is even more problematic when compliance involves choices to be made about the meaning of an act of consumption.

For the same reason we should not be surprised if there is not a rush, especially outside of the US, to embrace creative commons licensing. A defined legal identity may be a part of global citizenship. However the formal expression of legal identity is not essential to the network economy. And a law-free sign still has some currency in it, at least for now. It is one of the many identity choices we are still permitted to make and in the name of freedom, we should not abandon it too eagerly.

7

Participate/comply/resist

In December 2001 a Palestinian refugee, Aladdin Sisalem, sailed to Saiwai Island, an Australian territory in the Torres Strait. He approached Australian immigration officers there seeking asylum from persecution in Kuwait. Aladdin was flown to Thursday Island and interviewed by phone by immigration officials. He was then taken with 120 other asylum seekers back across the Torres Strait to Manus Island, Papua New Guinea, and placed in an Australian-funded detention centre there. There is also an Australian detention centre in Nauru. These centres are a consequence of the Australian government's 'Pacific Solution' to asylum seeking. As a signatory to the UN refugee convention, Australia is obliged to grant asylum to anyone who is a refugee and lands in the migration zone. But under the Pacific Solution asylum seekers who try to enter Australia by boat from the north are, so far as possible, prevented from entering Australian territorial waters. Several islands have also been excluded from the migration zone. As asylum seekers are detained in centres offshore, this makes it more difficult for refugees to access human rights advice, other services and community support within Australia that could assist them in making successful asylum applications. Unlike Aladdin, most of the other refugees taken to Manus Island had been prevented from entering Australian territory.

Two months after arriving on Manus Island, Aladdin noted that the other refugees' applications seemed to be proceeding. He however had had no news. When he asked about the progress of his case the Australian officials notified him that they did not have an application for him. Soon after most of the other refugees were resettled in New Zealand.

Then in July 2003 an Immigration Department press release was issued saying that the centre on Manus Island was being wound down. It was claimed that the last three residents had now been transferred to Australia. With this misinformation it is clear that Aladdin was to be left as the sole inmate in a centre built to house around 1,000 asylum seekers. Apart from guards, his only companion was a cat, called Honey.

Australian refugee policy utilises a strategy of preventing communication with refugees. As one reporter put it:

> The government has gone to extraordinary lengths to prevent Australians putting faces to those locked up in Australian detention centres. It would not do for voters to think they were normal, if desperate, human beings. On Nauru this policy is easy to enforce. Quite apart from isolation, lawyers, human rights advocates and journalists have been denied visas to Nauru.[1]

It is also argued that the 'privacy' concerns of refugees require that there be no access to journalists for interviews or generating publicity surrounding individual cases, regardless of the willingness of subjects to be interviewed.

Whilst in detention Aladdin spent most of his time on the computer, and although he was only permitted two phone calls each month, he had internet access:

> ALADDIN SISALEM: The internet is the only window I can look out from this detention centre. So I can spend all my day inside the room. Finding research for information, trying to find help outside, that's all that I can do here.[2]

It was through friendships made over the internet that journalists were eventually made aware of Aladdin's existence on Manus Island and pressure was placed on the Australian government to act. The Immigration Minister's initial suggestions that he had not requested a specific application form whilst on Australian territory, and later, that since he was now in PNG, he should have applied for refugee status there, were widely ridiculed. Aladdin was granted refugee status by the UNHCR whilst on Manus Island. A protest movement developed and the absurdity of the government's position in this case was highlighted. A tabloid newspaper pointed out that given the cost of maintaining the centre for a sole occupant, estimated to cost AU $1.4 million, it would be preferable to detain Aladdin in the Diplomatic suite at Sydney's Park Hyatt Hotel, with four private balconies, panoramic views of the Harbour Bridge and Opera House and, of course, a marble bathroom and security guard for AU $7,000 a night.

After 18 months in detention and ten months as a solitary detainee, Aladdin Sisalem was granted a five-year secondary-movement relocation visa, which allows him to live and work in Australia. Through the efforts of supporters, Honey was also later relocated to Australia.

In interviews Aladdin says that without internet access he would not have survived. It was being able to get his story out that saved his life.

This is not a new issue. In 1993 an African scholar, Olu Oguibe, was attending a conference in Mexico. He and other conference delegates noticed a small boy, scantily clad and crudely made up in the colours of an indigenous performer, gesticulating in the hotel lobby. The boy did not speak their language. He was offered money but refused it, and was then driven out of the lobby by hotel staff. It was then explained that the little boy had wanted water.

Oguibe uses this anecdote to reflect on debates about globalisation and the culture of digitisation:

> In our piety in that Guadalajara hotel that day, some of us offered the little boy money. Yet he had two very fundamental needs more crucial than money: namely, water, and the ability to communicate this most basic need to others. Amongst us, both conferees and tourists, there were probably dollars in their thousands, a good dozen, state-of-the-art digital equipment, expensive clothing, innumerable degrees and diplomas, millions of miles in travel and adventure, a good deal of enlightenment and knowledge of the arts and letters. There was goodwill too, and charitable disposition. Yet, of all these, two things which none of us was disposed to provide for a little, gesturing child: water, and understanding . . .
>
> I dwell on the boy in Guadalajara because his case has a relevance, and a resonance for me as an African and an outsider in the West, because his case has a relevance for the African condition in the cyber age. I dwell on him because he is a reminder of the implications of our complicity in the erection of a new frontier, even as we claim to have destroyed all frontiers; our role in the construction of a new border besides existing borders, a new line of demarcation which he, and many millions more like him, may not cross . . .
>
> Cyberspace, as we have seen, is not the new, free global democracy we presume and defend, but an aristocracy of location and disposition, characterized, ironically, by acute insensitivity and territorialist proclivities.[3]

In September 2004 it was reported that two Australian security guards had been kidnapped by the 'Horror Brigades of the Islamic Secret Army' in Iraq. In exchange the terrorists demanded withdrawal of Australian troops from Iraq. Security analysts advised that it could be a hoax as no video or photographs of the alleged kidnap victims had been circulated on the internet. It was reported two days later that a Muslim cleric with dual Australian and Iraq citizenship had been released by terrorists after private negotiations were instigated and a ransom had been paid, without Australian government involvement.

We are accustomed to the idea that globalisation is about mobilities, networks and liberating flows – of goods, services, information, data, and finances.

Communications technologies have created a new world order:

> The revolution in technology brought about by the rapid development of computer and video has created a new geography of power relations in the first world that could only be imagined as little as twenty years ago: people are reduced to data, surveillance occurs on a global scale, minds are melded to screenal reality, and an authoritarian power emerges that thrives on absence.[4]

In critical analyses of globalisation the authoritarian power that threatens citizens is no longer understood as the modern nation state. Critics link the power of nation state with the furthering of private corporate agendas and global ambitions.[5]

In the context of globalisation, the national economic interest has come to be identified with supporting the wealth creation strategies of big business. As Braithwaite and Drahos's study summarised it:

> Our data have demonstrated the unsurprising conclusion that many different kinds of actors have played important roles in the globalisation of business regulation. Some might read the data selectively as demonstrating the death of the nation-state. This would be an erroneous reading . . . if we asked the crude question, 'which is the type of actor that has had the greatest influence?', the answer is fairly clearly the nation-state. If we ask which single actor has had the greatest influence, that answer is even clearer – the US state.
>
> What has changed is the nature of state power . . . In the era of information capitalism and the new regulatory state, control from the nation's territory of abstract objects like patents is crucial to building the nation's wealth, as is embedding global principles of regulation that suit the wealth creators from the state's territory.[6]

With globalisation ICT is more than a tool of the state or a subject of social policy. It is a central instrument of expression, a ways and means, of a new distributed form of global power.

It is out of concern for the apparent unaccountability of this power that many lawyers have argued that we need to develop corresponding communications rights, that are expressive of citizenship in this new order. How can commercial concerns and respect for property be more fully reconciled with our needs as citizens? Can information ownership rights be 'balanced' with user rights and with privacy rights? Can legal tools be designed that

Law and Internet Cultures

foster individual informational autonomy, and what might that comprise? Is it possible to make ICT policy formation more democratic and on a global scale? These are preoccupations of much of the legal writing pertaining to 'internet policy'.

Radicals share a similar concern for the unaccountability of this new power. However compared to lawyers they have few, if any, positive expectations of law making a fundamental difference to existing and developing distributions of power. Law is generally presumed to be co-opted by the powers that be. Accordingly focus is on the need to continue to foster technological forms of resistance:

> Given increasing computer prevalence and the fact our political opponents are among the most wired in the world, it is foolish to ignore the computer. Rather, it is important to turn our attention toward the computer, to understand it, and to transform it into an instrument of resistance. For the luddites of the world who resist computers, consider using computers to resist.[7]

However amongst radicals there are different opinions surrounding how communications technologies should be used for purposes of resistance. Is a denial of service attack acceptable if the target is a global corporate or government entity with 'questionable' practices and/or strained community relations? Is it acceptable to create tools that undermine the efficacy of surveillance in an authoritarian state? Or in a democratic state? What if these tools are also used by terrorists or to circulate child pornography? How can and should resistance be expressed, and the tools perhaps regulated? What would be a legitimate cause for regulation? Who could be trusted? And as a practical matter, what do communication rights and technological resistance have to offer to those citizens – the majority – residing outside of an 'aristocracy of location and disposition'? Can resistance really foster new forms of community that house an emancipatory potential? And if so, what are the features that differentiate a radical, empowering use of communications networks, from a reactionary one?

A related consideration is of how the assertion of new rights and/or the need to resist and change the emerging order can be made meaningful in a communications system that facilitates the turning of politics into spectacle:

> Power itself is no longer primarily pedagogical or narrative but instead, itself performative. 'Nation' now works less through narrative or pedagogy but through the performativity of information and communication. Power works less through the linearity and the reflective argument of discourse or ideology than through the immediacy of information, of communications.[8]

A part of the problem for 'downsiders' is of visibility. Unless there is a virtual representation of a problem, with sufficient performative value that there is a desire to quickly and more broadly circulate an 'exceptional' and fascinating tale,[9] the fear is that the issue remains 'off the political radar'. For example, appreciating the effects of the Australian refugee policy on individual lives is deliberately frustrated by the state anticipating and managing the 'phenomenon' of concern for refugees through enforcing media restrictions and creating a range of obstacles for reporters. Yet it is only by placing the tragedy of a particular case on public display that intervention and political action are made possible. Where an instance of injustice becomes 'suddenly' visible through the media this can sometimes lead to intervention that brings about a 'successful' outcome in that instance. However there is a question about how public resolution to these particular 'exceptional' stories of injustice relate to dealing with the broader problem that remains for the invisible class – the indeterminate objects of the same unfair rules and devious, arbitrary practices. What needs to be considered is the way communications technologies are erecting a new political border or boundary, and how the demand we stage our politics in a spectacular manner affects the possibilities for resistance and action.

We do need new rights and more resistance to the narrow, economic ambitions of corporations and the nation state. However as part of this struggle we need to work with the political potential of *all* the new legal practices: the new 'theory' spaces that enable forms of community participation; the formal legal processes that facilitate corporate and other forms of compliance; and with opportunities to foster mainstream resistance to the culture dictated by the nation state and corporate powers through technologies and laws. Participate/consult/resist – a combination of strategies is required to combat this new globally distributed power. The ambition is to more fully appreciate and engage all the dimensions of the relationship between internet culture and the law.

Inhuman flows

The 'up-side' to globalisation is that through ICT we have faster, reliable contact across the globe:

> Simply put, globalization denotes the expanding scale, growing magnitude, speeding up and deepening impact of interregional flows and patterns of social interaction. It refers to a shift or transformation in the scale of human

social organization that links distant communities and expands the reach of power relations across the world's major regions and communities.[10]

The ability to send messages quickly across distance through the internet, for relatively small costs compared to using the phone line alone, is now something many of us in developed countries take so much for granted that disruption to service caused by viruses, worms and spam is now accepted as sufficient cause for regulation, including imposing criminal sanctions.

However it is not just concern for the functioning of the pipes that has inspired debate about the need for new laws. Sociologists argue that globalisation creates entirely new kinds of social relations. We are not just 'connecting people[TM]', as the Nokia advertising suggests.

From stones to chips, technology has always been a part of human relations. However global communications networks have created new ways of identifying, managing, disciplining and profiting from human relations with and through the use of the technologies that connect people:

> In both the optimistic and the pessimistic analyses, it is inhuman objects that reconstitute social relations. Such relations are made and remade through machines, technologies, objects, texts, images, physical environments and so on. Human powers increasingly derive from the complex interconnections of humans with material objects, including signs, machines, technologies, texts, physical environments, animals, plants, and waste products. People possess few powers which are uniquely human, while most can only be realised because of their connections with these inhuman components.[11]

Nikolas Rose focuses on the scary potential of this:

> In such a regime of control, Deleuze suggests, we are not dealing with 'individuals' but with 'dividuals': not with subjects with a unique personality that is the expression of some inner fixed quality, but with elements, capacities, potentialities. These are plugged into multiple orbits, identified by unique codes, identification numbers, profiles of preferences, security ratings and so forth: a 'record' containing a whole variety of bits of information on our credentials, activities, qualifications for entry into this or that network. In our societies of control, it is not a question of socialization and disciplining the subject ab initio.[12]

In the modern state, socialisation occurred in civil society – through the family, school, church, workplace and through welfare delivery. Delivering jobs, minimum wages and employment conditions, housing, schooling and welfare was part of the means of discipline that held the society together. It enabled social order and produced sufficient purchasing capacity for citizens to participate in consumption, driving ongoing local demand for manufactured products.[13] At the end of the twentieth century we have faced crises, breakdowns and withdrawal of many of these social institutions in our daily lives, and with that a weakening of the old, collective sources of identity.

The 'inhumanity' inherent in globalisation is not simply of ICT increasing social alienation or necessarily diminishing the agency of citizens or the state, though Urry does imply our technologically enhanced relationships are a problem:

> The ordering of social life is presumed to be contingent, unpredictable, patterned and irreducible to human subjects. Luhmann summarises: 'There can be no 'intersubjectivity' on the basis of the subject.'[14]

Given the 'absence' in many people's lives today of the authorities that were the hallmarks of the modern nation state there are concerns about the viability of 'society' as a group concept.[15] If the main source of connection is an 'inhuman network' criss-crossed at ever faster speeds,[16] and the state has lost capacity to regulate informally through socialisation and citizenship as it once did, what are the hallmarks of citizenship that now apply? Can a global expression of 'civil society' develop to contribute to global governance and moderate the power of corporations and the nation state?

Though driven from the US, the pursuit of a policy of 'innovation' and 'free trade' has become a pre-eminent directive of most governments of developed countries. Nation states are keen to 'harmonise' business regulation, financial regulation and intellectual property laws to further these objectives. There is regulation to prevent technological disruption to the data flows, but a reluctance to regulate the networks for other reasons. Even spam in the US, and national security, are regulated with an eye to harnessing the profit motive.

Given the development of globalisation, the concern is that the disciplinary state has been transformed into the surveillance state. 'Inhumanity' is referred to in order to highlight the winding down of control over citizens' lives once directly executed by the state and indirectly delivered through social institutions. This loss is, of course, not exactly mourned by all. However the greater fear is that a more intrusive, dehumanising, less visible or locatable form of surveillance has replaced it.

The old modern forms of social control were obscured by the liberal political fiction that all significant power was exercised by and through the nation state and its bureaucracies, and that these forces were able to be made accountable through legal processes.[17] Some abuses of power were made visible and able to be addressed through this means, but only some. However the new power is even more shadowy, diffuse and less visible than that preceding it. There are questions whether any of it is seriously able to be made accountable using the old processes. This new power is presumed to be the facility of global corporate forces working with the blessing of the nation state and supported by the new global institutions that have been sponsored to further their reach. Rather than controlling exercises of power, the suggestion is that these institutions only orchestrate further, ongoing corporate control of us, over and through the wires.

Data is collected, collated and transmitted. Data is used to identify us and speak for who we are. But our identity is only revealed through the databases largely generated by the records of our choices and actions. The related political concern here is that our agency or capacities as citizens have already become confined by and through these webs and networks. We cannot expect the state to intervene or act on our behalf, to address our other needs, interests or desires. The nation state will only identify us as consumers of services signified by the data that represents us, or see us as threats to the network, the state and ultimately other citizens, requiring a strategic political response. Though the US military initiated the technological developments that eventually led us to this virtual citizenship, the visibility of that source of direction has now receded. The future of the networks is driven by private development of these technologies.[18] These global networks are perceived as a new form of power, not of our own making and insensitive to other ideas or possibilities for society, order and control.

Participation and the new citizenship

As the role of the nation state has changed and modern notions of citizenship rights seem inadequate, there has been a push to develop international law and human rights to accommodate broader aspirations for all citizens of the globe:

> Individuals and organizations have increasing layers of legal rights that neither have their origin in the positive law of sovereign nation states, nor are exclusively exercisable before municipal courts. This phenomenon is intimately related to the corrosion of sovereignty: as states cease to be the sole source of legal rights, citizenship . . . is no longer monopolised by the laws of nation states.[19]

In the same way that the welfare state represented the constitutionization of the domestic economy in the sense of bringing a measure of equality of citizenship into its operations, human rights have the potential to infuse similar principles into the global domain.[20]

Both global institutions and national law are affected by this development. An example of human rights jurisprudence influencing domestic law can be seen from the Australian internet defamation case discussed earlier.[21] Justice Kirby linked interpretation of Mr Gutnick's right of reputation under state law to accommodating the realities of the impact of global communications networks on citizens, and the aspirations of the UN *International Covenant on Civil and Political Rights*.

Likewise, the Declaration of Principles and Plan of Action adopted at the first phase of the World Summit on the Information Society (WSIS) explicitly links the politics of internet governance and the development of the information society with adhering to the principles of the Charter of the United Nations and with the upholding of the Universal Declaration of Human Rights.[22] Some have optimistically anticipated that these meetings will lead to new international treaties on internet governance and communications rights.

The structure of WSIS seeks to harness 'civil society' in governance. That is, there is an attempt to engage non-governmental actors who represent various interest groups based on the NGO and UN models, to work alongside represented governments. This 'Civil Society Division' is separate to a 'Coordinating Committee of Business Interlocutors' representing the worldwide business community. These divisions and related voluntary bodies facilitate the input of a broad range of contributions into WSIS processes. Government delegates also have a role to play.

Out of concerns raised about lack of consultation and inclusion of the interests and participation of developing countries[23] the 2003 meeting requested a UN-based Working Group on Internet Governance (WGIG) report to the second phase 2005 meeting. As a Brazilian delegate attending an initial global forum hosted by the UN complained:

Internet governance should not be the prerogative of one group of countries or stakeholders, and the specific roles of all stakeholders should be defined. Governments also had a stake, and the concerns of developing countries should be taken into account.[24]

A High-Level Summit Organizing Committee (HLSOC) has also been established as part of the WSIS Secretariat, to co-ordinate the efforts and involvement of the numerous and diverse United Nations organisations.[25] The main three areas set down for discussion in 2005 relate to stocktaking on the implementation of the Plan of Action at national, regional and international levels, internet governance and financing.

WSIS: what to expect?

Selian argues:

> The period of preparation for the summit has permitted key national, regional, and global entities to struggle to assert their respective positions to 'govern' the many unwieldy subject areas and themes that comprise the famed 'information society'.[26]

All the stakeholders in this 'network' of representation are meant to make contributions to the development of a declaration and action plan. While such declarations do not possess the binding force of a treaty, they do have juridical significance and play a major role in the development of international law and, for example, in the preliminary work on treaties and conventions.[27]

However she notes that unlike previous global summits such as the Earth Summit in Rio in 1992, and the Fourth World Conference on Women in Beijing 1995, WSIS lacks a similar level of consensus about policy objectives. Further as with the other summits, the business community has not been particularly enthusiastically engaged with these processes. Selian concludes 'the lack of private-sector interest in and attendance at WSIS is nothing less than a statement of dissociation'.[28]

In many accounts of WSIS deliberations, the role of governments in seeking disproportionate representation to 'civil society' groups is criticised:

> The push of developing countries for a stronger role for governments is difficult to reconcile with the growing movement among NGOs, policy advocates, intellectuals, the scientific, academic and technical communities, and developed world governments for more influence for 'civil society'. Indeed, this contradiction seems strangely characteristic of the entire World Summit on the Information Society.
>
> The WSIS-CS (Civil Society) Internet Governance Caucus . . . called for equal representation on the WGIG for civil society, governments and the

private business sector, whereas most governments were asking that half the WGIG be made up of governmental representatives.[29]

Suspicion of government involvement is a well-rehearsed theme in rela- tion to critiques of ICANN. There have also been concerns over authoritarian practices in WSIS forums, where governments have refused to participate with civil society delegates being present. Apparently representatives from 'Reporters without Borders' and 'Human Rights China' were excluded from WSIS participation for having raised rights abuses by participating states.[30] These are genuine, well-grounded concerns.

However 'civil society' is really a governance concept best developed in relation to western liberal and postliberal democracies. From developing country perspectives there is a variable capacity for members represent- ing their 'civil society' to participate. These countries do not have equiv- alent educational, welfare and community sector organisations to those that assist civil governance in modern and postmodern states. Accordingly, greater encouragement, involvement and support via both national gov- ernments and NGOs to sponsor and develop these nations' capacities for 'civil society' representation is required. As Oguibe's anecdote shows, with developing countries it is especially not the case that left to their own devices underprivileged citizens will experience civil society as dynamic or housing the capacity to express communicative or any other form of freedom. African delegates have claimed that WSIS provided some useful impetus to facili- tate development and inclusion of civil society representation. Nonetheless observers have still identified the limited financial resources allocated to travel scholarships as an effective barrier to civil society representatives.[31]

There is already a relevant history here, not with WSIS, but with its original UN sponsor, the International Telecommunications Union (ITU). In a history of the ITU's own quest for more inclusive global governance Don MacLean argues:

> The ITU's diverse membership and extensive experience in attempting to enhance the roles of developing countries and nongovernmental actors in its decision-making processes place it among the leaders in the quest for inclusive governance models. However . . . in spite of the substantive differences that exist in structures, functions, and membership of the ITU, WTO, and ICANN, and in spite of the different policy and political forces to which they are subject, the three organizations face a common set of organizational challenges as they seek to construct governance arrangements that are more inclusive of developing countries, the private sector, and civil society.[32]

He concludes:

> Clearly, the successes and failures of the ITU's attempts over the past decade
> to develop more inclusive governance arrangements have important impli-
> cations for the future direction of the ITU reform movement . . .
> . . . the key to strengthening developing country participation in the gov-
> ernance of global ICTs lies in building technical and policy capacity at the
> national and regional levels; and second, that without this capacity changes
> to the governance structures and decision making processes of international
> organizations that are designed to create special spaces for developing coun-
> tries may mean very little in practice, even if they are potentially valuable. The
> ITU has a broad range of developing country participants from the public
> and private sectors, long experience in providing technical assistance, and a
> separate organizational sector devoted to development activities, and it has
> imposed development obligations on its regulatory and standardization func-
> tions. In spite of this, developing countries are far from being fully included in
> the ITU's principal governance activities, fundamentally because they often
> lack the capacity to participate effectively at every stage of the governance
> process, which includes technology assessment, issue identification, agenda
> setting, policy formulation, coalition building, negotiation, policy implemen-
> tation, and evaluation.[33]

Governance issues are practically separated from 'access' issues in developed countries and, though not always the case,[34] it is the former that
attracts most attention from civil society representatives. However the pre-
eminent concern of African countries remains the creation of a Digital
Solidarity Fund.[35] There are also North/South splits on the role of 'consensus language'. The fear of developing nations is that this will only result
in motherhood statements that 'invite all stakeholders to join in the digital
solidarity agenda,' but do not create funding obligations. Northern comfort
with 'civil consensus' and discomfort with rule by government also has a
neo-liberal ideological component. Whilst it is true that there are successful
global civil society institutions like the IETF, this is an unusual body with
strong, practical traditions that have served to hold participants together.
Its constitutional framework has worked to keep contentious issues off the
agenda.[36] The same management feat simply should not be considered as
a likely scenario for new, far more socially diverse, unwieldy bureaucratic
institutions like WSIS.

A lack of a common understanding or priorities can be seen within
the groups that make up the UN 'family' and are represented in the
HLSOC. There are real differences both within and between UN agencies

Table 10 *Comparative use of computers or the internet by indigenous persons in Australia, 2002–2003*

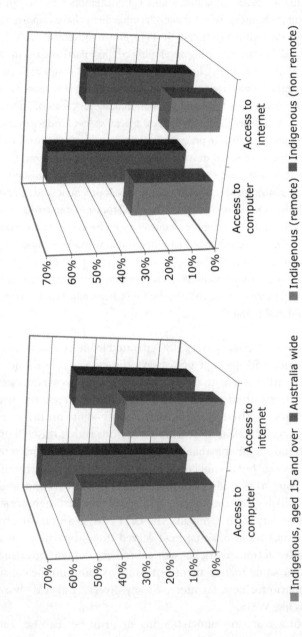

Reference: Australian Bureau of Statistics, *Household Use of Information Technology, Australia* (cat. no. 8146.0)

reflecting the varying political pressures exerted by nation states on them from time to time. WIPO, for example, has previously been sympathetic to developing country perspectives on intellectual property. It has also supported reflection on IP and traditional cultural expressions (TCEs), traditional knowledge (TK) and associated genetic resources.[37] However in 2004 WIPO resisted hosting a forum for debate about open source software and the information commons despite support by many concerned with equity and development issues.[38] Later that year the United Nations Development Programme (UNDP) established the International Open Source Network (IOSN), whose goal is to promote Free and Open Source software usage, especially in the Asia-Pacific region.[39] Given both of these organisations are represented on the HLSOC, how will these respective contributions be 'co-ordinated'?

The same discord is reproduced right across WSIS. For example, Alan Toner notes that language endorsing preferential use of free and open source software was excised from the Asian Regional Meeting for WSIS in Tokyo at the behest of the US government and Microsoft, though there is a growing agitation from civil society groups in the US and the EU encouraging global adoption of non-proprietary software models.[40] This leaves one to ponder the practicalities of the stated objective of WSIS to build 'a common vision and understanding of the information society'.[41]

Whilst human rights dialogue may be on the rise amongst civil society groups and participants in global forums, Drahos argues that it is a mistake to presume that we live in an era where multilateral treaties have displaced bilateral agreements and moderated the power of nation states such as the US. It was because developing countries were asserting independent agendas through WIPO, that the US began to advance its proprietary IP agenda through the WTO and TRIPS.[42] Drahos shows how bi-lateral agreements, such as free trade agreements (FTA) and bi-lateral investment treaties, are now being used to build even more extensive protection of IP rights than TRIPS had envisaged:

In bilateral trade negotiations between states involving a strong and weak state, generally speaking the strong state comes along with a prepared draft text which acts as a starting point for the negotiations. Bilateral negotiations are complex and lengthy affairs, features which make them costly even for strong states. In order to lower the transaction costs of bilateralism the US has developed models or prototypes of the kind of bilateral treaties it wishes to have with other countries. Once a model treaty is ratified by the Senate, US trade negotiators know that if they stick to its terms in other negotiations there is a good chance the treaties flowing from these negotiations will also be approved. For the US there are very strong incentives for a standardization of bilateral treaty standards.[43]

The capacity of 'civil society' or even national interest to be engaged in these negotiations can be seen from Australia's recent experience with the US–Australia FTA.[44]

Australia–US Free Trade Agreement

This agreement followed the Singapore–US FTA. Discussion began with American references to supposedly 'weak' Australian laws being reported in the press in 2003. Going into the negotiations the US's stated objectives included seeking 'to enhance the level of Australia's protection for intellectual property rights beyond TRIPS in new areas of technology' and 'to strengthen Australia's domestic enforcement procedures, such as increasing criminal penalties so that they are sufficient to have a deterrent effect on piracy and counterfeiting.' In the second media briefing, US Chief Negotiator Ralph Ives said 'the fundamental objective, I think both countries have, is to provide a high level of protection for intellectual property.'[45]

Whilst submissions were invited from interested Australian stakeholders, these submissions were not made available whilst negotiations were underway. The text of negotiations was not made publicly available. Comments by the Trade Minister Mark Vaile, that 'when we agree to it, we will not be undermining our ability to deliver good public policy in a number of areas, given the uniqueness of Australia and Australians',[46] did not allay many fears.

With respect to copyright the Australia–US Free Trade Agreement capitulated on a copyright term extension, ISPs liability, access to subscriber information where infringement is alleged and the import of DMCA-style anti-circumvention provisions.[47] Significant concessions were also made concerning patents, primarily restricting access to generic drugs that are an important component of the government's policy of providing cheaper access to medicines under the national Pharmaceutical Benefits Scheme.[48]

An exchange in the Australian Senate between Opposition Senators and Australian Chief Negotiator, Stephen Deady, over the copyright term extension reveals something of the spirit of those negotiations:

Senator CONROY – Was any analysis undertaken on the impact of this particular change? I appreciate this was a bit rushed at the end and it was pretty cold over in Washington, but did you get a chance to look at the consequences of this?

Mr DEADY – We have not done any particular work on this question of copyright extension . . . It is an on-balance question. The costs are difficult to really measure.[49]

The Australian government had previously commissioned an inquiry which included a detailed economic analysis of a term extension. The Intellectual Property and Competition Review Committee could find no empirical evidence to support an extension of the copyright term. Accordingly, the Committee recommended that there would be no justification to change the existing copyright term.[50]

> Senator COOK– Were you aware of the Australian Intellectual Property and Competition Review Committee's recommendation on this point when we agreed to it?
>
> Mr DEADY – In negotiating this whole agreement – certainly this IP chapter – we were . . . given a mandate by the government to take this thing forward. The copyright extension was an issue that the Americans put on the table. It was an issue that went right through the negotiations. In the context of the overall deal and the balance that was struck, the government decided to agree, as part of the FTA, to align our copyright term more closely with the United States term. That was a decision on the balance of the agreement with the United States.
>
> Senator COOK – I am not blaming you, Mr Deady, because you cannot be expected to have read every damn thing and you are in a position where you need to be advised on some of the finer details of some of these things. My question was: were you aware of that recommendation when we reached this agreement?
>
> Mr DEADY – I was not aware of that recommendation, but that is not to say that members of the team were not. I assume they probably were . . . these were decisions that were taken as part of the overall package. The government agreed, as part of the overall deal, to this extension. So I am not sure of the relevance of a recommendation that there should be some review before this decision was taken.[51]

In a forum to discuss the deals done, Peter Coreneos, CEO, Australian Internet Industry Association, noted that in relation to the changes to ISP liability for copyright infringement by subscribers, there was extensive consultation with his organisation and members but 'they were basically presented with a fait accompli.'[52] Likewise, in a Government Standing Committee hearing, David Herd, Screen Producers Association of Australia, noted:

We just wanted to get on the record that, despite the fact that the national interest analysis talks about the consultation that was undertaken with the sector, we agreed that there was a lot of talking, but what we saw at the end of the agreement is way past what the sector was consulted about. In fact the deal that was done in Washington earlier this year is not what the sector supported and it was not discussed with the sector at all by the Department of Foreign Affairs and Trade.

Mr WILKIE – Were sector representatives invited to Washington to be part of the negotiations?

Mr HERD – No. And that, as we say in our submission, stands in stark contrast with what we believe the level of consultation was with the American cultural sector.[53]

Whilst there was a space made for US government and particular global owner interests to assert their preferences, there was no corresponding respect for unwelcome Australian perspectives from civil society interest groups like the Electronic Frontiers Australia (EFA), Australian Digital Alliance, Australian Consumers Association, Australian Library and Information Association, local free software and open source advocates, IP academics, or even passing reference to the findings of the government's own IP expert committees.

Perhaps we should not expect a different outcome from civil society participation through WSIS.

Globalised law-making

In 1993 and in relation to the EU Neil MacCormick argued that:

> Wherever there is law, there is normative order; wherever there is normative order institutionalised, there is law. Law is about institutional normative relations between normatively recognised persons of sorts. Law is about rights and duties and, therefore, liberties and no rights.[54]

In Australia debates about the emerging international legal order led to an argument by lawyers that participating in the global economy requires 'harmonisation' of our laws with essential global norms and principles. As with developing countries, this led to the adoption of minimum standards via the TRIPS Agreement. There were also changes to comply with new and old WIPO treaties.[55] What we have now seen is that, in terms of furthering the advance of particular US corporate interests, pertinent minimum global standards are then extended through bi-lateral negotiations. The US is currently engaged in negotiating an FTA with Thailand.

Drahos reminds us that we should not consider the global 'normative' processes and setting of minimum standards as significant initiatives in themselves. These are only one component of a broader strategy that secures the future development and extends the global reach of big business. Where standard-setting encounters 'difficulties' the US, and to a lesser extent the EU, has embarked on a process of forum shifting leading to the co-ordination of bi-lateral and multilateral strategies. The end result has been a continual ratchetting up of IP laws globally.[56]

WSIS groups may be able to deliver some consensus on ICT policy, however the likelihood is that what will be able to be agreed upon are rather empty norms, motherhood statements: the vague consensus it is possible to gain international agreement on. This would still be a favourable outcome for big business. Vacant norms pose no practical obstacles and there is no need to flesh out more specific legal obligations. Where more detail is necessary bi-lateral agreements can provide enough specifics to keep corporate agendas moving and block the entrenching of unwelcome new ideas and programs.

For developing countries, the consequences of the inability to enact practically meaningful obligations is quite different. Accordingly a strategy that anticipates this likely outcome needs to be considered. As appealing as the focus on better global norms is for many, especially those keen to distance themselves from the evil global corporate lawyer stereotype, development of global norms is irrelevant when the reality of the postmodern nation state and US power is not *always fully accepted* as intersecting with this new normativity.

This does not mean that it is a waste of time and energy for WSIS civil society groups to continue to advocate for better policies that seek to 'balance' corporate/nation state influence. Further continual pressure on global bodies like WIPO, challenging the current maximalist IP mission and work program for WIPO, is worthwhile.[57] These symbolic efforts should be supported, however, not because it follows that these efforts actually address the current unequal global distribution of communications technologies or render economic power more accountable on the international stage.

Rather, support that strengthens the profile and role of select US civil society groups globally can contribute to the moderation of some of the more objectionable current policies advocated by the US government, such as the global advocacy of proprietary models of software protection and strong patent rights. Arguably it is only changes to US domestic policy that will moderate further global IP rights advancement. Indirectly it is these changes that are more likely to benefit developing and other countries in the longer term. Accordingly, though an enhanced civil society role in global governance does disproportionately little for developing countries, it is important that critics work with, and not alienate or marginalise, US-based civil society groups. Even if civil society groups are insensitive to the practical realities of developing countries (and not all are equally so), it is changes generated within the powerful states that can shift the political pressures and expectations currently exerted on developing nations and global institutions. For this reason alone, there needs to be some sophistication in developing and supporting the global perspectives of some of the more powerful civil society groups. Perhaps not all groups necessarily need to profile the global inhumanity of current policies, if such focus is not a major concern in the political circles they move in, within the US.

Compliance with cyberlaw activism

This said, what are the current achievements of civil society-inspired communications-information policy advocacy?

There is little empirical research on civil society advocacy.[58] It is probably not possible to acknowledge all the diverse groups that are, or have been active even in one jurisdiction. There are also huge differences in scale and resources, even amongst bodies with similar objectives. For example, the Electronic Frontiers Foundation (EFF) based in San Francisco has premises, paid and unpaid staff, a strong donor program, significant high-profile tech-industry, lawyer and academic support, facilitates pro bono legal work, holds regular meetings, and conferences, and participates in court cases. The EFF acknowledges other like-minded organisations such as the American Civil Liberties Union (ACLU), the Electronic Privacy Information Center (EPIC), Public Citizen, the Online Policy Group (OPG), and the Privacy Rights Clearinghouse (PRC). Though not affiliated to the EFF, Electronic Frontiers Australia (EFA) has very similar civil rights objectives it seeks to advance in the Australian context. However the EFA cannot afford premises or paid staff. It is a shoestring operation that mainly responds to government policy initiatives. Through the efforts of a small committed number of volunteers the EFA has maintained and increased its local profile over a decade. However there is no comparative nexus of support from other civil society groups such as exists in the US. The only official link the EFA notes is membership of Global Internet Liberty Campaign (GILC), an international coalition of organisations working to protect and enhance online civil liberties and human rights, a body virtually unknown in Australia. GILC was formed at the annual meeting of the Internet Society in Montreal in 1996.

Most advocacy is localised. Groups have defensively responded to regulatory initiatives by domestic legislatures and courts (and to a far lesser extent, standard-setting bodies). The overriding concern has been that the shift from an apparent absence of regulation to an emerging body of cyberlaw carries with it a corresponding erosion of previously held freedoms. Advocacy is not simplistically anarchist, but rather seeks to raise the profile of the civil and human rights implications of various legislative initiatives. Where the US constitution enshrines certain civil rights, this creates an avenue to moderate or overturn 'bad' law. In Australia, the EFA is accepted as an interested stakeholder in public political debates, but there is no equivalent constitutional mandate to develop in an online context, or to enforce in the courts.

Roughly categorised, cyberlaw activism has focused on a number of regulatory concerns:

- content restrictions e.g. obscene publications such as restricted material, child pornography, Nazi propaganda and memorabilia, defamation, digital copyright controls;
- conduct restrictions e.g. new cybercrimes related to hacking, interference with data, denial of service attacks, virus, worms;
- telecommunications standards e.g. service provider responsibility in dealing with client information;
- e-commerce rules e.g. spam, authenticated electronic transactions, e-signatures;
- engineering protocols and standards e.g. cryptography, key escrow, Pretty Good Privacy (PGP), Platform for Privacy Preferences (P3P);
- data surveillance e.g. data management and smart card devices, electronic eavesdropping;
- security e.g. export restrictions affecting personal encryption standards and IP, search warrant and seizure procedures, anti-terrorism initiatives.

Clearly many of the political concerns raised by these issues overlap.

It is not my purpose to refer to the specifics of any particular Australian or US laws. They differ, not just in subject matter, but in approach. Many significant differences can be attributed to the constitutional possibilities of the particular political framework (federal and state powers), the need to mesh new regulation with existing laws dealing with the subject, established administrative expertise, practice and competence with oversight of the issue, funding allocated etc. The domestic political context of the time also needs to be considered. For example, Australia has unique 'symbolic' legislation in the area of online content restrictions and online gambling.

The regulation is ineffective in restricting user access to pornography or online gaming services from Australia, although regulation affects and burdens service providers and certain businesses located within the jurisdiction. These laws were enacted in response to perceived conservative community demand for 'strong government' to protect vulnerable members of the community.[59]

There are however some similarities in civil society approaches to cyber-regulation that can generally be considered. Specific proposals are usually evaluated against an expectation that *the internet can or should deliver something more, or something different.* There is usually an idealism underpinning analyses, suggestive of the ideological agenda of such groups. Ideology is not necessarily openly engaged, but expressed in the optimism and pessimism driving assessments.

The optimistic desire is always to better advance freedom, liberty, expression and creativity, and make life easier with less complicated, but effective, freedom-enhancing technology and regulation. This is frequently related to a pessimism, expressed in terms of perceived failings of law regulating power – the capture of technology decision-making by large, self-interested corporations, leading to less than the best solution being advanced, and leading to government inaction in the creation of new civility rights.

For example, in relation to privacy it is argued that market-based approaches to regulation, that rely on user 'choices' to accept cookies, pre-select privacy preferences, or opt-out of spam are inadequate. In response to the industry standard-setting group W3C's P3P standard, civil society groups, EPIC and Junkbusters assessed:

> P3P fails to comply with baseline standards for privacy protection. It is a complex and confusing protocol that will make it more difficult for Internet users to protect their privacy . . . earlier versions of P3P were withdrawn because the developers recognized that the proposed negotiation process was too burdensome for users and that the automatic transfer of personal information would be widely opposed. . . . The report concludes that there is little evidence to support the industry claim that P3P will improve user privacy citing the widely accepted Fair Information Practices.[60]

The argument for 'baseline standards' is mirrored in academic overviews of privacy law, where it is argued that constitutional values and rights conducive to online freedom should include defined obligations with respect to use of personal data, transparent processing systems, procedural rights, and the capacity for external oversight.[61] Julie Cohen argues that:

Conventional understandings of ownership, liberty, and expression do not easily stretch to accommodate informational privacy rights, but not because of any inherent incompatibility between privacy and ownership, or between privacy and economic or expressive freedom. Rather, the disjunct arises because these understandings are grounded in a theory of self-actualization based on exchange – designed to minimize transaction costs and other obstacles to would-be traders, and thus systematically, inevitably biased toward facilitating trade in personally-identified information. They are grounded, as well, in a theory of the social role of information that conceives information primarily as a lubricant to trade, and that seeks revealed truth about human potential (to be translated into trade advantage) in the rationalized, regularized processing of observed facts.[62]

She goes on to note that whilst the protocol might be better than none, what needs to be considered are the structural choices that are foreclosed by adopting 'privacy-as-choice'. She argues for the development of a jurisprudence that does not automatically oppose property and speech in a war of rights.

Where civil society criticism is reflected on or picked up in academic circles, there are clearly synergies and advantages for developing a new jurisprudence. Further, given the weaker basis for developing civic rights in some jurisdictions, and the deafness of some governments, such as the Australian government, to academic advice that conflicts with dictated political outcomes, perhaps spreading models based on US civil society and academic leadership makes more sense. We have seen this attraction expressed in Australia most recently with affiliating with US 'Creative Commons' initiatives, and invitations to profile civil society IP celebrity spokespeople such as Larry Lessig and Richard Stallman. The presumption is that the Australian situation is enhanced by mimicking emerging US jurisprudence that looks attractive – encouraging the market 'choice' of new de facto global standards for copy-left[63] (but not for spam or privacy where models are considered as too pro-market).

In view of the strategic issues and local limitations outlined above, there are certain practicalities in adopting this approach. However there is also considerable cause for unease. Because compared to local circumstance, US civil society groups and academics seem so well organised, funded, vibrant, and one might add entrepreneurial – Australians tend to assume that this (eventually) corresponds with political success in the US and ultimately abroad. Whilst US experiments in developing civic rights cybernorms are more advanced than our efforts, that advance has been best secured where it has been related to more traditional constitutional jurisprudence on speech rights and conventional IP practice. My worry is that we are being mesmerised by the show, and forget the local obstacles. Despite US influence, Australia has quite different constitutional 'baselines', legal cultures and political circumstance. Some of the US initiatives will also work here, but complying with US jurisprudence, and seemingly prioritising these efforts, is servile. For my tastes, it all too hopefully overstates the degree of the advance achieved or achievable based on the US jurisprudence underpinning these 'new' rights. For me the dilemma is the need to support US developments that may eventually lead to changes in US domestic law and corresponding changes in the international context, whilst still keeping alive a more independent space for local reflection, and targeted action and inaction.

'Be Alert, But Not Alarmed'[64]

Terrorist groups were not the first to use the internet as a political tool. Internet technology and policy have always been integral to advancing the national security and foreign policy interests of nation states, especially of the US state:

> At a time when the US style of competitive market capitalism attracts the world's attention – even its envy – and US computer firms dominate the global marketplace, it is difficult to recall and acknowledge that the federal government has played a major role in launching and giving momentum to the computer revolution, which now takes pride of place among the nation's recent technological achievements. Federal funding not only financed development of most of the nation's early digital computers, but also has continued to enable breakthroughs in areas as wide ranging as computer time-sharing, the Internet, artificial intelligence, and virtual reality as the industry has matured. Federal investment also has supported the building of physical infrastructure needed for leading-edge research and the education of undergraduate and graduate students who now work in industry and at academic research centers.[65]

In his 'Baghdad Blog', Salam Pax discusses the US reporting of an email that circulated in Iraq in early January 2003. The email, written in Arabic, was sent to Iraq email account users, urging recipients to send information to an address about weapons stored in their homes, and not to show resistance in the event of the coming attack. The mail was sent at 00:00, and fifteen minutes later the mail server was shut down:

I'm trying to find someone who has the email, but isn't afraid to admit that he still has not deleted it.

UPDATE: Well, the 'Washington Post' knows: 'US government Starts E-mail Campaign to Key Iraqis'. So does 'ABC Online': 'US sends Iraqis anti-Saddam e-mails'. The title of the Washington Post article is not exactly correct. My friend is not a 'key Iraqi', whatever that means. Anyone who downloaded their email around 12 got that message.

AUTHORITIES BLOCK EMAIL SERVICE

Iraqis began to receive the e-mail last week, visitors there said. The state-controlled e-mail service is only available to a small number of Iraqis, mainly government officials, senior public servants, academics and scientists.

That is also not quite correct. All you need is an ID, a phoneline and cash. It's the cash that gets in the way of people getting the e-mail service. And the fact that Iraq is not a very computer literate land. Importing computers is banned by the sanctions committee. We get smuggled equipment, which is much more expensive. The people mentioned in the article get their service for free; that is what should have been said. And whilst they get it for free, we pay an arm and a leg.[66]

The use of propaganda in the advance of a military campaign is not remarkable. What is noteworthy is the framing of the political issue by the US press coverage. The assumed framework is of authoritarian government, in the absence of established communicative rights giving special communication privileges to state functionaries, severely restricting more democratic citizen access to services, and monitoring and censoring the use and content of the technology. This projects a fantasy of untrammelled political and communicative freedom existing in democratic states, and attributes the denial of those 'corresponding' rights exclusively to the political program of the opposing evil empire. The simplistic implication is that civil society is strengthened by rights creating more liberal access to communications technology. There is an uncritical adoption of civil society idealism here, as the relevant analytical tool.

Saddam's Iraq was clearly an authoritarian state, however the problems facing Iraqi citizens are hardly reducible to a problem of a lack of 'rights'. In his blog Salam frequently notes the discordant interest in postings from the US attending to matters of 'freedom', without any corresponding level of interest or concern for more concrete and immediate matters of 'survival' as a consequence of the US and allied presence and ongoing military conflict, not to mention awareness of the way the invasion has spread a fundamentalism, especially amongst a previously less-interested middle class, that is somewhat hostile to civil rights.

The 'Reporters without Borders' study *Internet Under Surveillance* (2004)[67] notes:

> On 10 September 2001, the Internet was still a place of hopes and dreams that was going to give everyone access to impartial information and undermine dictatorships. A few days later, it had became a lawless place where Al-Qaeda had managed to plan and coordinate its attacks. The Internet began to frighten people. 10 September was the last day of a golden age of free online expression. Since then, Big Brother has loomed ever closer.

The report has an impressive documentation of online censorship on a country basis and concludes that 'Censorship is growing, often without public protest or interest, even in countries that usually respect freedom of expression.'

One cause of concern they note relates to the role of US businesses in facilitating the penetration of internet censorship. In the report on China they note:

> China today has nearly 600,000 websites that have been approved by the authorities, a 60 per cent increase over 2002. Internet businesses are also booming. Sina.com, China's biggest portal, announced turnover of more than 30 million euros for the fourth quarter of 2003, a 197 per cent increase on the same period in 2002. While western Internet firms are struggling to emerge from the crisis, China looks like El Dorado and is the source of envy.
>
> To keep its foothold in this market, Yahoo! agreed to censor the Chinese version of its search engine and to control its discussion forums. So, if you enter 'Taiwan independence' into its search engine, you get no results. If you try to post a message on this subject in a discussion forum, it never appears online. The US giant is ready to do anything to conquer the Chinese Internet market and is buying up Chinese companies such as the search engine 3721.com, for which it paid 120 million dollars. With all this money at stake, human rights and freedom of expression are brushed aside.

Likewise they note that Cisco Systems sold China several thousand routers and provided Cisco engineers to help build the regime's surveillance infrastructure. The technology allows identification of visitors to banned sites and the source of transmission of 'dangerous' email messages, as well as screening data transmitted on the internet to spot 'subversive' key words.

Whilst civil society groups such as 'Peek-a-booty.org' will continue to create anti-censorship tools, and the Berkman Center for Internet & Society will continue to study and document filtering and screening technologies in places such as China and Saudi Arabia, the Berkman Center suggest an emerging trend is that US legislatures are experimenting with adopting the censorship tools and approaches that have proven effective in authoritarian regimes.[68] In view of these ongoing developments, we need to be particularly alert to superficial comparisons of democracy and authoritarianism, freedom and oppression, in a global context.

Resistance

Throughout the 1990s cyberactivism, culture jamming, politically motivated hacktivism, cyberprotest emerged. These are all terms for forms of protest to globalisation, US power, capitalism, media concentration, and corporate or state control over communications.[69] Well-known actions include orchestrating disruption and organising protests against the WTO, and supporting an alternative internet-based free press in Belgrade during the Milosevic regime and thereafter. With its origins in notions of the internet as a source of technological freedom, activism is grounded in the notion that, given the right tools, surveillance can be exposed, censorship averted and avoided, data dead ends routed around.[70] Of course, the political risks to activists are distributed somewhat unequally, in that the risks and consequences to Chinese, Iraqis or Iranians engaging in 'cyberactivism' are not of the same order to those residing in the West.

Most recently there has been some revision and far less optimism surrounding this politics. Jordan and Taylor ask:

> What use is an online mass action? Who knows it has occurred? Are not some of the most powerful uses of mass demonstrations – the sense of being on the march with so many others – simply absent online? . . . Mass action hactivism might, in this way, simply be inventing alienated civil disobedience, while simultaneously refusing the power cyberspace does offer . . . Their acceptance of hacking's identification of means with ends is simply an acceptance of how things work in cyberspace.[71]

Tiziana Terranova's assessment of 'information politics' sounds similar:

The appearance of the modern informational problematic . . . is related to a conception of communication as an operational problem dominated by the imperatives of the channel and the code rather than by a concern with exchange of ideas, ethical truth or rhetorical confrontation (a definition that dominates the liberal and enlightened concept of communications). It is not about signs, but about signals.[72]

She goes on to argue that:

There is nothing inherently technological here, in the modern sense of a Frankenstein monster which has been created by human will but which is now threatening to destroy it. It is not so much a question of technology as of techniques and forms of knowledge that all converge – through a variety of media and channels – on the basic problem of how to clear out a space and establish a successful contact.[73]

Rose argues:

The notion of resistance, at least as it has conventionally functioned within the analyses of self-proclaimed radicals, is too simple and flattening . . . It is merely the obverse of a one-dimensional notion of power as domination.

It is too tied to 'spectacle', 'agency', 'courage and bravery' but remiss in attending to local conditions and practical obstacles:

If one were trying to characterise the creativity of what one might term . . . 'minority' politics . . . one would examine the ways in which creativity arises out of the situation of human beings engaged in particular relations of force and meaning, and what is made out of the possibilities of that location. These minor engagements do not have the arrogance of programmatical politics – perhaps even refuse their designation as politics at all. They are cautious, modest, pragmatic, experimental, stuttering, tentative. They are concerned with the here and now, not with some fantasized future, with small concerns, petty details, the everyday and not the transcendental.[74]

Lovink says:

There is a need for contemporary forms of organization, such as global (online) labor unions, networks of immigrants, refugee tongs, free association of digital artisans. The question here is how to go beyond the exchange of information.[75]

This brings us back to a question about the nature of agency in a global order that houses no singular form of power or rationality. For citizens there is a recurring problem of visibility, of telling their stories *and* making a difference, in relation to the establishment of broader possibilities for order and action. It is a problem of constituting community.

Reconciling law and internet culture

This book primarily focuses on legal community in relation to the internet, considering the old modern, new and emerging forms of regulation. This is because I think that, however acute descriptions of this new modality of power – of Empire[76] – are, we need to do more than explore the phenomenon from the position of the postcolonial, postmodern and postimperialist subject. Whilst sociologists, communications and cultural studies commentators, technologists, political theorists and philosophers have all used their respective disciplines and approaches to diagnose the general crises of unaccountable and invasive forms of network power, they seem to have brushed over the implication of it being primarily within the legal arenas that the power to change things is most accessibly and visibly located. Law creates and denies possibilities of community. It sets standards and many of the communication rules. But law is not an omnipotent or singular force.

With globalisation we have seen the emergence of a lot of new legal communities and organisations that are driving the direction, dissemination and availability of information and communications technologies. These groups influence the realm of possibility for law-making by nation states. They impact on the capacity of citizens as legal subjects to act creatively, whether that be in terms of working in the arts or sciences or some other kind of endeavour. These legal spaces do deserve better and further 'pragmatic, experimental, stuttering, tentative' consideration. Not all legal spaces offer the same possibilities for engagement or participation. Interventionist strategies would not apply across the board. But they do offer sites for our participation, compliance and resistance. They house some capacity to make things change.

Notes

1 Defining internet law

1 S. Bradner, 'RFC 2026 Internet Standards Process – Revision 3', October 1996, 3.
2 J. Reynolds and J. Postel, 'RFC 1000 The Request for Comments Guide', August 1987.
3 Richard Barbrook and Andy Cameron, 'Californian Ideology: critique of West Coast cyberlibertarianism', <http://www.hrc.westminster.ac.uk/hrc/theory/californianideo/index/t.4.html>.
4 RFC-ignorant.org is at <http://www.rfc-ignorant.org/>.
5 See IETF at <http://www.ietf.org/> and RFC's Homepage at <http://www.rfc-editor.org/>.
6 The new draft WHOIS Protocol Specification, RFC 3912, designed to make obsolete RFC 954, was released in September 2004.
7 See <http://www.mail-abuse.com/>.
8 Dow Jones & Company Inc. v Gutnick [2002] 194 ALR 433; see also Brian Fitzgerald, 'Dow Jones & Co v Gutnick. Negotiating "American Legal Hegemony" in the Transnational World of Cyberspace', *Melbourne University Law Review*, 27:2 (2003), 590.
9 SriMedia, '*Dow Jones v Gutnick*: Australian Court on a very slippery slope to totalitarianism?' at <http://www.srimedia.com/artman/publish/article_317.shtml>.
10 Felicity Barringer, 'Internet Makes Dow Jones Open to Suit in Australia', *New York Times*, 11 December 2002. For an interesting alternative view see Michael Geist, 'In Web disputes, U.S. law rules the world', *Toronto Star*, 24 February 2003.
11 For a history of the global regulation of the domain name system see Milton Mueller, *Ruling the Root: internet governance and the taming of cyberspace* (Cambridge, Mass.; London: MIT Press, 2002).
12 For a critical overview of the history of its democratic processes see Dan Hunter, 'ICANN and the concept of Democratic Deficit', *Loyola of Los Angeles Law Review*, 36 (2003), 1149.
13 ICANN, 'Staff Manager's Issues Report on Privacy Issues Related to Whois', 13 May 2003 at <http://www.icann.org/gnso/issue-reports/whois-privacy-report-13may03.htm>.
14 Interestingly there was no mention of IETF's work – perhaps reflecting a bureaucratic political concern about how to relate to expertise provided by an 'open' body, where information is provided by a self-selecting community of peers rather than by experts who are formally appointed.
15 Geert Lovink, *My First Recession. Critical Internet Culture in Transition* (Rotterdam: V2 Publications, 2003). See also Geert Lovink, *Dark Fiber. Tracking Critical Internet Culture* (Cambridge, Mass.; London: MIT Press, 2002).

16 Ibid., 10.
17 See David Silver, 'Looking Backwards, Looking Forwards: Cyberculture Studies, 1990–2000', in David Gauntlett (ed.), *web.studies* (London: Arnold, 2000), 19–30.
18 Foucault was not the only influence on new critical studies in law. For an American perspective where cultural studies influence was perhaps strongest, see generally Rosemary Coombe, 'Contingent Articulations: A Critical Cultural Studies of Law', in Austin Sarat and Jonathon Simon (eds), *Law in the Domains of Culture* (Ann Arbor: University of Michigan Press, 1998), 21–64.
19 Michel Foucault, *Discipline and Punish: The Birth of the Prison*, trans. Alan Sheridan (New York: Pantheon Books, 1977), 194.
20 See Alan Hunt and Gary Wickham, *Foucault and Law: Towards a New Sociology of Law as Governance* (London; Boulder, Colo: Pluto, 1994).
21 Ibid. Also Brendan Edgeworth, *Law, Modernity, Postmodernity* (Aldershot: Ashgate, 2003), 207–223.
22 Austin Sarat and Jonathon Simon, 'Cultural Analysis, Cultural Studies, and the Situation of Legal Scholarship', in Austin Sarat and Jonathon Simon (eds), *Cultural Analysis, Cultural Studies, and the Law: Moving beyond Legal Realism* (Durham: Duke University Press, 2003), 9.
23 With respect to intellectual property analysis of a cultural kind, the most influential works are those of Rosemary Coombe, *The Cultural Life of Intellectual Properties: Authorship, Appropriation and the Law* (Durham; London: Duke University Press, 1998) and Jane Gaines, *Contested Culture. The Image, The Voice and The Law* (Chapel Hill; London: University of North Carolina Press, 1991).
24 Sarat and Simon, 'Cultural Analysis', 13.
25 Maureen Cain, 'The Symbol Traders', in Maureen Cain and Christine Harrington (eds), *Lawyers in a Postmodern World: Translation and Transgression* (Buckingham: Open University Press, 1994), 39.
26 Sarat and Simon, 'Cultural Analysis', 4.
27 Naomi Mezey, 'Law as Culture', in Austin Sarat and Jonathon Simon (eds), *Cultural Analysis, Cultural Studies, and the Law: Moving beyond Legal Realism* (Durham: Duke University Press, 2003), 37.
28 Coombe, 'Contingent Articulations', 21.
29 Ibid.
30 This is the subtitle of the book by Sarat and Simon, *Cultural Analysis*.
31 Lawrence Lessig, *Code and other laws of cyberspace* (New York: Basic Books, 1999), 6.
32 See also Lawrence Lessig, *The Future of Ideas: the fate of the commons in a connected world* (New York: Random House, 2001).
33 The notion of 'internet community' is taken up in the following chapter.
34 Coombe, 'Contingent Articulations', 32.

2 Defining internet cultures

1 Gilles Deleuze and Felix Guattari, *A Thousand Plateaus. Capitalism and Schizophrenia*, trans. Brian Massumi (London: Athlone Press, 1988).
2 For an overview of globalisation literature generally see David Held and Anthony McGrew, 'The Great Globalisation Debate: An introduction', in David Held and Anthony McGrew (eds), *The global transformations reader: an introduction to the*

globalization debate (Malden, Mass.: Polity Press, 2000), 1–45. See also David Harvey, *The Condition of Postmodernity. An Enquiry into the Origins of Cultural Change* (Oxford; Cambridge, Mass.: Blackwell, 1990); John Bird et al. (eds), *Mapping the Future. Local cultures, global change* (London; New York: Routledge, 1993); John Urry, 'Inhuman globalisation', in his *Sociology beyond Societies. Mobilities for the twenty-first century* (London: Routledge, 2000), 12–18.

3 Denis Wood, *The Power of Maps* (New York: Guilford Press, 1992), 7.

4 For a reflection on the relation between modern imperialism and the new form of Empire, described in terms of dispersed network power without a grounded territorial base, and challenging the ability of nation states to shape events, see Michael Hardt and Antonio Negri, *Empire* (Cambridge, Mass.; London: Harvard University Press, 2000).

5 Jean-François Lyotard, *The Postmodern Condition: A Report on Knowledge*, trans. Geoffrey Bennington and Brian Massumi (Manchester: Manchester University Press, 1984), 15.

6 For example, Luce Irigaray, *This sex which is not one*, trans. Catherine Porter (Ithaca, N.Y.: Cornell University Press, 1985); Judith Butler, *Gender Trouble. Feminism and the Subversion of Identity* (New York: Routledge, 1990); Trinh Minh-ha, *Woman, Native, Other* (Bloomington: Indiana University Press, 1989).

7 See Clifford Geertz, *Local Knowledge: Further Essays in Interpretative Anthropology* (New York: Basic Books, 1983); Bill Ashcroft, Gareth Griffiths and Helen Tiffin (eds), *The Post-Colonial Studies Reader* (New York: Routledge, 1995).

8 He goes on to cite the following passage: 'It is obvious that "man" holds the majority, even if he is less numerous than mosquitoes, children, women, blacks, peasants, homosexuals etc. That is because he appears twice, once in the constant and again in the variable from which the constant is extracted. Majority assumes a state of power and domination, not the other way around.' (Deleuze and Guattari, *A Thousand Plateaus*, 291), in Paul Patton, *Deleuze and the Political* (London; New York: Routledge, 2000), 47.

9 The authority of the speaker's voice is explored in Michel Foucault, 'What is an author?', in J. V. Harari (ed.), *Textual Strategies: Perspectives in Poststructuralist Criticism* (Ithaca, N.Y.: Cornell University Press, 1979), 141, and Roland Barthes, *Image-Music-Text*, trans. Stephen Heath (New York: Noonday Press, 1988).

10 Samuel R. Smith, 'Postmodernism is Dead. Now what? Distributed Culture and the Rise of the Network Age', *Intelligent Agent*, 1 (2003), 1.

11 The world wide web (http) is perhaps the best known manifestation of the internet, but there are also DNS, ftp, telnet, email, smpt etc.

12 For example, David Held and Anthony McGrew write: 'the constraints of social time and geographical space, vital coordinates of modern social life, no longer appear to impose fixed barriers to many forms of social interaction or organization, as the existence of the World Wide Web and round the clock trading in global financial markets attests', 'The Great Globalisation Debate', 3.

13 For example, Arjun Appadurai, 'Disjuncture and Difference in the Global Cultural Economy', in David Held and Anthony McGrew (eds), *The global transformations reader: an introduction to the globalization debate* (Malden, Mass.: Polity Press, 2000), 230. The concept has been appropriated and transformed from that developed by Benedict Anderson in his *Imagined Communities. Reflections on the origin and the spread of nationalism* (London: Verso, 1983).

14 Ibid., 231.
15 See, for example, the way identity is represented in the collection by David Bell and Barbara M. Kennedy (eds), *The Cybercultures Reader* (New York: Routledge, 2000); Marc Smith and Peter Kollock (eds), *Communities in Cyberspace* (New York: Routledge, 1999). See also Paulina Borsook, *Cyberselfish: A Critical Romp through the Terribly Libertarian Culture of High Tech* (New York: Public Affairs, 2000).
16 John Friedman, *The Monstrous Races in Medieval Art and Thought* (Cambridge, Mass.: Harvard University Press, 1981), 12.
17 Ibid., 25.
18 '22. How men know through the idol if sick men will die or not; of the people of different shapes, and very ugly; and of the monks who give their alms to baboons, monkeys and marmosets', in *The Travels of Sir John Mandeville*, trans. C. W. R. D. Moseley (New York: Penguin, 1983), 137.
19 Moseley, 'Introduction', in *The Travels*, 14.
20 Ibid., 9–39.
21 Stephen Greenblatt, *Marvelous Possessions, The Wonder of the New World* (Chicago: University of Chicago Press, 1991), 26–51.
22 Robert Appelbaum, 'Anti-geography', *Early Modern Literary Studies* 4:2 Special Issue 3 (1998), 12.1–17. See <http://www.shu.ac.uk/emls/04-2/appeanti.htm>.
23 Sebastian I. Sobecki, 'Mandeville's Thought of the Limit: The Discourse of Similarity and Difference in *The Travels of Sir John Mandeville*', *The Review of English Studies*, New Series 53 (211) (2002), 330.
24 Moseley, 'Introduction', *The Travels*, 16–17. See also Mary Campbell, '"That othere half". Mandeville Naturalizes the East', in her *The Witness and The Other World. Exotic European Travel Writing, 400–1600* (Ithaca: Cornell University Press, 1988), 158–159.
25 Greenblatt, *Marvelous Possessions*, 34–35.
26 The Second (1598) Edition of Hakluyt's *Principal Navigations* dropped all of the material he had previously published in 1587 from Mandeville's *Travels*. See Appelbaum, 'Anti-geography', 6; and Greenblatt, *Marvelous Possessions*, 30ff.
27 Giles Milton, *The Riddle and the Knight. In search of Sir John Mandeville* (London: Sceptre, 2001), 57.
28 Moseley, 'Introduction', in *The Travels*, 29.
29 Gustav Jahoda, *Images of Savages. Ancient Roots of modern prejudice in western culture* (London; New York: Routledge, 1999).
30 Italo Calvino, *If on a Winter's Night a Traveller*, trans. William Weaver (London: Picador, 1982), 11–12.
31 Ibid., 166.
32 For example, John C. Dvorak, 'Flawed Thinking And Dot-Com Death', *Forbes.com*, 13 November 2000; Philip J. Kaplan, *F'd Companies, Spectacular Dot Com Flameouts* (New York: Simon & Schuster, 2002); Geert Lovink, 'Anatomy of Dotcom mania: overview of recent literature', in his *My First Recession. Critical Internet Culture in Transition* (Rotterdam: V2 Publications, 2003), 56–85.
33 Department of Communications and Information Technology and the Arts, *An overview of the Australian ICT Industry and Innovation Base* (Commonwealth of Australia, 2003), 4.
34 For a sophisticated analysis see John Braithwaite and Peter Drahos, *Global Business Regulation* (Cambridge: Cambridge University Press, 2000). For a more

simplistic analysis see the 'Foreign Policy Globalisation Index' at <http://www.foreignpolicy.com/wwwboard/g-index.php>.

35 R. W. McChesney, *Rich Media, Poor Democracy: Communication Politics in Dubious Times* (Urbana: University of Illinois Press, 1999).

36 See, for example, Screen Producers Association Of Australia, 'A Submission To The Intellectual Property & Competition Review Committee', Intellectual Property Review Committee, Interim Report, June 2000.

37 For a good overview of these issues see Diana Crane, 'Culture and Globalisation', in Diana Crane, Noboko Kawashima and Ken'ichi Kawasaka (eds), *Global Culture. Media, Arts, Policy and Globalisation* (New York; London: Routledge, 2001), 1–25.

38 John Cassidy, *Dot con: The real story of why the internet bubble burst* (New York: Harper Collins, 2002), 174ff.

39 This is discussed in Howard Kurtz, 'Who Blew the Dot-Com Bubble? The Cautionary Tale of Henry Blodget', *Washington Post*, 12 March 2001, C01.

40 Standard Schaefer, 'Tech Bubble: Who Benefited?: An Interview with Michael Hudson', *CounterPunch*, August 30 2003 at <http://www.counterpunch.org/schaefer08302003.html>.

41 Cassidy, *Dot con*, 268ff.

42 Ibid., 327–328.

43 Ibid., 246–248.

44 Carlotta Mast, 'Living Through the Death of a Dot-Com', *Business Week Online*, 13 December 2000.

45 Cassidy, *Dot con*, 320.

46 See, for example, Jim Puplava's *Financial Sense Newsletter*, 'Trains, Planes and Dot coms revisited . . . the end of an era', 20 December 2000 at <http://www.financialsense.com/newsletter/revisited.htm>.

47 Framework for the Future Steering Committee, 'Enabling our Future: A Framework for the information and communications technology industry' (Commonwealth of Australia: Department of Communications and Information Technology and the Arts, 2003), 20.

48 David Mitsuo Nixon, 'The Matrix Possibility', in William Irwin (ed.), *The Matrix and Philosophy: Welcome to the Desert of the Real* (Chicago: Open Court, 2002), 36.

49 See 'Inhuman flows', Chapter 7, 176.

50 Guy Debord, 'Comments on the Society of the Spectacle' (1988), trans. Malcolm Imrie at <http://www.notbored.org/commentaires.html>.

3 Universal standards and the end of the universe

1 Arthur C. Clarke, 'The Nine Billion Names of God', republished in Alberto Manguel (ed.), *White Fire: Further Fantastic Literature* (London: Picador, 1990), 920–927.

2 Milton Mueller in Geert Lovink, 'Interview with Milton Mueller', *<nettime>*, 25 November 2003.

3 These are explored in a volume dedicated to internet governance, *Loyola of Los Angeles Law Review*, 36 (2003).

4 ICANN is at <http://www.icann.org>. For the pre-history see Milton Mueller, *Ruling the Root, Internet Governance and the Taming of Cyberspace* (Cambridge, Mass.: MIT Press, 2002), 74–103.

5 Mueller, in Lovink, 'Interview', 7–8.

6 See Chapter 2, 41.

7 Only a few remain today. See Irational.org Trade Mark club at <http://www.irational.org/tm/clubcard/>.

8 <http://www.icannwatch.org>.

9 <http://www.ideography.co.uk/wsis-focus/index.html/>.

10 World Summit on the Information Society, 'Basic Information: About WSIS', at <http://www.itu.int/wsis/basic/about.html>.

11 <http://www.itu.int/wsis/geneva/index.html>.

12 See Chapter 7, WSIS: What to expect?, 181.

13 See Chapter 1, 16.

14 'Internet History: Important People' at <http://www.unc.edu/depts/jomc/academics/dri/pioneers2c.html>.

15 <http://www.ibiblio.org/pioneers/cerf.html>.

16 See 'All about the Internet Society: In memory of internet pioneer. Jon Postel' at <http://www.isoc.org/postel/index.shtml>; RFC 2468, 'I remember IANA' at <http://www.faqs.org/rfcs/rfc2468.html>.

17 <http://www.w3.org/History.html>.

18 This is noted in passing in Bruno Latour, 'Technology is society made durable', trans. Gabrielle Hecht, in John Law (ed.), *A Sociology of Monsters: Essays on power, technology and domination* (New York: Routledge, 1991), 111.

19 Peter Galison, 'The Collective Author', in Mario Biagioli and Peter Galison (eds), *Scientific Authorship. Credit and Intellectual Property in Science* (New York; London: Routledge, 2003), 325.

20 Ibid., 351.

21 Ibid., 352.

22 Ibid., 353.

23 See also Mario Biagioli, 'Aporias of Scientific Authorship. Credit and Responsibility in Contemporary Biomedicine' in Mario Biagioli (ed.), *The science studies reader* (New York: Routledge, 1999), 12.

24 IETF Credo, attributed to David Clark, in Gary Kessler, 'IETF – History, Background, and Role in Today's Internet' (1996) at <http://www.garykessler.net/library/ietf_hx.html>, 5.

25 Vint Cerf, 'IETF and ISOC' (1995) at <http://www.isoc.org/isoc/related/ietf>.

26 RFC 3160 'The Tao of IETF' at <http://www.ietf.org/tao.html>.

27 Ibid.

28 Michael Froomkin, 'Habermas @ Discourse.Net: Toward a Critical Theory of Cyberspace', *Harvard Law Review*, 116 (2003), 749 at 787–788.

29 Ibid., 786–793.

30 See, for example, RFC 1000, Chapter 1, 1.

31 Patricia Owen, 'Hannah Arendt and the Public Sphere: Model for a Global Public?', Conference Paper, International Studies Association Conference, New Orleans, 24–27 March 2002 at <http://www.isanet.org/noarchive/Owens.html>.

32 Froomkin, 'Habermas', 803–804.

33 For a concise description of Foucault's concept of biopolitics see <http://www.generation-online.org/c/cbiopolitics.htm>.

34 Pierre Bourdieu, 'The Specificity of the Scientific Field and the Social Conditions of the Progress of Reason', in Mario Biagioli (ed.), *The science studies reader* (New York: Routledge, 1999), 31.

35 Ibid., 35.
36 See Chapter 1, 12.
37 Hannah Arendt, *The Human Condition* (Chicago: University of Chicago Press, 1958). See also Owen, 'Hannah Arendt'.
38 Nancy Fraser, 'Rethinking the Public Sphere', in her *Justice interruptus: Critical reflections on the 'postsocial' condition* (New York: Routledge, 1997), 70.
39 RFC 3271 in Froomkin, 'Habermas', 811.
40 Ibid., 810.
41 Ibid., 811.
42 Owen, 'Hannah Arendt'.
43 See also Fraser, 'Rethinking the Public Sphere', 76.
44 Ibid., 80.
45 See Chapter 2, 24. Also Seyla Benhabib, *The reluctant modernism of Hannah Arendt* (Lanham, Md.: Rowman & Littlefield, 2000), 200.
46 Fraser, 'Rethinking the Public Sphere', 86.
47 's51. The Parliament shall, subject to this Constitution, have power to make laws for the peace, order, and good government of the Commonwealth with respect to:-(xviii) Copyrights, patents of inventions and designs, and trade marks.'
48 See Chapter 7, 186.
49 See, for example, Keith Aoki, 'Considering Multiple and Overlapping Sovereignties: Liberalism, Libertarianism, National Sovereignty, "Global" Intellectual Property and the Internet', *Indiana Journal of Global Legal Studies*, 5 (1998), 443; Doris Estelle Long, '"Democratising Globalisation": Practising the Policies of Cultural Inclusion', *Cardozo Journal of International Law*, 10 (2002), 217; Michael Ryan, *Knowledge Diplomacy. Global competition and the politics of intellectual property* (Washington, DC: Brookings Institution Press, 1998); Susan K. Sell, *Private Power, Public Law, The Globalization of Intellectual Property Rights* (Cambridge: Cambridge University Press, 2003); Shelley Wright, *International Human Rights, Decolonisation and Globalisation: Becoming Human* (London; New York: Routledge, 2001).
50 This was not historically the case, see George Armstrong, 'From the Fetishism of Commodities to the Regulated Market: The Rise and Decline of Property', *Northwestern University Law Review*, 82 (1987), 79.
51 See, for example, in relation to patenting life-forms, David Kell, 'The Furore over the patenting of Animals: Animal Legal Defense Fund v Quigg', *European Intellectual Property Review*, 8 (1992), 279.
52 See generally Peter Drahos and Ruth Mayne (eds), *Global Intellectual Property Rights* (Basingstoke: Palgrave Macmillan, 2002); Christopher May, 'Why IPRS are a Global Political Issue', *European Intellectual Property Review*, 25:1 (2003), 1; Seth Shulman, *Owning the Future* (Boston: Houghton Mifflin, 1999).
53 Tim Berners-Lee, 'Patent Policy Working Group Face-to-Face Meeting Summary, 15–17 October 2001, Cupertino, CA USA' at <http://www.w3.org/2001/10/ppwg-cupertino-ftf-summary.html>.
54 IETF Intellectual Property Rights Notices at <http://www.ietf.org/ipr.html>; see also IETF Internet Draft: Guidelines for Working Groups on Intellectual Property Issues, Scott Brim, 11-Jun-03. <http://www.ietf.org/internet-drafts/draft-ietf-ipr-wg-guidelines-05.txt>; IETF Internet Draft: Intellectual Property Rights in IETF Technology, Scott Bradner, <21-Oct-03. http://www.ietf.org/internet-drafts/draft-ietf-ipr-technology-rights-12.txt>; IETF Internet Draft: IETF Rights

in Contributions, Scott Bradner, 21-Oct-03; <http://www.ietf.org/internet-drafts/draft-ietf-ipr-submission-rights-08.txt>.

55 IETF Internet Draft: Guidelines for Working Groups on Intellectual Property Issues, Scott Brim, 11-Jun-03.

56 For a critical view of RAND licensing, see generally 'Patents and Open Standards', *Cover Pages: Online Resource for markup language technologies* at <http://xml.coverpages.org/patents.html#RAND>.

57 Competition reviews of intellectual property are becoming more common. See US Federal Trade Commission, *To Promote Innovation: The Proper Balance of Competition and Patent Law and Policy*, October 2003 at <http://www.ftc.gov/os/2003/10/innovationrpt.pdf>; also see coverpages.org: 'US Federal Trade Commission Report Calls for Patent Law and Policy Reform' at <http://xml.coverpages.org/ni2003-11-11-a.html>; in the Australian context see *Intellectual Property Competition Review* Australia, 2000 at <http:www.ipcr.gov.au>.

58 For practical guidelines for working groups in this context, see IETF Internet Draft: Guidelines for Working Groups on Intellectual Property Issues, Scott Brim, 11-Jun-03.

59 IETF Internet Draft: Intellectual Property Rights in IETF Technology, Scott Bradner, 21-Oct-03.

60 Eolas stands for Embedded Objects Linked Across Systems and the company claims the word is also the Gaelic word for knowledge, though perhaps the usual meaning is not in the context of asserting private ownership of knowledge? *Eolas Technologies, Inc. And The Regents Of The University Of California v. Microsoft Corporation* N.D. Ill. 11 August 2003 U.S. Dist. LEXIS 13482.

61 The fragility of digital data is explored in Brian Bergeron, *Dark Ages II. When the Digital Data Die* (Upper Saddle River, NJ: Prentice Hall PTR, 2002).

62 Letter from Tim Berners-Lee (W3C) to James E. Rogan (USPTO) at <http://www.w3.org/2003/10/27-rogan.html>.

63 See, for example, coverpages.org: 'W3C Presents Prior Art Filing to USPTO and Urges Removal of Eolas Patent' at <http://xml.coverpages.org/ni2003-10-28-b.html#reexam>.

4   Linux is a registered trademark of Linus Torvalds

* Thanks to Martin Hardie for our discussions about the free software movement.

1 George Orwell, *Nineteen Eighty Four* (Harmondsworth: Penguin, 1974 edition), 47.

2 Ibid., 45.

3 Ibid., 199.

4 The concept of personal detachment in contract is critically explored in Anthony Bellia, 'Promises, Trust, And Contract Law', *American Journal of Jurisprudence*, 47 (2002), 25–40 at 29. See also Dori Kimel, 'Neutrality, Autonomy, and Freedom of Contract', *Oxford Journal of Legal Studies*, 21 (2001), 473–494 at 490–491.

5 <http://www.opensource.org>.

6 Whatis.com provides the following definition: 'The kernel is the essential center of a computer operating system, the core that provides basic services for all other parts of the operating system. A synonym is nucleus. A kernel can be contrasted with a shell, the outermost part of an operating system that interacts with user commands. Kernel and shell are terms used more frequently in Unix operating systems than

in IBM mainframe or Microsoft Windows systems.' At <http://whatis.techtarget. com/definition/0,289893,sid9_gci212439,00.html>.

7   For a history of its development see <http://en.wikipedia.org/wiki/Linux_kernel>. See also Eric S. Raymond, 'The Cathedral and the Bazaar' at <http://www. firstmonday.org/issues/issue3_3/raymond/>.

8   Gary Rivlin, 'Leader of the Free World', *Wired*, 11 (11) (2003) at <http://www.wired. com/wired/archive/11.11/linus.html>.

9   See <http://opensource.org/trademarks/>.

10 See <http://creativecommmons.org>.

11 <http://www.ggpl.org/>.

12 Richard Stallman, 'Why "Free Software" is better than "Open Source"', in Joshua Gay (ed.), *Free Software, Free Society: selected essays of Richard Stallman* (Boston: GNU Press, 2002), 55. Also at <http://www.gnu.org/philosophy/free-software-for-freedom.html>.

13 Ibid., 57.

14 Joanne Richardson, 'Free Software & GPL Society. Stefan Merten of Oekonux interview' at <http://subsol.c3.hu/subsol_2/contributors0/mertentext.html>. See also Martin Hardie, 'Floss and the Crisis? Foreigner in a Free Land', *Sarai Reader 2004: Crisis/Media*, 384–397; J. J. King, 'The Packet Gang: Openness and its Discontents', *Mute*, 27 (2004), 80.

15 See, for example, Rishab Aiyer Ghosh, 'Clustering and dependencies in free/open source software development: Methodology and tools', *First Monday*, 8 (4) (2003) at <http://firstmonday.org/issues/issue8_4/ghosh/index.html>; David Lancashire, 'Code, Culture and Clash. The Fading Altruism of open source development', *First Monday*, 6 (12) (2001) at <http://firstmonday.org/issues/issue6_12/lancashire/ index.html>.

16 Gilberto Camara, 'Open Source Software Production: Fact & Fiction', *Mute*, 27 (2004), 74.

17 In part this work could be interpreted as an empirical response to Eric Raymond's influential piece 'The Cathedral and the Bazaar'. In this paper the greatness of the open source way is explained as that there is no unidirectional forward planning by committee as is the case with the development of the mega proprietary corporations. There are several versions of this text. See Eric Raymond, 'The Cathedral and the Bazaar' (Beijing; Cambridge, Mass.: O'Reilly, 2001); *First Monday*, 3 (3) (1998) at <http://www.firstmonday.dk/issues/issue3_3/raymond/>; <http://www.catb.org/ ~esr/writings/cathedral-bazaar/>.

18 Richard Gabriel and Ron Goldman (Sun Microsystems), 'Open source: Beyond the Fairytales', 17 September 2002 at <http://opensource.mit.edu/ papers/gabrielgoldman.pdf>; See also Simon Phipps, 'Free speech, free beer and free software', *CNET*, 20 August 2002 at <http://news.com.com/2010-1071-954384. html>.

19 <http://zdnet.com.com/2100-1104_2-5157655.html>.

20 Eric S. Raymond, 'Open letter to Sun: Let Java Go', 12 February 2004 at <http://www. catb.org/~esr/writings/let-java-go.html>; see also Eric S. Raymond, 'Let Java Go, Round 2', 19 February 2004 at <http://www.catb.org/esr/writings/let-java-go-2.html>.

21 'Sun's Simon Phipps Answers ESR's Call to Open Source Java: Doesn't Hold Water', O'Reilly's OSDir.com, http://news.osdir.com/article451.html

22 Eric S. Raymond, 'Let Java Go, Round 2', 19 February 2004 at <http://www.catb.org/esr/writings/let-java-go-2.html>.

23 The concept of 'Other' is briefly discussed in Chapter 2, 25.

24 Mike Ricciuti, 'Open source: Rebels at the gate', *CNET News.com* 14 October 2002 at <http://news.com.com/2009-1001-961354.html>.

25 This is acknowledged in a set of documents leaked from Microsoft in October 1998, about Redmond's strategy against Linux and Open Source software, called the 'Halloween documents'. See <http://www.opensource.org/halloween/>.

26 The signatories were Richard Stallman, Free Software Foundation; Eric Raymond, Open Source Initiative; Linus Torvalds, Creator of the Linux Kernel; Miguel de Icaza, GNOME GUI Desktop Project; Larry Wall, Creator of the Perl Language; Guido van Rossum, Creator of the Python Language; Tim O'Reilly, Publisher; Bob Young, Co-Founder, Red Hat; Larry Augustin, CEO, VA Linux Systems. See Bruce Perens, 'Free Software Leaders Stand Together' at <http://perens.com/Articles/StandTogether.html>.

27 Toni Solo, 'Misery and Intellectual Property Rights Trashing Free Software', *CounterPunch.com* 10 October 2003 at <http://www.counterpunch.org/solo10102003.html>.

28 Jonathan Krim, 'The Quiet War Over Open-Source', *Washington Post*, 21 August 2003 at <http://www.washingtonpost.com/ac2/wp-dyn/A23422-2003Aug20>.

29 Peter Galli, 'SCO Group Launches Broadside Against GPL', *EWeek*, 4 December 2003 at <http://www.eweek.com/article2/0,1759,1404303,00.asp>; Matt Hicks, 'SCO Goes to Washington in Linux Battle', *EWeek*, 21 January 2004 at <http://www.eweek.com/article2/0,4149,1455175,00.asp>.

30 Steve Lohr, 'Microsoft Said to Encourage Big Investment in SCO Group', *New York Times*, 12 March 2004; Keith Regan, 'Leaked E-Mail Fuels Microsoft-SCO Conspiracy Theories', *Linux News*, 20 March 2004 at <http://www.linuxinsider.com/perl/story/33051.html>. Public speculation about Microsoft conspiracies is discussed further in Chapter 5.

31 E.g. Lawrence Lessig, *The Future of Ideas* (New York: Random House, 2001); Lawrence Lessig, *Free Culture: How Big Media Uses Technology and the Law to Lock Down Culture and Control Creativity* (New York: Penguin, 2004); Jessica Litman, *Digital Copyright* (Amherst, NY: Prometheus Books, 2001).

32 <http://www.debian.org/social_contract.html>.

33 John Gava and Janey Greene, 'Do We Need A Hybrid Law Of Contract? Why Hugh Collins Is Wrong And Why It Matters' (*Cambridge Law Journal*, 63 (3) (2004) 605–31); Hugh Collins, *Regulating Contracts* (Oxford; New York: Oxford University Press, 1999).

34 Interview, Eben Moglen, 3 March 2004.

35 The proprietary movement itself has acknowledged the customer relations problems and business costs associated with compliance with licenses. For example, Microsoft trialled selling software by subscription in Australia, New Zealand and Brazil but reportedly abandoned the scheme because of customer confusion and concern about what the scheme entailed. Microsoft marketing managers have also acknowledged that other licenses have been too complex and difficult for their customers to engage every time they want to upgrade. See Ian Grayson, Tessa Denton and Simon Hayes, 'License to bill: Microsoft plan row', *The Australian IT* , 2 July 2002; Bill Bennett, 'Trial period over', *The Age*, 19 November 2002, at <http://www.theage.com.au/articles/2002/11/19/1037490107674.html> and Adam

Turner, 'Time Bombs Ticking in the Cupboard', *The Age* 3 June, 2003 at <http://www.theage.com.au/articles/2003/06/02/1054406119566.html>.

36 This is discussed in Roger Cotterrell, 'Trusting in Law', *Current Legal Problems*, 46 (2) (1993), 75–95.

37 Ibid., 78.

38 This is in relation to indigenous property claims, see *Bulun Bulun v. R & T Textiles Pty Ltd* [1998] 41 IPR 513. Also Kathy Bowrey, 'The Outer Limits Of Copyright Law – Where Law Meets Philosophy and Culture', *Law and Critique*, 12 (1) (2001), 1–24.

39 This is discussed in Chapter 3 of Brad Sherman and Lionel Bently, *The Making of Modern Intellectual Property* (Cambridge: Cambridge University Press, 1999).

40 Quoted in Matthew Rimmer, 'The dead poets society: the copyright term extension and the public domain', *First Monday*, 8 (6) (2003), n 17.

41 See Alain Pottage, 'Instituting Property', *Oxford Journal of Legal Studies*, 18 (1988), 331–344, especially 338.

42 Cotterrell, 'Trusting in Law', 81.

43 See Pottage, 'Instituting Property'.

44 I am grateful to Valerie Kerruish for these points.

45 Interview, Eben Moglen, 3 March 2004.

46 *Eldred v Ashcroft* (2003) 123 S. Ct. 769.

47 *Eldred v Ashcroft* (2003) 123 S. Ct. 769, 785.

48 *Eldred v Ashcroft* (2003) 123 S. Ct. 769, 786.

49 *Eldred v Ashcroft* (2003) 123 S. Ct. 769, 786. Notes omitted.

50 This is discussed further in Kathy Bowrey and Matthew Rimmer, 'Rip, Mix, Burn, Rip, Mix, Burn: The Politics of Peer to Peer', *First Monday*, 7 (8) (2002) at 'A Different Kind of Politics'; with the argument extended in relation to the Eldred case in Matthew Rimmer, 'The dead poets society: the copyright term extension and the public domain', *First Monday*, 8 (6) (2003).

51 Lawrence Lessig, 'The Architecture of Innovation', *Duke Law Journal*, 51 (2002), 1788.

52 Michael Hardt and Antonio Negri, *Empire* (Cambridge, Mass.; London: Harvard University Press, 2000), 302.

5   In a world without fences who needs Gates?

1 Mark Stefik, *Internet Dreams. Archetypes, Myths and Metaphors* (Cambridge, Mass.; London: MIT Press, 1996), xxii.

2 Ibid., 176.

3 Ibid., 177.

4 Italo Calvino, 'The Argentine Ant', trans. Archibald Colquhoun, in Alberto Manguel (ed.), *Black Water. The Anthology of Fantastic Literature* (London: Picador, 1983), 440–469.

5 Ibid., 460.

6 Ibid., 461.

7 Satirewire.com, 'It's Official: Everybody Hates Microsoft' (2000) at <http://www.satirewire.com/news/0008/satire-microsofthated.shtml>.

8 *Forbes Magazine* Lists. See <http://www.forbes.com/lists/>.

9 There are many books from journalists and economists dealing with the Microsoft antitrust litigation. See for example, Ken Auletta, *World War 3.0. Microsoft and*

its enemies (New York: Random House, 2000); John Heilemann, *Pride Before the Fall. The Trial of Bill Gates and the end of the Microsoft era* (New York: Perennial, 2002); Stan Liebowitz and Stephen Margolis, *Winners, Losers and Microsoft. Competition and AntiTrust in High Technology* (Oakland, CA: Independent Institute, 2001).

10 Bill Gates, *The Road Ahead* (London; New York: Penguin, 1996), 6.

11 Bill Gates, *Business @ the Speed of Thought* (London; New York: Penguin, 1999), xx.

12 See Chapter 2, 26.

13 See David Silver, 'Looking Backwards, Looking Forwards, Cyberculture Studies, 1990–2000', in David Gauntlett (ed.), *web.studies* (Arnold, 2000), 19–30; Richard Barbrook and Andy Cameron, 'The Californian Ideology', *Mute* 3, Autumn 1995 available at <http://www.hrc.wmin.ac.uk/theory-californianideology.html>.

14 Gates, *The Road Ahead*, 181.

15 Ibid., 207.

16 Bill Gates, Statement to Committee on the Judiciary, US Senate 3 March 1998.

17 See 'Moore's law' at <http://whatis.techtarget.com/definition/0,,sid9_gci212591,00. html>; *Scientific American Interview: Gordon E. Moore,* September 1997 at <http:// www.sciam.com/interview/moore/092297moore1.html>.

18 He calls this the 'Company's stark rallying cry.' Bill Gates, Statement to Committee on the Judiciary, US Senate 3 March 1998.

19 Gates, *The Road Ahead*, 321.

20 Gates, *Business @ the Speed of Thought*, 185.

21 Heilemann, *Pride Before the Fall*, 63.

22 James Boyle, 'Missing the point on Microsoft', *Salon.com* 7 April 2000 at <http://dir.salon.com/tech/feature/2000/04/07/greenspan/index.html>.

23 Gates, *Business @ the Speed of Thought*, 43.

24 Rachel Burstein, 'Overseas Invasion', *Mother Jones,* January/February 1998 at <http://www.motherjones.com/news/feature/1998/01/burstein.html>.

25 See Chapter 4, 82–3.

26 James Fallow, 'Inside the Leviathan', *The Atlantic Monthly,* February 2000. Available at <http://www.theatlantic.com/issues/2000/02/002/fallows.htm>.

27 See, for example, KMFMS, 'What's So Bad About Microsoft?' available at <http://www.kmfms.com/whatsbad.html>.

28 See, for example, Dan Schiller, 'Brought to you by . . .', in *Digital Capitalism. Networking the Global Market System* (Cambridge, Mass.; London: MIT Press, 1999); Andrew L. Shapiro, 'Where Do You Want To Go Today?', in *The Control Revolution How the Internet is Putting Individuals in Charge and Changing the World We Know* (New York: Public Affairs/The Century Foundation, 1999).

29 The Department of Justice had commenced an action against Microsoft for unlawfully maintaining a monopoly in its operating system in 1994, but a trial was avoided by the parties entering a consent decree. See *United States v Microsoft Corp* 56 F3d 1448 (DC Cir 1995). It was allegedly violating the provisions of the decree that initiated further inquiry and action by the Department of Justice in 1997/98.

30 See Donald Norman, *The Invisible Computer* (Cambridge, Mass.: MIT Press, 1998), 79.

31 Ibid. See also Geoffrey Moore, *Crossing the Chasm* (New York: Harper Business, 2002).

32 Liebowitz and Margolis, *Winners, Losers and Microsoft*, 4. See also Carl Shapiro and Hal Varian, *Information Rules* (Boston, Mass.: Harvard Business School Press, 1999), 103–104.

33 Ibid., 9. See also Shapiro & Varian, *Information Rules*, 183ff.

34 Norman, *The Invisible Computer*, 172.

35 This discussion focuses on the District Court 'Findings of Fact' and 'Conclusions of Law' by Justice Jackson, *United States v Microsoft Corp.* 84 F.Supp.2d 9 (DDC 1999); *United States v Microsoft Corp.* 87 F.Supp.2d 30 (DDC 2000) and the subsequent appeal, *United States v Microsoft Corp.* 253 F.3d 34 (DC Cir. 2001). For a fuller consideration of the many complicated legal actions and settlements see US Department of Justice: Microsoft case at <http://www.usdoj.gov/atr/cases/ms_index.htm>; and Microsoft Legal News at <http://www.microsoft.com/presspass/legalnews.asp>.

36 *United States v Microsoft Corp.* 84 F.Supp.2d 9, 20 (DDC 1999).

37 *United States v Microsoft Corp.* 84 F.Supp.2d 9, 21 (DDC 1999).

38 *United States v Microsoft Corp.* 84 F.Supp.2d 9, 26 (DDC 1999).

39 *United States v Microsoft Corp.* 84 F.Supp.2d 9, 43 (DDC 1999).

40 *United States v Microsoft Corp.* 84 F.Supp.2d 9, 29 (DDC 1999).

41 *United States v Microsoft Corp.* 84 F.Supp.2d 9, 31 (DDC 1999).

42 *United States v Microsoft Corp.* 84 F.Supp.2d 9, 32 (DDC 1999).

43 *United States v Microsoft Corp.* 84 F.Supp.2d 9, 33 (DDC 1999).

44 *United States v Microsoft Corp.* 84 F.Supp.2d 9, 33 (DDC 1999).

45 *United States v Microsoft Corp.* 84 F.Supp.2d 9, 45 (DDC 1999).

46 *United States v Microsoft Corp.* 84 F.Supp.2d 9, 48 (DDC 1999).

47 *United States v Microsoft Corp.* 84 F.Supp.2d 9, 49 (DDC 1999).

48 *United States v Microsoft Corp.* 84 F.Supp.2d 9, 50 (DDC 1999).

49 *United States v Microsoft Corp.* 84 F.Supp.2d 9, 52–3 (DDC 1999).

50 *United States v Microsoft Corp.* 84 F.Supp.2d 9, 81 (DDC 1999).

51 *United States v Microsoft Corp.* 84 F.Supp.2d 9, 85 (DDC 1999).

52 *United States v Microsoft Corp.* 84 F.Supp.2d 9, 101–2 (DDC 1999).

53 *United States v Microsoft Corp.* 87 F.Supp.2d 30, 38–9 (DDC 2000).

54 *United States v Microsoft Corp.* 87 F.Supp.2d 30, 40 (DDC 2000).

55 *United States v Microsoft Corp.* 87 F.Supp.2d 30, 41 (DDC 2000).

56 *United States v Microsoft Corp.* 87 F.Supp.2d 30, 44 (DDC 2000).

57 *United States v Microsoft Corp.* 97 F.Supp.2d 59 (DDC 2000).

58 *United States v Microsoft Corp.* 253 F.3d 34, 83 (DC Cir. 2001); 346 US App.DC 330, 379.

59 *United States v Microsoft Corp.* 253 F.3d 34, 90 (DC Cir. 2001); 346 US App.DC 330, 386.

60 *United States v Microsoft Corp.* 253 F.3d 34, 49 (DC Cir. 2001); 346 US App.DC 330, 345.

61 *United States v Microsoft Corp.* 253 F.3d 34, 49–50 (DC Cir. 2001); 346 USA pp.DC 330, 345–6.

62 *Copyright Act 1968* (Cth) s10(1).

63 *Data Access Corporation v Powerflex Services Pty Ltd* (1999) 45 IPR 353.

64 Liebowitz and Margolis, *Winners, Losers and Microsoft*, 255.

65 Ian Eagles and Louise Longdin, 'The Microsoft Appeal: Different Rules for Different Markets?', *New Zealand Business Law Quarterly*, 7, November 2001, 303.

66 See Chapter 2, 24; Chapter 7, 176–7.

67 See Chapter 2, 108.

68 John Seely Brown and Paul Duguid, *The Social Life of Information* (Cambridge, Mass.: Harvard Business School Press, 2000), 244.

69 *United States v Microsoft Corp.* 253 F.3d 34, 107–112 (DC Cir. 2001); 346 US App. DC 330, 403–8. Notes omitted.

70 *United States v Microsoft Corp.* 253 F.3d 34, 115 (DC Cir. 2001); 346 US App. DC 330, 411.

71 John Heilemann, 'Fear and Trembling in Silicon Valley', *Wired*, 8 (3) (2000).

72 The *Wired* magazine articles, 'Fear and Trembling in Silicon Valley' and 'The Truth, The Whole Truth, and Nothing But The Truth', *Wired*, 8 (11) (2000), were expanded to form the basis of Heilemann's book *Pride Before the Fall*.

73 Heilemann, 'Fear and Trembling in Silicon Valley'.

74 Final Judgment, *United States v Microsoft Corp.* CA No. 98–1232 (CKK), filed 12 November 2002 (DDC 2002).

75 Ronald Rotunda, 'Judicial Comments on Pending Cases: the Ethical Restrictions and the Sanctions. A Case Study of the Microsoft Litigation', *University of. Illinois Law Review*, 611 (2001), 621.

76 Final Judgment, *United States v Microsoft Corp.*, CA No. 98–1232 (CKK), filed 12 November 2002 (DDC 2002).

77 European Commission, 'Press Release: Commission concludes on Microsoft investigation', 24 March 2004.

78 Senator Bill Frist, 'Press Release: Frist Comments On European Union Ruling Against Microsoft', 24 March 2004.

79 'EU's ruling a blow to globalization', *Tucson Citizen*, 25 March 2004.

80 Islam Online.net. 'Anti-Globalization Forum Moots Alternative to WTO', 17 January 2004, available at <http://www.islamonline.net/English/News/2004-01/17/article06.shtml>. See also 'Anti globalization march brings Mumbai to a standstill', *The Guardian*, 21 January 2004 at <http://www.guardian.co.uk/globalisation/story/0,7369,1128030,00.html>.

81 Kaushik Basu, 'The politics of business outsourcing', 10 December 2003 available at <http://www.rediff.com/money/2003/dec/10guest2.htm>.

82 Schiller, 'Brought to you by . . .', 42.

83 Ibid., 208.

84 Ashok Deo Bardhan, Dwight Jaffee and Cynthia Kroll, *Globalization and a High-Tech Economy* (Boston; New York; Dordrecht: Kluwer, 2004), 57.

85 Ibid., 92.

86 Ibid., 108.

87 Ibid., 178.

88 Ibid., 179

89 Ibid., 180.

90 Ashok Deo Bardhan and Cynthia Kroll, 'Research Report: The New Wave of Outsourcing', Fisher Center for Real Estate and Urban Economics, University of California, Berkeley, Fall 2003, 2.

91 Peter Zvalo, 'Does Globalization Spell Trouble for Technical Writers?', *Business Word*, Fall 2001.

92 Naomi Klein, *No Logo. Taking Aim at the Brand Bullies* (New York: Picador, 1999), 250.

93 Kim Peterson, 'Microsoft workers vent over cuts in benefits', *Seattle Times*, 26 May 2004.

94 David Beckman, 'Is Microsoft Sending Core Development to India?', *WashTech News*, 15 June 2004.

95 Alorie Gilert, 'Protesters picket US outsourcing powwow', *ZDNet*, 17 September 2003.

96 'Shipping Out White-Collar Jobs', *The Christian Science Monitor*, 17 February 2004.

97 'New Study Documents Systematic Attempt by offshore Contractors to Target State Government Work', *WashTech News*, 14 July 2004.

98 See, for example, World Bank Research Report, *Globalisation, Growth and Poverty: Building an Inclusive World Economy* (New York: Oxford University Press, 2002).

99 Nick Couldry, 'The productive "consumer" and the dispersed "citizen"', *International Journal of Cultural Studies*, 7 (1) (2004), 21, 22.

6   Telling tales

1 This chapter draws upon my earlier work, 'Ethical Boundaries And Internet Cultures', in L. Bently and S. Maniatis (eds), *Intellectual Property and Ethics, Vol. IV, Perspectives in Intellectual Property* (London: Sweet & Maxwell, 1998), 3–36; 'Intellectual property, peer to peer and resistance to regulation' [2001], *CyberLRes* 5; 'Retrospective Futures? Law, Technology and Copyright Control in Cyberspace', *Media and Arts Law Review*, 6 (4), September 2001, 181–191; Kathy Bowrey and Matthew Rimmer, 'Rip, Mix, Burn: The Politics of Peer to Peer and Copyright Law', *First Monday*, 7 (8) (2002), and Matthew Rimmer, 'The dead poets society: The copyright term and the public domain', *First Monday*, 8 (6) (2003).

2 Richard Forno, 'High-Tech Heroin', 9 December 2003, available at <http://www.infowarrior.org>.

3 Quoted in Jessica Litman, *Digital Copyright* (Amherst, NY: Prometheus Books, 2001), 151.

4 Forno, 'High-Tech Heroin'.

5 Ibid.

6 Lawrence Lessig, *The Future of Ideas: the fate of the commons in a connected world* (New York: Random House, 2001).

7 Lawrence Lessig, *Free Culture: How Big Media uses Technology and the Law to Lock Down Culture and Control Creativity* (New York: Penguin, 2004).

8 Lessig, *The Future of Ideas*, 9.

9 Ibid., 11.

10 Ibid., 10.

11 Ibid., 11.

12 This is critically explored in Geoff Airo-Farulla, 'Politics and Markets. What are they good for?', *Griffith Law Review*, 8 (1) (1999), 1–27.

13 In the US the first sale doctrine allows the owner of any particular lawful copy of a copyrighted work to resell, rent, lend, or give away that copy without the copyright owner's permission. For a discussion of implications for digital works see R. Anthony Reese, 'The First Sale Doctrine in the Era of Digital Networks', *Boston College Law Review*, 44 (2003), 577.

14 For a discussion of the success of inefficient technologies see Clay Shirky, 'File-sharing Goes Social', *Networks, Economics, and Culture: Mailing list,* 12 October 2003 available at <http://www.shirky.com/writings/file-sharing_social.html>.

15 Zygmunt Bauman, *Culture as Praxis* (London; Boston: Routledge and Kegan Paul, 1973).

16 Michel Foucault, *Discipline and Punish: The Birth of the Prison,* trans. Alan Sheridan (New York: Pantheon Books, 1977).

17 Jacques Donzelot, *The Policing of Families,* trans. Robert Hurley (New York: Pantheon Books, 1979).

18 Robin West, 'Economic Man and Literary Woman. One Contrast', in Leonora Ledwon (ed.), *Law and Literature, Text and Theory* (New York: Garland Publishing, 1996), 127–38 at 128.

19 Jean Baudrillard, *The System of Objects,* trans. James Benedict (London; New York: Verso, 1996), 164.

20 Richard Sherwin, *When Law Goes Pop. The Vanishing Line between Law and Popular Culture* (Chicago: University of Chicago Press, 2000), 10.

21 Ibid., 5.

22 Gayatri Chakravorty Spivak quoted in Steve Redhead, *Unpopular Cultures. The birth of law and popular culture* (Manchester; New York: Manchester University Press, 1995), 1.

23 Sherwin, *When Law Goes Pop,* 19.

24 Ibid., 7.

25 Greg Milner, 'Anarchy from the U.K.', *Spin* (September 2000), 165. Napster was purchased by Roxio, and launched as a legitimate music service in October 2003.

26 With peer-to-peer technology your computer storage, cycles and content are made available because the PC via modem becomes a node that operates outside the DNS system, having significant autonomy from central servers with the ability to be accessed by other users. It is file sharing on the internet that occurs outside of the traditional forms of file transfer – http and ftp. There is some centralisation that allows the network to function, however applications differ in this regard. At its simplest peer-to-peer creates an alternate file trading channel to the web or a black market where what is traded is 'free' but users of the network are subjected to shared codes of conduct. See Clay Shirky, 'What is P2P and What Isn't', O'Reilly Network at <http://www.openp2p.com/pub/a/p2p/2000/11/24/shirky1-whatisp2p.html>; Andy Oram (ed.), *Peer-to-Peer, Harnessing the Power of Disruptive Technologies* (Cambridge, Mass.: O'Reilly, 2001)

27 Damien Riehl, 'Peer to Peer Distribution Systems: Will Napster, Gnutella and Freenet create a Nirvana or Gehenna?', *William Mitchell Law Review,* 27 (2001), 1761.

28 Clay Shirky, 'Smuggled in Under Cover of Darkness', O'Reilly Network at <http://www.openp2p.com/pub/a/p2p/2001/02/14/clay_darkness.html>.

29 See John Perry Barlow, 'The Economy of Ideas: A Framework for Rethinking patents and copyright in the Digital Age', *Wired,* 2 (3) (March 1994), 84.

30 Ibid.

31 Ibid.

32 Critical Arts Ensemble, 'Utopian Plagiarism, Hypertextuality, and Electronic Cultural Production', in *The Electronic Disturbance* (New York: Autonomedia, 1996), 89.

33 'The Thinker: Doug Carlston', in John Brockman (ed.), *Digerati* (London: Orion, 1996), 41.
34 'The Marketer: Ted Leonsis', in John Brockman (ed.), *Digerati* (London: Orion, 1996), 240.
35 Marshall McLuhan, 'The Typewriter: Into the Age of the Iron Whim', in *Understanding Media* (London: Sphere Books first edition, 1967), 279.
36 Tom Standage, *The Victorian Internet* (London: Weidenfeld & Nicolson, 1998).
37 Martha Woodmansee, *The Author, Art & the Market* (New York: Columbia University Press, 1994).
38 Martha Woodmansee and Peter Jaszi (eds), *The Construction of Authorship: Textual Appropriation in Law and Literature* (Durham; London: Duke University Press, 1994).
39 Rosemary Coombe, *The Cultural Life of Intellectual Properties. Authorship, Appropriation and the Law* (Durham; London: Duke University Press, 1998).
40 Jane Gaines, *Contested Culture. The Image, The Voice and The Law* (Chapel Hill: University of North Carolina Press, 1991).
41 Celia Lury, *Cultural Rights. Technology, Legality and Personality* (London: Routledge, 1993).
42 Ronald V. Bettig, *Copyrighting Culture: The Political Economy of Intellectual Property* (Boulder, CO: Westview, 1996).
43 Alvin Toffler, *Future Shock* (London: The Bodley Head, 1970).
44 This is an established idea of the legal realist movement that dates from the 1920s in the US. See 'Legal realism' at <http://en.wikipedia.org/wiki/Legal_realism>; see also Chapter 1, 16.
45 The Nebula Awards™ are voted on by the Science Fiction and Fantasy Writers of America. Its membership includes most of the leading writers of science fiction and fantasy in the US. As well as writing science fiction, Levinson is Professor of Mass Communications at Fordham University.
46 Paul Levinson, *Bestseller: Wired, Analog and digital writings* (Mill Valley, CA: Pulpless.com, 1999), 69.
47 Siva Vaidhyanathan, *The Anarchist in the Library* (New York: Basic Books, 2004), xi.
48 Ibid., xvii.
49 Ibid., 21.
50 Ibid., 22–23.
51 Brendan Edgeworth, *Law, Modernity, Postmodernity: legal change in the contracting state* (Aldershot: Ashgate, 2003), 137.
52 Maureen Cain, 'The Symbol Traders' in Maureen Cain and Christine Harrington (eds), *Lawyers in a Postmodern World: Translation and Transgression* (Buckingham: Open University Press, 1994), 33.
53 Quoted in Ian Parsons, 'Copyright and Society' in Asa Briggs (ed.), *Essays in the History of Publishing* (London: Longman, 1974), 42.
54 See Kathy Bowrey, 'Chapter Four: The case for romantic authorship', in 'Don't Fence Me In: The Many Histories of Copyright' (SJD thesis, University of Sydney, 1994).
55 Lionel Bently, 'Copyright And The Victorian Internet: Telegraphic Property Laws In Colonial Australia' *Loyola Los Angeles Law Review* (forthcoming, 2004).
56 Ibid.
57 Sherwin, *When Law Goes Pop*, 42.

58 *A&M Records Inc and others v Napster Inc and Does 1-100*, Case No 99-5183-MHP, Complaint for Contributory and Vicarious Copyright Infringement, Violations of California Civil Code Section 980(a)(2), and Unfair Competition. (N.D. Cal. 2000) at #1, 2. Hereafter 'Napster Complaint'. My emphasis.

59 Ibid. at #30, 7

60 *A&M Records Inc v Napster Inc*, 114 F. Supp. 2d 896 2000 U.S. Dist. LEXIS 11862 (N.D. Cal. 2000) 908.

61 *A&M Records Inc v Napster Inc*, 114 F. Supp. 2d 896 2000 U.S. Dist. LEXIS 11862 (N.D. Cal. 2000) 903.

62 *A&M Records Inc v Napster Inc*, 114 F. Supp. 2d 896 2000 U.S. Dist. LEXIS 11862 (N.D. Cal. 2000) 913.

63 Continuity with this legal narrative can be seen in the Eldred case. See Rimmer, 'The dead poets society', and Chapter 4, 97–8.

64 *Metro-Goldwyn-Mayer Studios, Inc., et al. v. Grokster Ltd., et al.* 259 F. Supp. 2d 1029 (C.D. Cal., April, 2003) aff'd F.3d (9th Cir., Aug. 19, 2004). Hereafter *Grokster II*.

65 *Grokster II*, at 11730.

66 *Sony Corp. of America v Universal City Studios, Inc.* 464 US 417 (1984).

67 *Grokster II*, at 11736.

68 *Grokster II*, at 11737.

69 Quoting *Grokster I*, 259 F. Supp. 2d at 1041 in *Grokster II*, at 11739.

70 *Grokster II*, at 11740.

71 *Grokster II*, at 11741.

72 *Grokster II*, at 11741.

73 *Grokster II*, at 11743–4.

74 *Grokster II*, at 11745.

75 *Grokster II*, at 11746–7.

76 See Chapter 5, 122–4.

77 See Linda Colley, *Captives. Britain, Empire and the World 1600–1850* (London: Pimlico, 2003); Niall Ferguson, *Empire. How Britain Made the Modern World* (London: Penguin, 2004); Diana Preston and Michael Preston, *A Pirate of Exquisite Mind: Explorer, Naturalist, and Buccaneer. The Life of William Dampier* (New York: Doubleday, 2004).

78 The technical distinction between a privateer and a pirate was the grant of a letter of marque and reprisal. This was an official warrant or commission from the government that authorised the private ship owner to prey on enemy shipping during time of war. See <http://en.wikipedia.org/wiki/Privateer>.

79 Franz Kafka, 'Before the Law', in *The Trial* (New York: Vintage Books ed , 1969), 267–268.

80 See Electronic Frontiers Foundation, 'Prelude to a fake complaint', September 2004 at <http://www.eff.org/IP/Apple_Complaint.php>.

81 *Universal Music Australia Pty Ltd and Others v Sharman License Holdings Ltd and Others*, No. N110 of 2004.

82 Nick Couldry, 'The Productive "consumer" and the dispersed "citizen"', *International Journal of Cultural Studies* (2004), 7 (1), 21, 22.

83 There is a good overview of this concept in Stephen Kline, Nick Dyer-Witherford and Greig de Peuter (eds), *Digital Play: the interaction of technology, culture and marketing* (Montreal: McGill-Queens University Press, 2003), 66ff.

84 Ibid., 67–68.

85 Ibid., 66.

86 This argument draws heavily on the insights of Keith Negus, 'Culture, industry, genre: conditions of musical creativity', in his *Music Genres and Corporate Cultures* (London: Routledge, 1999), 14–30.

87 Lester Haines, 'iPod: this season's must-have for muggers', *The Register* 30 (March 2004). Available at <http://www.theregister.co.uk/2004/03/30/ipod_this_seasons_musthave/>.

88 The industry source on successful legitimate services is <http://www.ifpi.org>.

89 <http://www.apple.com/ipod/>.

90 See 'Popular music', *Wikipedia*. Available at <http://en.wikipedia.org/wiki/Popular_music>. An excellent brief introduction to commodification and popular music is Keith Negus, 'Between corporation and consumer: culture and conflict in the British Record Industry', in Simon Frith (ed.), *Popular Music. Critical concepts in media and cultural studies* Vol. 2: The Rock Era (London: Routledge, 2003), 24–41. See also Negus, 'Culture, industry, genre'.

91 Sherwin, *When Law Goes Pop*, 4–5.

92 Roland Barthes, 'From Work to Text', in *Image, Music, Text*, trans. S. Heath (New York: Noonday Press, 1977), 160.

93 For an excellent discussion on the complexity of music consumption see Will Straw, 'Consumption', in Simon Frith, Will Straw and John Street (eds), *The Cambridge Companion to Pop and Rock* (Cambridge: Cambridge University Press, 2001), 53–73.

94 RIAA website, *It's all about the Music* 2003.

95 This is discussed in relation to hacker culture in Amanda Chandler, 'The Changing Definition and Image of Hackers in Popular Discourse', *International Journal of the Sociology of Law*, 24 (2) (1996), 229–251.

96 See, for example, Andy Boon, Steve Greenfield and Guy Osborn, 'Complete Control? Judicial and Practical Approaches to the Negotiation of Music Contracts', *International Journal of the Sociology of Law*, 24 (2) (1996), 89–115.

97 Baudrillard, quoted in Sherwin, *When Law Goes Pop*, 29.

98 Global Information Inc, 'Youth Mobile Products Market Analysis, Data & Figures': Press Release 7 May 2003. Available at <http://www.gii.co.jp/press/w2f1333_en.shtml>; Robin Robertson, 'Moving pictures to crackle open youth market', *Australian Financial Review*, 6 March 2003.

99 'Conflict over MP3', *The Korea Herald*, 7 May 2004.

100 See Andrew Orlowski, 'EC Launches Microsoft DRM Probe', *The Register*, 25 August 2004 at <http://www.theregister.co.uk/2004/08/25/ec_ms_drm_probe/>.

101 Jon Casimir, 'Four apparently Air-less places – the bizarre, illogical world of copy-controlled CDs', *Sydney Morning Herald*, 13 March 2004.

102 David Vaver, 'Need Intellectual Property Law be Everywhere? Against Ubiquity and Uniformity', *The Dalhousie Law Journal*, 25 (1) (2002), 1, 12.

103 This dynamic is discussed in the Australian case *Campomar v Nike International Ltd* (2000) 202 CLR 45. For critical views of this development see Coombe, *The Cultural Life of Intellectual Properties*; Gaines, *Contested Culture*; Naomi Klein, *No Logo. Taking Aim at the Brand Bullies* (New York: Picador, 1999); Kalle Lasn, *Culture Jam. The Uncooling of America*[TM] (New York: Eagle Brook, 1999).

104 Copyright Law Review Committee, *Copyright and Contract* (Commonwealth of Australia, 2002).

105 Lessig, *Free Culture*, 282.

106 Ibid., 283–284.

107 Available at <http://www.aesharenet.com.au/ffe/>.

108 See Brian Fitzgerald, 'Creative Commons Update', *Media and Arts Law Review*, 9 (2) (2004), 137. The license is available at <http://creativecommons.org/projects/international/au/>.

109 For a brief history of the movement see <http://creativecommons.org/learn/aboutus/>.

110 With the development of the information economy, US thinkers like Richard Stallman and Larry Lessig have been very effective in promulgating the freedom of the internet in terms of free speech. As Stallman explains, '"Free software" is a matter of liberty, not price. To understand the concept, you should think of "free" as in "free speech," not as in "free beer"'. See Joshua Gay (ed.), *Free Software, Free Society: selected essays of Richard Stallman* (Boston: GNU Press, 2002), 41.

111 Geert Lovink, *My First Recession: Critical Internet Culture in Transition* (Rotterdam: V2-NAi Publishers, 2003), 55.

112 Lessig, *Free Culture*, 304–306.

113 See Peter Drahos, *Information Feudalism* (London: Earthscan, 2002); Vaver, 'Need Intellectual Property Law be Everywhere?'.

114 West, 'Economic Man and Literary Woman', 129.

115 See David Throsby and Virginia Hollister, *Don't give up your day job: an economic study of professional artists in Australia* (Australia Council, 2003); DCITA, *Report of the Contemporary Visual Arts & Crafts Inquiry: The Myer Report* (Commonwealth of Australia, 2002). Available at <http://www.dcita.gov.au/Article/0,,0_1-2_15-4_111225,00.htm>.

116 See Chapter 7, 'Culture as Anarchy', in Vaidhyanathan, *The Anarchist in the Library*, 97–114.

117 See Jane Anderson, 'The Production of Indigenous Knowledge in Intellectual Property Law' (PhD thesis, UNSW, 2004).

7 Participate/comply/resist

1 Russell Skelton, *The Australian*, quoted in Sarah Stephen, 'Horror on Manus Island', *Green Left Weekly*, 20 August 2003.

2 Olivia Rousset, 'Last Man on Manus Island', *Dateline*, SBS, 31 March 2004.

3 Olu Oguibe, 'Forsaken Geographies: Cyberspace and the New World "Other"', *5th International Conference on Cyberspace*, 6–9 June 1996. Available at <eserver.org/internet/oguibe>.

4 Critical Arts Ensemble, *The Electronic Disturbance* (New York: Autonomedia, 1994), 3.

5 See, for example, John Braithwaite and Peter Drahos, *Global Business Regulation* (Cambridge; Melbourne: Cambridge University Press, 2000); Peter Drahos with John Braithwaite, *Information Feudalism: Who Owns the Knowledge Economy?* (London: Earthscan, 2002); Susan Sell, *Private Power, Public Law: The Globalization of Intellectual Property Rights* (Cambridge: Cambridge University Press, 2003).

6 Braithwaite and Drahos, *Global Business Regulation*, 475.

7 S. Wray, quoted in Tim Jordan and Paul A. Taylor, *Hactivism and Cyber wars. Rebels With A Cause?* (London: Routledge, 2004), 17.

8   S. Lash, quoted in ibid., 149.

9   This dynamic is discussed in relation to economic data in Chapter 2, 31.

10 David Held and Anthony McGrew, 'The Great Globalisation Debate: An introduction', in David Held and Anthony McGrew (eds), *The global transformations reader: an introduction to the globalization debate* (Malden, Mass.: Polity Press, 2000), 4.

11 John Urry, *Sociology beyond Societies. Mobilities for the twenty-first century* (London: Routledge, 2000), 14.

12 Nikolas Rose, *Powers of Freedom: reframing political thought* (Cambridge: Cambridge University Press, 1999), 234.

13 For a brief account see Kline et al., *Digital Play: the interaction of technology, culture and marketing* (Montreal: McGill-Queens University Press, 2003), 61–69. For a fuller discussion see Brendan Edgeworth, *Law, Modernity, Postmodernity* (Aldershot: Ashgate, 2003).

14 Urry, *Sociology beyond Societies*, 16.

15 See also Chapter 2, 25.

16 Urry, *Sociology beyond Societies*, 15.

17 See Chapter 1, 16.

18 See Chapter 3.

19 Edgeworth, *Law, Modernity, Postmodernity*, 192. See also Shelley Wright, *International human rights, decolonisation and globalisation: becoming human* (London: Routledge, 2001).

20 Ibid., 277.

21 See Chapter 1, 11.

22 See Chapter 3, 52.

23 See 'UN Global Forum on Internet Governance', *Circle ID*, 30 March 2004.

24 Ibid.

25 The HLSOC includes a representative of the UN Secretary-General and Executive Heads of the UN Food And Agriculture Organization, International Atomic Energy Agency, International Civil Aviation Organization, International Labour Organization, International Maritime Organization, International Telecommunications Union, UN Regional Economic Commissions, UN Conference On Trade And Development, UN Development Programme, UN Environment Programme, UNESCO, UN Population Fund, UN High Commissioner For Human Rights, UNHCR (UN Refugee Agency), UN Industrial Development Organization, UN University, Universal Postal Union, UN World Food Programme, World Health Organization, World Intellectual Property Organization, World Meteorological Organization, World Bank and the World Trade Organization (WTO). The Organization For Economic Co-Operation And Development (OECD), Inter-American Development Bank, UN Institute For Training And Research and UN Volunteers have observer status. See <http://www.itu.int/wsis/basic/roles.html>.

26 Audrey Selian, 'The World Summit on the Information Society and Civil Society Participation', *The Information Society*, 20, 201–215 (2004), 202.

27 Ibid., 203.

28 Ibid., 204.

29 Milton Mueller, 'WGIG will Reassess – or Reassert? – Governments' Role in Internet', *ICANNWatch*, 21 September 2004.

30 Anriette Esterhuysen, 'Whose "Information Society"? Or: Was WSIS worth it?' (Heinrich-Boll Foundation, 23 March 2004). See also IP Justice Report, 'World

Summit on the Information Society' (WSIS)', 21 December 2003 available at< http://www.ipjustice.org/WSIS/IPJ_WSIS_Report.html>.

31 See ibid.

32 Don MacLean, 'The Quest for Inclusive Governance of Global ICTs: Lessons from the ITU in the Limits of National Sovereignty', *Information Technologies and International Development*, 1 (1) Fall 2003, 1–18 at 3.

33 Ibid., 16–17.

34 The US-based Consumer Project on Technology is one notable exception.

35 'North-South And South-South Perspectives On The Information Society: Discussion on Digital Solidarity Agenda and Finance', (Heinrich-Boll Foundation, 25 September 2003).

36 See Chapter 3.

37 See WIPO, 'Emerging issues in IP', at <http://www.wipo.int/about-ip/en/studies/index.html>.

38 See Consumer Project on Technology, 'Request for WIPO Meeting on Collaborative Development Models', available at <http://www.cptech.org/ip/wipo/openwipo.html>; Lawrence Lessig, *Free Culture: How Big Media uses Technology and the Law to Lock Down Culture and Control Creativity* (New York: Penguin, 2004), 262–8. See also Chapter 4, 91.

39 See <http://www.iosn.net/>.

40 Alan Toner, 'Unzipping the World Summit on the Information Society', *Metamute* 26, Summer/Autumn 2003. See also IP Justice Report, 'World Summit on the Information Society (WSIS)', 21 December 2003 available at <http://www.ipjustice.org/WSIS/IPJ_WSIS_Report.html>.

41 Resolution adopted by the General Assembly 56/183, World Summit on the Information Society.

42 See Michael Ryan, *Knowledge Diplomacy. Global Competition and the Politics of Intellectual Property* (New York: Brookings Institute, 1998); 'Chapter 7: Agendas and Agenda-setters: The Multilateral Game', Drahos with Braithwaite, *Global Business Regulation*.

43 Peter Drahos, 'The New Bilateralism in Intellectual Property' (Oxfam GB, December 2001) available at <http://www.maketradefair.org/assets/english/bilateralism.pdf>.

44 For a fuller account of this see Kathy Bowrey, 'Can we afford to think about copyright in a global marketplace?', in Fiona MacMillan (ed.), *New directions in Copyright Law* (Cheltenham: Edward Elgar, 2004).

45 Australian Government, Department of Foreign Affairs and Trade (2003)

46 ABC Radio, *PM Program*, 13 November 2003.

47 See generally Chapter 17 Intellectual Property Rights available at <http://www.dfat.gov.au/trade/negotiations/us_fta/text/index.html>.

48 See P. Drahos, T. Faunce, M. Goddard and D. Henry, 'The FTA and the PBS: a submission to the Senate Select Committee on the US-Australia Free Trade Agreement', available at <http://www.aph.gov.au/library/pubs/RN/2004-05/05rn03.pdf>.

49 Foreign Affairs, Defence and Trade Legislation Committee 2004, *Estimates*, available at <http://www.aph.gov.au/hansard/senate/committee/S7431.pdf>, 16.

50 Australian Government, Intellectual Property and Competition Review (IPCR) Final Report (September 2000), available at <http://www.ipcr.gov.au/>.

51 Foreign Affairs, Defence and Trade Legislation Committee 2004, 19.

52 *The US-Australia Free Trade Agreement and Intellectual Property – A Symposium*, Baker & McKenzie Cyberspace Law and Policy Centre, UNSW Law Faculty, 28 April 2004.

53 Joint Standing Committee on Treaties 2004, 63–64.

54 Neil MacCormick, 'Beyond the Sovereign State', *Modern Law Review*, 56 (1) (1993), 11.

55 For example, the moral rights legislation was finally introduced into Australia, but not in the US. Amendments were made to comply with the WIPO Copyright Treaty and the WIPO Performances and Phonograms Treaty.

56 Drahos, 'The New Bilateralism in Intellectual Property', 9.

57 See Consumer Project on Technology, 'Geneva Declaration on the Future of the World Intellectual Property Organization', <http://www.cptech.org/ip/wipo/genevadeclaration.html>. See also James Boyle, 'A Manifesto on WIPO and the Future of Intellectual Property' (2004), *Duke Law and Technology Review* at <http://www.law.duke.edu/journals/dltr/articles/2004dltr0009.html>.

58 For one empirical study of US involvement see Milton Mueller, Christine Pagé and Brenden Kuerbis, 'Civil Society and the Shaping of Communication-Information Policy: Four Decades of Advocacy', *The Information Society*, 20 (2004), 169–185.

59 See Carolyn Penfold, 'World Leader or Village Idiot? An Examination of Internet Content Regulation in Australia' (LLM thesis, UNSW, 2004).

60 EPIC, 'Pretty poor privacy: An assessment of P3P and Internet Privacy', June 2000, available at <http://www.epic.org/reports/prettypoorprivacy.html>.

61 See, for example, Paul M. Schwartz, 'Privacy and Democracy In Cyberspace', *Vanderbilt Law Review*, 52 (1999), 1609.

62 See Julie Cohen, 'Examined Lives: Informational Privacy and the Subject as Object', *Stanford Law Review*, 52 (2000), 1373, 1375–1376.

63 See <http://en.wikipedia.org/wiki/Copyleft>.

64 Australian Government, *Let's Look Out For Australia*, Anti-Terrorism Kit for Australian Householders, February 2003. The campaign is best remembered for the associated fridge magnets to combat terror.

65 Computer Science and Telecommunications Board, *Funding a Revolution: Government Support for Computing Research* (Washington, DC: National Academy Press, 1999), 1. Available at <http://www7.nationalacademies.org/cstb/pub_revolution.html>. See also Office of International Affairs, *The Pervasive Role of Science, Technology, and Health in Foreign Policy: Imperatives for the Department of State* (Washington, DC: National Academy Press, 1999).

66 Salam Pax, *Baghdad Blog* (Melbourne: Text Publishing Company, 2003), 73–74.

67 <http://www.rsf.org>.

68 See Jonathon Zittrain, 'Internet Points of Control' (*Boston College Law Review*, forthcoming). Available at <http://ssrn.com/abstract_id = 388860>.

69 See Geert Lovink, 'An insider's guide to tactical media', in *Dark Fiber. Tracking Critical Internet Culture* (Cambridge, Mass.; London: MIT Press, 2002); Graham Meikle, *Future Active. Media Activism and the Internet* (London; New York: Routledge, 2002); Wim van de Donk, Brian D. Loder, Paul G. Nixon and Dieter Rucht (eds), *Cyberprotest. New Media, citizens and social movements* (London: Routledge, 2004).

70 See Michael Froomkin, 'The Internet as a source of Regulatory Arbitrage', in Brian Kahin and Charles Nesson (eds), *Borders in Cyberspace: Information Policy and the Global Information Infrastructure* (Cambridge, Mass.: MIT Press, 1997), 129–163.

71 Jordan and Taylor, *Hactivism and Cyber Wars*, 168.
72 Tiziana Terranova, *Network Culture. Politics for the Information Age* (London: Pluto Press, 2004), 15–16.
73 Ibid., 17.
74 Rose, *Powers of Freedom*, 279–280.
75 Lovink, 'An insider's guide to tactical media', 261.
76 Michael Hardt and Antonio Negri, *Empire* (Cambridge, Mass.; London: Harvard University Press, 2000).

Bibliography

Airo-Farulla, Geoff, 'Politics and Markets. What are they good for?', *Griffith Law Review* (1999), 8 (1), 1–27

Anderson, Benedict, *Imagined Communities. Reflections on the origin and the spread of nationalism* (London: Verso, 1983)

Anderson, Jane, 'The Production of Indigenous Knowledge in Intellectual Property Law' (PhD thesis, UNSW, 2004)

Anon., 'North-South And South-South Perspectives On The Information Society: Discussion on Digital Solidarity Agenda and Finance' (Heinrich-Boll Foundation, 25 September 2003)

Aoki, Keith, 'Considering Multiple and Overlapping Sovereignties: Liberalism, Libertarianism, National Sovereignty, "Global" Intellectual Property and the Internet', *Indiana Journal of Global Legal Studies*, 5 (1998), 443

Appadurai, Arjun, 'Disjuncture and Difference in the Global Cultural Economy', in Held, David, and McGrew, Anthony (eds), *The global transformations reader: an introduction to the globalization debate* (Malden, Mass.: Polity Press, 2000), 230

Appelbaum, Robert, 'Anti-geography', *Early Modern Literary Studies*, 4 (2), Special Issue 3 (1998), 12.1

Arendt, Hannah, *The Human Condition* (Chicago: University of Chicago Press, 1958)

Armstrong, George, 'From the Fetishism of Commodities to the Regulated Market: The Rise and Decline of Property', *Northwestern University Law Review*, 82 (1987), 79

Ashcroft, Bill, Gareth Griffiths and Helen Tiffin (eds), *The Post-Colonial Studies Reader* (New York: Routledge, 1995)

Auletta, Ken, *World War 3.0. Microsoft and its enemies* (New York: Random House, 2000)

Australian Government, *Intellectual Property and Competition Review* (IPCR) Final Report (September 2000)

Barbrook, Richard, and Andy Cameron, 'The Californian Ideology', *Mute* 3, Autumn 1995

Bardhan, Ashok Deo, Jaffee, Dwight and Kroll, Cynthia, *Globalization and a High-Tech Economy* (Boston; New York; Dordrecht: Kluwer, 2004)

Bardhan, Ashok Deo, Jaffee, Dwight and Kroll, Cynthia, 'Research Report: The New Wave of Outsourcing', Fisher Center for Real Estate and Urban Economics, University of California, Berkeley, Fall 2003

Barlow, John Perry, 'The Economy of Ideas: A Framework for Rethinking patents and copyright in the Digital Age', *Wired*, 2 (3), (1994), 84

Barthes, Roland, *Image-Music-Text*, trans. Stephen Heath (New York: Noonday Press, 1988)

Baudrillard, Jean, *The System of Objects*, trans. James Benedict (London; New York: Verso, 1996)

Bauman, Zygmunt, *Culture as Praxis* (London; Boston: Routledge and Kegan Paul, 1973)

Basu, Kaushik, 'The politics of business outsourcing', 10 December 2003 available at <http://www.rediff.com/money/2003/dec/10guest2.htm>

Beckman, David, 'Is Microsoft Sending Core Development to India?', *WashTech News* 15 June 2004

Bell, David, and Barbara M. Kennedy (eds), *The Cybercultures Reader* (New York: Routledge, 2000)

Bellia, Anthony, 'Promises, Trust, And Contract Law', *American Journal of Jurisprudence*, 47 (2002), 25

Benhabib, Seyla, *The reluctant modernism of Hannah Arendt* (Lanham, Md.: Rowman & Littlefield, 2000)

Bently, Lionel, 'Copyright And The Victorian Internet: Telegraphic Property Laws In Colonial Australia', *Loyola Los Angeles Law Review* (forthcoming, 2004)

Bergeron, Brian, *Dark Ages II. When the Digital Data Die* (Upper Saddle River, NJ: Prentice Hall PTR, 2002)

Berners-Lee, Tim, 'Patent Policy Working Group Face-to-Face Meeting Summary, 15–17 October 2001, Cupertino, CA USA', at <http://www.w3.org/2001/10/ppwg-cupertino-ftf-summary.html>

Berners-Lee, Tim, Letter to James E. Rogan (USPTO) at <http://www.w3.org/2003/10/27-rogan.html>

Bettig, Ronald V., *Copyrighting Culture: The Political Economy of Intellectual Property* (Boulder, CO: Westview, 1996)

Bettig, Ronald V. and Lynn Hall, Jeanne, *Big Media, Big Money: Cultural Texts and Political Economics* (Lanham, Md.: Rowman & Littlefield, 2003)

Biagioli, Mario, 'Aporias of Scientific Authorship. Credit and Responsibility in Contemporary Biomedicine' in Biagioli, Mario (ed.), *The science studies reader* (New York: Routledge, 1999)

Bird, John, et al. (eds), *Mapping the Future. Local cultures, global change* (London; New York: Routledge, 1993)

Boon, Andy, Steve Greenfield and Guy Osborn, 'Complete Control? Judicial and Practical Approaches to the Negotiation of Music Contracts', *International Journal of the Sociology of Law*, 24 (2) (1996), 89–115

Borsook, Paulina, *Cyberselfish: A Critical Romp through the Terribly Libertarian Culture of High Tech* (New York: Public Affairs, 2000)

Bourdieu, Pierre, 'The Specificity of the Scientific Field and the Social Conditions of the Progress of Reason', in Biagioli, Mario (ed.), *The science studies reader* (New York: Routledge, 1999)

Bowrey, Kathy, 'Can we afford to think about copyright in a global marketplace?', in Fiona MacMillan (ed.), *New directions in Copyright Law* (Cheltenham: Edward Elgar, 2004)

Bowrey, Kathy, 'Chapter Four: The case for romantic authorship', in 'Don't Fence Me In: The Many Histories of Copyright' (SJD thesis, University of Sydney, 1994)

Bowrey, Kathy, 'Ethical Boundaries And Internet Cultures', in L. Bently and S. Maniatis (eds), *Intellectual Property and Ethics, Vol. IV, Perspectives in Intellectual Property* (London: Sweet & Maxwell, 1998), 3–36

Bowrey, Kathy, 'Intellectual property, peer to peer and resistance to regulation' [2001], *CyberLRes* 5 available at <www.austlii.edu.au/au/other/CyberLRes/2001/5>

Bowrey, Kathy, 'The Outer Limits Of Copyright Law – Where Law Meets Philosophy and Culture', *Law and Critique,* 12 (1) (2001), 1–24

Bowrey, Kathy, 'Retrospective Futures? Law, Technology and Copyright Control in Cyberspace', *Media and Arts Law Review,* 6 (4), 2001, 181–191

Bowrey, Kathy and Rimmer, Matthew, 'Rip, Mix, Burn, Rip, Mix, Burn: The Politics of Peer to Peer', *First Monday,* 7 (8) (2002)

Boyle, James, 'A Manifesto on WIPO and the Future of Intellectual Property' (2004), *Duke Law & Technology Review* 0009

Boyle, James, 'Missing the point on Microsoft', *Salon.com* 7 April, 2000 at <http://dir.salon.com/tech/feature/2000/04/07/greenspan/index.html>

Bradner, S., 'RFC 2026 Internet Standards Process – Revision 3' (October 1996)

Braithwaite, John, and Peter Drahos, *Global Business Regulation* (Cambridge; Melbourne: Cambridge University Press, 2000)

Brockman, John (ed.), *Digerati* (London: Orion, 1996)

Brown, John Seely and Duguid, Paul, *The Social Life of Information* (Boston, Mass.: Harvard Business School Press, 2000)

Burstein, Rachel, 'Overseas Invasion', *Mother Jones* January/February 1998 at <http://www.motherjones.com/news/feature/1998/01/burstein.html>

Butler, Judith, *Gender Trouble. Feminism and the Subversion of Identity* (New York: Routledge, 1990)

Cain, Maureen, 'The Symbol Traders', in Maureen Cain and Christine Harrington (eds), *Lawyers in a Postmodern World: Translation and Transgression* (Buckingham: Open University Press, 1994)

Calvino, Italo, 'The Argentine Ant', trans. Archibald Colquhoun, in Alberto Manguel (ed.), *Black Water. The Anthology of Fantastic Literature* (London: Picador, 1983), 440–469

Calvino, Italo, *If on a Winter's Night a Traveller,* trans. William Weaver (London: Picador, 1982)

Camara, Gilberto, 'Open Source Software Production: Fact & Fiction', *Mute* 27 (2004), 74

Campbell, Mary, '"That othere half". Mandeville Naturalizes the East', in Mary Campbell, *The Witness and The Other World. Exotic European Travel Writing, 400–1600* (Ithaca, N.Y.: Cornell University Press, 1988), 122–161

Casimir, Jon, 'Four apparently Air-less places – the bizarre, illogical world of copy-controlled CDs', *Sydney Morning Herald,* 13 March 2004

Cassidy, John, *Dot con: The real story of why the internet bubble burst* (New York: Harper Collins, 2002)

Cerf, Vint, 'IETF and ISOC', (1995) at <http://www.isoc.org/isoc/related/ietf>

Chandler, Amanda, 'The Changing Definition and Image of Hackers in Popular Discourse', *International Journal of the Sociology of Law,* 24 (2) (1996), 229–251

Clarke, Arthur C., 'The Nine Billion Names of God', republished in Alberto Manguel (ed.), *White Fire: Further Fantastic Literature* (London: Picador, 1990)

Cohen, Julie, 'Examined Lives: Informational Privacy and the Subject as Object', *Stanford Law Review,* 52 (2000), 1375–1376

Colley, Linda, *Captives. Britain, Empire and the World 1600–1850* (London: Pimlico, 2003)

Collins, Hugh, *Regulating Contracts* (Oxford; New York: Oxford University Press, 1999)

Computer Science and Telecommunications Board, *Funding a Revolution: Government Support for Computing Research* (Washington, DC: National Academy Press,. 1999) 1, available at <http://www7.nationalacademies.org/cstb/pub_revolution.html>

Consumer Project on Technology, 'Geneva Declaration on the Future of the World Intellectual Property Organization', <http://www.cptech.org/ip/wipo/genevadeclaration.html

Consumer Project on Technology, 'Request for WIPO Meeting on Collaborative Development Models', available at <http://www.cptech.org/ip/wipo/openwipo.html>

Coombe, Rosemary, 'Contingent Articulations: A Critical Cultural Studies of Law', in Austin Sarat and Jonathon Simon (eds), *Law in the Domains of Culture* (Ann Arbor: University of Michigan Press, 1998), 21–64

Coombe, Rosemary, *The Cultural Life of Intellectual Properties: Authorship, Appropriation and the Law* (Durham; London: Duke University Press, 1998)

Copyright Law Review Committee, *Copyright and Contract* (Commonwealth of Australia, 2002)

Cotterrell, Roger, 'Trusting in Law', *Current Legal Problems*, 46 (2) (1993), 75–95

Couldry, Nick, 'The Productive "consumer" and the dispersed "citizen"', *International Journal of Cultural Studies*, 7 (1) (2004), 21

coverpages.org, 'US Federal Trade Commission Report Calls for Patent Law and Policy Reform', at <http://xml.coverpages.org/ni2003-11-11-a.html>

coverpages.org, 'W3C Presents Prior Art Filing to USPTO and Urges Removal of Eolas Patent', at <http://xml.coverpages.org/ni2003-10-28-b.html#reexam>

Crane, Diana, 'Culture and Globalisation', in Diana Crane, Noboko Kawashima and Ken'ichi Kawasaka (eds), *Global Culture. Media, Arts, Policy and Globalisation* (New York; London: Routledge, 2001)

Critical Arts Ensemble, *The Electronic Disturbance* (New York: Autonomedia, 1994)

Critical Arts Ensemble, 'Utopian Plagiarism, Hypertextuality, and Electronic Cultural Production', in *The Electronic Disturbance* (New York: Autonomedia, 1996)

Debord, Guy, 'Comments on the Society of the Spectacle' (1988), trans. Malcolm Imrie, at < http://www.notbored.org/commentaires.html>

Deleuze, Gilles and Guattari, Felix, *A Thousand Plateaus. Capitalism and Schizophrenia*, trans. Brian Massumi (London: Athlone Press, 1988)

Department of Communications and Information Technology and the Arts, *Report of the Contemporary Visual Arts & Crafts Inquiry: The Myer Report*, Commonwealth of Australia (2002)

Department of Communications and Information Technology and the Arts, *An overview of the Australian ICT Industry and Innovation Base*, Commonwealth of Australia, (2003)

Department of Communications and Information Technology and the Arts, Framework for the Future Steering Committee, *Enabling our Future: A Framework for the information and communications technology industry'*, Commonwealth of Australia, (2003)

Donzelot, Jacques, *The Policing of Families*, trans. Robert Hurley (New York: Pantheon Books, 1979)

Dossani, Rafiq and Kenney, Martin, '"Lift and Shift": Moving the Back Office to India', *Information Technologies and International Development*, 1 (2) (2003), 21–37

Drahos, Peter, 'The New Bilateralism in Intellectual Property' (Oxfam GB, December 2001) available at <http://www.maketradefair.org/assets/english/bilateralism.pdf>

Drahos, Peter, and Ruth Mayne (eds), *Global Intellectual Property Rights* (Basingstoke: Palgrave Macmillan, 2002)

Drahos, Peter with John Braithwaite, *Information Feudalism: Who Owns the Knowledge Economy?* (London: Earthscan, 2002)

Dvorak, John C., 'Flawed Thinking And Dot-Com Death', *Forbes.com* (13 November 2000)

Eagles, Ian and Longdin, Louise, 'The Microsoft Appeal: Different Rules for Different Markets?', *New Zealand Business Law Quarterly* 7, Nov 2001, 303

Edgeworth, Brendan, *Law, Modernity, Postmodernity* (Aldershot: Ashgate, 2003)

Electronic Frontiers Foundation, 'Prelude to a fake complaint', September 2004 at <http://www.eff.org/IP/Apple_Complaint.php>

EPIC, 'Pretty poor privacy: An assessment of P3P and Internet Privacy', June 2000 available at <http://www.epic.org/reports/prettypoorprivacy.html>

Esterhuysen, Anriette, 'Whose "Information Society"? Or: Was WSIS worth it?', (Heinrich-Boll Foundation, 23 March 2004)

'EU's ruling a blow to globalization', *Tucson Citizen*, 25 March 2004

Fallow, James, 'Inside the Leviathan', *The Atlantic Monthly* February 2000, available at <http://www.theatlantic.com/issues/2000/02/002/fallows.htm>

Ferguson, Niall, *Empire. How Britain Made the Modern World* (London: Penguin, 2004)

Fitzgerald, Brian, 'Dow Jones & Co v Gutnick. Negotiating "American Legal Hegemony" in the Transnational World of Cyberspace', *Melbourne University Law Review* 27 (2) (2003), 590

Fitzgerald, Brian, 'Creative Commons Update' *Media and Arts Law Review*, 9 (2) (2004), 137

Forno, Richard, 'High-Tech Heroin', 9 December 2003, available at <http://www.infowarrior.org>

Foucault, Michel, *Discipline and Punish: The Birth of the Prison*, trans. Alan Sheridan (New York: Pantheon Books, 1977)

Foucault, Michel, 'What is an author?', in J. V. Harari (ed.), *Textual Strategies: Perspectives in Poststructuralist Criticism* (Ithaca, N.Y.: Cornell University Press, 1979)

Fraser, Nancy, 'Rethinking the Public Sphere' in Fraser, Nancy, *Justice interruptus: Critical reflections on the 'postsocial' condition* (New York: Routledge, 1997)

Friedman, John, *The Monstrous Races in Medieval Art and Thought* (Cambridge, Mass.: Harvard University Press, 1981)

Froomkin, Michael, 'Habermas @ Discourse.Net: Toward a Critical Theory of Cyberspace', *Harvard Law Review*, 116 (2003), 749

Froomkin, Michael, 'The Internet as a source of Regulatory Arbitrage', in Brian Kahin and Charles Nesson (eds), *Borders in Cyberspace: Information Policy and the Global Information Infrastructure* (Cambridge, Mass.: MIT Press, 1997), 129–163

Gabriel, Richard and Goldman, Ron (Sun Microsystems), 'Open source: Beyond the Fairytales', 17 Sept 2002 at <http://opensource.mit.edu/papers/gabrielgoldman.pdf>

Gaines, Jane, *Contested Culture. The Image, The Voice and The Law* (Chapel Hill; London: University of North Carolina Press, 1991)

Galison, Peter, 'The Collective Author' in Mario Biagioli and Peter Galison (eds), *Scientific Authorship. Credit and Intellectual Property in Science* (New York; London: Routledge, 2003)

Gates, Bill, *The Road Ahead* (London; New York: Penguin, 1996)

Gates, Bill, *Business @ the Speed of Thought* (London, New York: Penguin, 1999)

Gava, John, and Janey Greene, 'Do We Need A Hybrid Law Of Contract? Why Hugh Collins Is Wrong And Why It Matters', *Cambridge Law Journal* 63 (3) (2004) 605–31

Gay, Joshua (ed.), *Free Software, Free Society: selected essays of Richard Stallman* (Boston: GNU Press, 2002)

Geertz, Clifford, *Local Knowledge: Further Essays in Interpretative Anthropology* (New York: Basic Books, 1983)

Geist, Michael, 'In Web disputes, U.S. law rules the world', *Toronto Star*, 24 February 2003

Ghosh, Rishab Aiyer, 'Clustering and dependencies in free/open source software development: Methodology and tools', *First Monday* 8 (4) (2003)

Global Information Inc, 'Youth Mobile Products Market Analysis, Data & Figures', Press Release 7 May 2003 available at <http://www.gii.co.jp/press/w2f1333_en.shtml>

Greenblatt, Stephen, *Marvelous Possessions, The Wonder of the New World* (Chicago: University of Chicago Press, 1991)

Haines, Lester, 'iPod: this season's must-have for muggers', *The Register*, 30 March 2004

Hardie, Martin, 'Floss and the Crisis? Foreigner in a Free Land', *Sarai Reader: Crisis/Media*, (2004), 384–397

Hardt, Michael and Negri, Antonio, *Empire* (Cambridge, Mass.; London: Harvard University Press, 2000)

Harvey, David, *The Condition of Postmodernity. An Enquiry into the Origins of Cultural Change* (Oxford; Cambridge, Mass.: Blackwell, 1990)

Heilemann, John, 'Fear and Trembling in Silicon Valley', *Wired* 8 (3) (2000)

Heilemann, John, *Pride Before the Fall. The Trial of Bill Gates and the end of the Microsoft era* (New York: Perennial, 2002)

Held, David and McGrew, Anthony, 'The Great Globalisation Debate: An introduction' in Held, David and McGrew, Anthony (eds), *The global transformations reader: an introduction to the globalization debate* (Malden, Mass.: Polity Press, 2000)

Hunt, Alan and Wickham, Gary, *Foucault and Law: Towards a New Sociology of Law as Governance* (London; Boulder, Colo.: Pluto, 1994)

Hunter, Dan, 'ICANN and the concept of Democratic Deficit', *Loyola of Los Angeles Law Review*, 36 (2003), 1149–1160

ICANN, 'Staff Manager's Issues Report on Privacy Issues Related to Whois' 13 May 2003 at <http://www.icann.org/gnso/issue-reports/whois-privacy-report-13may03.htm>

IETF Internet Draft: Guidelines for Working Groups on Intellectual Property Issues, Scott Brim, 11-Jun-03. http://www.ietf.org/internet-drafts/draft-ietf-ipr-wg-guidelines-05.txt

IETF Internet Draft: Intellectual Property Rights in IETF Technology, Scott Bradner, <21-Oct-03. http://www.ietf.org/internet-drafts/draft-ietf-ipr-technology-rights-12.txt>

IETF Internet Draft: IETF Rights in Contributions, Scott Bradner, 21-Oct-03; <http://www.ietf.org/internet-drafts/draft-ietf-ipr-submission-rights-08.txt>

IETF Internet Draft: Guidelines for Working Groups on Intellectual Property Issues, Scott Brim, 11-Jun-03

IP Justice Report, 'World Summit on the Information Society (WSIS)', 21 December 2003 available at <http://www.ipjustice.org/WSIS/IPJ_WSIS_Report.html>

Irigaray, Luce, *This sex which is not one*, trans. Catherine Porter (Ithaca, N.Y.: Cornell University Press, 1985)

Jahoda, Gustav, *Images of Savages. Ancient Roots of modern prejudice in western culture* (New York: Routledge, 1999)

Jordan, Tim and Taylor, Paul A., *Hactivism and Cyber wars. Rebels With A Cause?* (London: Routledge, 2004)

Kafka, Franz, 'Before the Law' in *The Trial* (New York: Vintage Books ed., 1969), 267–268

Kaplan, Philip J., *F'd Companies, Spectacular Dot Com Flameouts* (New York: Simon & Schuster, 2002)

Kell, David, 'The Furore over the patenting of Animals: Animal Legal Defense Fund v Quigg', *European Intellectual Property Review*, 8 (1992), 279

Kessler, Gary, 'IETF – History, Background, and Role in Today's Internet' (1996) at <http://www.garykessler.net/library/ietf_hx.html>

Kimel, Dori, 'Neutrality, Autonomy, and Freedom of Contract', *Oxford Journal of Legal Studies*, 21 (2001), 473

King, J. J., 'The Packet Gang: Openness and its Discontents', *Mute* 27 (2004), 80

Klein, Naomi, *No Logo. Taking Aim at the Brand Bullies* (New York: Picador, 1999)

Kline, Stephen, Nick Dyer-Witherford and Greig de Peuter (eds), *Digital Play: the interaction of technology, culture and marketing* (Montreal: McGill-Queens University Press, 2003)

KMFMS, 'What's So Bad About Microsoft?' available at <http://www.kmfms.com/whatsbad.html>

Krim, Jonathan, 'The Quiet War Over Open-Source', *Washington Post*, 21 August, 2003 at <http://www.washingtonpost.com/ac2/wp-dyn/A23422-2003Aug20>

Kurtz, Howard, 'Who Blew the Dot-Com Bubble? The Cautionary Tale of Henry Blodget', *Washington Post*, 12 March 2001, C01

Lancashire, David, 'Code, Culture and Clash. The Fading Altruism of open source development', *First Monday* 6 (12) (2001)

Lasn, Kalle, *Culture Jam. The Uncooling of America*™ (New York: Eagle Brook, 1999).

Latour, Bruno, 'Technology is society made durable', trans. Gabrielle Hecht, in John Law (ed.), *A Sociology of Monsters: Essays on power, technology and domination* (New York: Routledge, 1991), 103

Lessig, Lawrence, 'The Architecture of Innovation', *Duke Law Journal*, 51 (2002), 1783

Lessig, Lawrence, *Code and other laws of cyberspace* (New York: Basic Books, 1999)

Lessig, Lawrence, *Free Culture: How Big Media Uses Technology and the Law to Lock Down Culture and Control Creativity* (New York: Penguin, 2004)

Lessig, Lawrence, *The Future of Ideas: the fate of the commons in a connected world* (New York: Random House, 2001)

Levinson, Paul, *Bestseller: Wired, Analog and digital writings* (Mill Valley, CA: Pulpless. com, 1999)

Liebowitz, Stan, and Stephen Margolis, *Winners, Losers and Microsoft. Competition and AntiTrust in High Technology* (Oakland, CA: Independent Institute, 2001)

Litman, Jessica, *Digital Copyright* (Amherst, NY: Prometheus Books, 2001)

Lohr, Steve, 'Microsoft Said to Encourage Big Investment in SCO Group', *New York Times*, 12 March, 2004

Long, Doris Estelle, '"Democratising Globalisation": Practicing the Policies of Cultural Inclusion' *Cardozo Journal of International Law*, 10 (2002), 217

Lovink, Geert, *Dark Fiber. Tracking Critical Internet Culture* (Cambridge, Mass.; London: MIT Press, 2002)

Lovink, Geert, 'Interview with Milton Mueller', <nettime> (25 November 2003)

Lovink, Geert, *My First Recession. Critical Internet Culture in Transition* (Rotterdam: V2-NAi Publishers, 2003)

Lury, Celia, *Cultural Rights. Technology, Legality and Personality* (London: Routledge, 1993)

Lyotard, Jean-François, *The Postmodern Condition: A Report on Knowledge* (trans. Geoffrey Bennington and Brian Massumi (Manchester: Manchester University Press, 1984)

MacCormick, Neil, 'Beyond the Sovereign State', *Modern Law Review*, 56 (1) (1993) 1, 11

MacLean, Don, 'The Quest for Inclusive Governance of Global ICTs: Lessons from the ITU in the Limits of National Sovereignty', *Information Technologies and International Development* 1(1) Fall 2003, 1–18 at 3

Mandeville, Sir John, *The Travels of Sir John Mandeville*, trans. C. W. R. D. Moseley (New York: Penguin, 1983)

Mast, Carlotta, 'Living Through the Death of a Dot-Com', *Business Week Online*, 13 December 2000

May, Christopher, 'Why IPRS are a Global Political Issue', *European Intellectual Property Review*, 25 (1) (2003), 1

McChesney, R. W., *Rich Media, Poor Democracy: Communication Politics in Dubious Times* (Urbana: University of Illinois Press, 1999)

McLuhan, Marshall, 'The Typewriter: Into the Age of the Iron Whim', in *Understanding Media* (London: Sphere Books first edition, 1967), 279

Meikle, Graham *Future Active. Media Activism and the Internet* (London; New York: Routledge, 2002)

Mezey, Naomi, 'Law as Culture', in Austin Sarat and Jonathon Simon (eds), *Cultural Analysis, Cultural Studies, and the Law: Moving beyond Legal Realism* (Durham: Duke University Press, 2003), 37

Milner, Greg, 'Anarchy from the U.K.', *Spin* (September 2000), 165

Milton, Giles, *The Riddle and the Knight. In search of Sir John Mandeville* (London: Sceptre, 2001)

Minh-ha, Trinh, *Woman, Native, Other* (Bloomington: Indiana University Press, 1989)

Moore, Geoffrey, *Crossing the Chasm* (New York: Harper Business, 2002)

Moseley, C. W. R. D., 'Introduction', in *The Travels of Sir John Mandeville*, trans. C. W. R. D. Moseley (New York: Penguin, 1983)

Mueller, Milton, *Ruling the Root: internet governance and the taming of cyberspace* (Cambridge, Mass.; London: MIT Press, 2002)

Mueller, Milton, 'WGIG will Reassess – or Reassert? – Governments' Role in Internet', *ICANNWatch*, 21 September 2004

Mueller, Milton, Pagé, Christine and Kuerbis, Brenden, 'Civil Society and the Shaping of Communication-Information Policy: Four Decades of Advocacy', *The Information Society*, Vol 20 (2004), 169–185

Negus, Keith, 'Between corporation and consumer: culture and conflict in the British Record Industry', in Simon Frith (ed.), *Popular Music. Critical concepts in media and cultural studies* Vol 2: The Rock Era (London: Routledge, 2003), 24–41

Negus, Keith, 'Culture, industry, genre: conditions of musical creativity', in his *Music Genres and Corporate Cultures* (London: Routledge, 1999), 14–30

'New Study Documents Systematic Attempt by offshore Contractors to Target State Government Work', *WashTech News*, 14 July 2004

Nixon, David Mitsuo, 'The Matrix Possibility', in William Irwin (ed.), *The Matrix and Philosophy: Welcome to the Desert of the Real* (Chicago: Open Court, 2002)

Norman, Donald, *The Invisible Computer* (Cambridge, Mass.: MIT Press, 1998)

Office of International Affairs, *The Pervasive Role of Science, Technology, and Health in Foreign Policy: Imperatives for the Department of State* (National Academy Press, 1999)

Oguibe, Olu, 'Forsaken Geographies: Cyberspace and the New World "Other"', *5th International Conference on Cyberspace* 6–9 June 1996, available at <eserver.org/internet/oguibe>

Oram, Andy (ed.), *Peer-to-Peer, Harnessing the Power of Disruptive Technologies* (Cambridge, Mass.: O'Reilly, 2001)

Orlowski, Andrew, 'EC Launches Microsoft DRM Probe', *The Register*, 25 August 2004 at <http://www.theregister.co.uk/2004/08/25/ec_ms_drm_probe/>

Orwell, George, *Nineteen Eighty Four* (Harmondsworth: Penguin, 1974 edition)

Owen, Patricia, 'Hannah Arendt and the Public Sphere: Model for a Global Public?', *Conference Paper, International Studies Association Conference*, New Orleans, March 24–27, 2002, at <http://www.isanet.org/noarchive/Owens.html>

Parsons, Ian, 'Copyright and Society', in Asa Briggs (ed.), *Essays in the History of Publishing* (London: Longman, 1974)

Patton, Paul, *Deleuze and the Political* (London; New York: Routledge, 2000)

Pax, Salam, *Baghdad Blog* (Melbourne: Text Publishing Company, 2003)

Penfold, Carolyn, *World Leader or Village Idiot? An Examination of Internet Content Regulation in Australia* (LLM Thesis, UNSW, 2004)

Perens, Bruce, 'Free Software Leaders Stand Together', at <http://perens.com/Articles/StandTogether.html>

Peterson, Kim, 'Microsoft workers vent over cuts in benefits', *Seattle Times*, 26 May 2004

Phipps, Simon, 'Free speech, free beer and free software', *CNET*, 20 August 2002, at <http://news.com.com/2010-1071-954384.html>

Pottage, Alain, 'Instituting Property', *Oxford Journal of Legal Studies*, 18 (1988), 331

Preston, Diana, and Michael Preston, *A Pirate of Exquisite Mind: Explorer, Naturalist, and Buccaneer: The Life of William Dampier* (New York: Doubleday, 2004)

Raymond, Eric, *The Cathedral and the Bazaar* (Beijing; Cambridge, Mass.: O'Reilly, 2001)

Raymond, Eric S., 'Open letter to Sun: Let Java Go', 12 February 2004 at <http://www.catb.org/~esr/writings/let-java-go.html>

Raymond, Eric S., 'Let Java Go, Round 2', 19 February 2004 at <http://www.catb.org/esr/writings/let-java-go-2.html>

Redhead, Steve, *Unpopular Cultures. The birth of law and popular culture* (Manchester: Manchester University Press, 1995)

Reese, R. Anthony, 'The First Sale Doctrine in the Era of Digital Networks', *Boston College Law Review*, 44 (2003), 577

Regan, Keith, 'Leaked E-Mail Fuels Microsoft-SCO Conspiracy Theories', *Linux News* 20 March 2004, at <http://www.linuxinsider.com/perl/story/33051.html>

Reynolds, J., and J. Postel, 'RFC 1000 The Request for Comments Guide' (August 1987)

Ricciuti, Mike, 'Open source: Rebels at the gate', *CNET* News.com 14 October, 2002, at <http://news.com.com/2009-1001-961354.html>

Richardson, Joanne, 'Free Software & GPL Society. Stefan Merten of Oekonux interview', at <http://subsol.c3.hu/subsol_2/contributors0/mertentext.html>

Riehl, Damien, 'Peer to Peer Distribution Systems: Will Napster, Gnutella and Freenet create a Nirvana or Gehenna?', *William Mitchell Law Review*, 27 (2001) 1761

Rimmer, Matthew, 'The dead poets society: the copyright term extension and the public domain', *First Monday*, 8 (6) (2003)

Rivlin, Gary, 'Leader of the Free World', *Wired*, 11:11 (2003), at <http://www.wired.com/wired/archive/11.11/linus.html>

Robertson, Robin, 'Moving pictures to crackle open youth market', *Australian Financial Review*, 6 March 2003

Rose, Nikolas, *Powers of Freedom: reframing political thought* (Cambridge: Cambridge University Press, 1999)

Rotunda, Ronald, 'Judicial Comments on Pending Cases: the Ethical Restrictions and the Sanctions. A Case Study of the Microsoft Litigation', *University of Illinois Law Review*, 611 (2001), 621

Rousset, Olivia, 'Last Man on Manus Island', *Dateline*, SBS, 31 March 2004

Ryan, Michael, *Knowledge Diplomacy. Global competition and the politics of intellectual property* (Washington, DC: Brookings Institution Press, 1998)

Sarat, Austin, and Jonathon Simon, 'Cultural Analysis, Cultural Studies, and the Situation of Legal Scholarship' in Sarat, Austin and Simon, Jonathon (eds), *Cultural Analysis, Cultural Studies, and the Law: Moving beyond Legal Realism* (Durham: Duke University Press, 2003)

Schaefer, Standard, 'Tech Bubble: Who Benefited?: An Interview with Michael Hudson', *CounterPunch*, 30 August 2003 at <http://www.counterpunch.org/schaefer08302003.html.>

Schiller, Dan, 'Brought to you by . . .', in *Digital Capitalism. Networking the Global Market System* (Cambridge, Mass.; London: MIT Press, 1999)

Schwartz, Paul M., 'Privacy and Democracy In Cyberspace', *Vanderbilt Law Review*, 52 (1999), 1609

Selian, Audrey, 'The World Summit on the Information Society and Civil Society Participation', *The Information Society*, 20 (2004), 201–215

Sell, Susan K., *Private Power, Public Law, The Globalization of Intellectual Property Rights* (Cambridge: Cambridge University Press, 2003)

Shapiro, Andrew L., 'Where Do You Want To Go Today?' in *The Control Revolution. How the Internet is Putting Individuals in Charge and Changing the World We Know* (New York: Public Affairs/The Century Foundation, 1999)

Shapiro, Carl, and Hal Varian, *Information Rules* (New York: Harvard Business School Press, 1999)

Sherman, Brad, and Lionel Bently, *The Making of Modern Intellectual Property* (Cambridge: Cambridge University Press, 1999)

Sherwin, Richard, *When Law Goes Pop. The Vanishing Line between Law and Popular Culture* (Chicago: University of Chicago Press, 2000)

Shirky, Clay, 'File-sharing Goes Social', *Networks, Economics, and Culture: Mailing list*, 12 October 2003, available at <http://www.shirky.com/writings/file-sharing_social.html>

Shirky, Clay, 'Smuggled in Under Cover of Darkness', O'Reilly Network at <http://www.openp2p.com/pub/a/p2p/2001/02/14/clay_darkness.html>

Shirky, Clay, 'What is P2P and What Isn't', O'Reilly Network at <http://www.openp2p.com/pub/a/p2p/2000/11/24/shirky1-whatisp2p.html>

Shulman, Seth, *Owning the Future* (Boston: Houghton Mifflin, 1999)

Silver, David, 'Looking Backwards, Looking Forwards, Cyberculture Studies, 1990–2000', in David Gauntlett (ed.), *web.studies* (London: Arnold, 2000), 19–30

Smith, Marc, and Peter Kollock (eds), *Communities in Cyberspace* (New York: Routledge, 1999)

Smith, Samuel R., 'Postmodernism is Dead. Now what? Distributed Culture and the Rise of the Network Age', *Intelligent Agent*, 1 (2003)

Sobecki, Sebastian I., 'Mandeville's Thought of the Limit: The Discourse of Similarity and Difference in *The Travels of Sir John Mandeville*', *The Review of English Studies*, New Series 53 (2002), 211

Solo, Toni, 'Misery and Intellectual Property Rights Trashing Free Software', CounterPunch.com October 10, 2003 at <http://www.counterpunch.org/solo10102003.html>

SriMedia, '*Dow Jones v Gutnick*: Australian Court on a very slippery slope to totalitarianism?' at <http://www.srimedia.com/artman/publish/article_317.shtml>

Stallman, Richard, 'Why "Free Software" is better than "Open Source"', in Joshua Gay (ed.), *Free Software, Free Society: selected essays of Richard Stallman* (Boston: GNU Press, 2002), 55

Standage, Tom, *The Victorian Internet* (London: Weidenfeld & Nicolson, 1998)

Stefik, Mark, *Internet Dreams. Archetypes, Myths and Metaphors* (Cambridge, Mass.: MIT Press, 1996)

Stephen, Sarah, 'Horror on Manus Island', *Green Left Weekly*, 20 August 2003

Stone, Brad, 'Linux Killer', *Wired*, 12 (7) (2004), 134

Straw, Will, 'Consumption', in Simon Frith, Will Straw and John Street (eds), *The Cambridge Companion to Pop and Rock* (Cambridge: Cambridge University Press, 2001), 53–73

Terranova, Tiziana, *Network Culture. Politics for the Information Age* (London: Pluto Press, 2004)

Throsby, David, and Virginia Hollister, *Don't give up your day job: an economic study of professional artists in Australia* (Australia Council, 2003)

Toffler, Alvin, *Future Shock* (London: The Bodley Head, 1970)

Toner, Alan, 'Unzipping the World Summit on the Information Society', *Metamute*, 26, Summer/Autumn 2003

Urry, John, *Sociology beyond Societies. Mobilities for the twenty-first century* (London: Routledge, 2000)

US Federal Trade Commission, *To Promote Innovation: The Proper Balance of Competition and Patent Law and Policy*, October 2003, at <http://www.ftc.gov/os/2003/10/innovationrpt.pdf>

Vaidhyanathan, Siva, *The Anarchist in the Library* (New York: Basic Books, 2004) van de Donk, Wim, Brian D. Loder, Paul G. Nixon and Dieter Rucht (eds), *Cyberprotest. New Media, citizens and social movements* (London: Routledge, 2004)

Vaver, David, 'Need Intellectual Property Law be Everywhere? Against Ubiquity and Uniformity', *The Dalhousie Law Journal*, 25 (1) (2002), 1

West, Robin, 'Economic Man and Literary Woman. One Contrast', in Leonora Ledwon (ed.), *Law and Literature, Text and Theory* (New York: Garland Publishing, 1996), 127–138

Wood, Denis, *The Power of Maps* (New York: Guilford Press, 1992)

Woodmansee, Martha, *The Author, Art & the Market* (New York: Columbia University Press, 1994)

Woodmansee, Martha, and Peter Jaszi (eds), *The Construction of Authorship: Textual Appropriation in Law and Literature* (Durham; London: Duke University Press, 1994)

World Bank Research Report, *Globalisation, Growth and Poverty: Building an Inclusive World Economy* (New York: Oxford University Press, 2002)

World Summit on the Information Society, 'Basic Information: About WSIS', at <http://www.itu.int/wsis/basic/about.html>

Wright, Shelley, *International Human Rights, Decolonisation and Globalisation: Becoming Human* (London; New York: Routledge, 2001)

Zittrain, Jonathon, 'Internet Points of Control', *Boston College Law Review* (forthcoming).

Zvalo, Peter, 'Does Globalization Spell Trouble for Technical Writers?', *Business Word*, Fall 2001

Case law

A&M Records Inc and others v Napster Inc and Does 1–100, Case No 99-5183-MHP, Complaint for Contributory and Vicarious Copyright Infringement, Violations of California Civil Code Section 980(a)(2), and Unfair Competition. (N.D. Cal. 2000) at #1, 2

A&M Records Inc v Napster Inc 114 F. Supp. 2d 896 2000 U.S. Dist. LEXIS 11862 (N.D. Cal. 2000) 908

Bulun Bulun v. R & T Textiles Pty Ltd [1998] 41 IPR 513

Campomar v Nike International Ltd (2000) 202 CLR 45

Data Access Corporation v Powerflex Services Pty Ltd (1999) 45 IPR 353

Dow Jones & Company Inc. v Gutnick [2002] 194 ALR 433.

Eldred v Ashcroft (2003) 123 S. Ct. 769

Eolas Technologies, Inc. And The Regents Of The University Of California v. Microsoft Corporation N.D. Ill. 11 August 2003 U.S. Dist. LEXIS 13482

Metro-Goldwyn-Mayer Studios, Inc., et al. v. Grokster Ltd., et al. 259 F. Supp. 2d 1029 (C.D. Cal., April, 2003) aff'd F.3d (9th Cir., Aug. 19, 2004)

Sony Corp. of America v Universal City Studios, Inc. 464 U.S. 417 (1984)

United States v Microsoft Corp. 56 F3d 1448 (DC Cir. 1995)

United States v Microsoft Corp. 84 F.Supp.2d 9 (DDC 1999)

United States v Microsoft Corp. 87 F.Supp.2d 30 (DDC 2000)

United States v Microsoft Corp. 97 F.Supp.2d 59 (DDC 2000)

United States v Microsoft Corp. 253 F.3d 34 (DC Cir. 2001); 346 U.S. App. D.C. 330

United States v Microsoft Corp. CA No 98-1232 (CKK), filed Nov. 12, 2002 (DDC 2002)

Universal Music Australia Pty Ltd and Others v Sharman License Holdings Ltd and Others, No. N110 of 2004.

Index